SAP® ERP HCM Performance Management

 **PRESS**

Christian Krämer, Sven Ringling, and Song Yang
Mastering HR Management with SAP
2007, 630 pp.
1-59229-050-7

Hans-Jürgen Figaj, Richard Haßmann, and Anja Junold
HR Reporting with SAP
2007, approx. 430 pp.
978-1-59229-172-4

Satish Badgi
Practical SAP US Payroll
2007, 324 pp.
978-1-59229-132-8

Satish Badgi
Configuring SAP US Benefits
2007, approx. 85 pp.
1-978-159229-164-9

Jeremy Masters, Christos Kotsakis

SAP® ERP HCM Performance Management

From Design to Implementation

Galileo Press

Bonn • Boston

ISBN   978-1-59229-124-3

1st edition 2008

Editor Jenifer Niles
Copy Editor Julie McNamee
Cover Design Silke Braun
Layout Design Vera Brauner
Production Vera Brauner
Typesetting DREI-SATZ, Husby
Printed and bound in Germany

Contents at a Glance

Contents

PART II Performance Management: System Functionality and Implementation

11 Portal Configuration 199

Foreword

There is a special culture here at JetBlue Airways. An intense energy radiates within our organization where a strong sense of community binds together our employees (whom we term "Crewmembers"). The company's Values (Safety, Caring, Integrity, Fun, and Passion) are taken very seriously, and we work hard to live by them every day. Whether it's a gate agent in Boston, a flight attendant based out of Long Beach, or a reservations specialist working in their home in Salt Lake City, each and every Crewmember has come to embody the unusual spirit for which this airline was created. Our fresh marketing and low prices are leading the market, but what brings our customers back over and over is their first-rate experience with our Crewmembers. Our strong relationship with our customers has proven to be the key differentiator in our industry. JetBlue Crewmembers repeatedly delivering the "JetBlue Experience" through the Values and their personal sense of accountability and responsibility.

Getting to where we are now was not easy, but it started from the top of the organization. JetBlue's strategic goals are supported within our company's "Flight Plan" — a charter delineating those corporate goals sustained by three pillars: *People*, *Product*, and *Performance,* which, when taken together, help achieve financial *Prosperity*. Stated as a simple formula: Great *People* delivering an innovative *Product* and executing strong *Performance* will drive *Prosperity* for our company, our Crewmembers, and our shareholders.

Last year, a newly implemented talent management system changed how we manage Crewmember performance. A fundamental transformation was made in the process: We replaced year-end, "after-the-fact" performance assessments with an objective setting performance plan, where individual objectives were jointly created and monitored by the Crewmember and his/her Crewleader (i.e., manager). This agreement serves as the mechanism to track and support Crewmember performance throughout the year. But the other critical change in this process is that the Crewmembers' individual objectives are more closely aligned to department and corporate goals, which makes our company's "Flight Plan" more pertinent and tangible throughout all levels of the organization.

This is done using system tools that allow Crewleaders to more effectively create and maintain goals that support the company strategy. Each Crewleader must work with their own Crewleader to ensure that goals are cascaded and ultimately support the three pillars and the "Flight Plan" to achieve *Prosperity* for JetBlue. Crewleaders work hand in hand with their Crewmembers throughout the annual cycle to maintain that alignment to the company's goals even in a fluid environment. If corporate goals evolve during the year, the objectives mapped to those goals can be recalibrated to more accurately reflect how the Crewmember will achieve them.

I am proud to be a part of an organization that so highly values the importance of culture and employee performance management. From all levels of the organization, we continue to cultivate an environment that instills pride in our Crewmembers and high levels of satisfaction in our customers. Our recent technology enhancements have greatly strengthened our performance management processes — helping to model behaviors that are being recognized and rewarded by leadership. A strong commitment to performance management, along with the processes and tools to make it a reality, is an absolute necessity for us to continue to deliver the high levels of customer service that our customers expect and our Crewmembers exhibit throughout the organization. And that is what will carry us into the next wave of *Prosperity* for our airline.

Vincent Stabile

Senior Vice President of People
JetBlue Airways

Preface

After years of working together on HR transformation and systems implementation projects, we noticed a recurring theme with our customers: although performance management was a burgeoning discipline within the talent management space, documentation on best practices, lessons learned, and process improvement using SAP's tools was lacking. Furthermore, the complexities inherent within the configuration and programming caused many clients to look for guidance on its design, build, and deployment.

As a result of this demand, we decided to embark on a book that would satisfy both functional and technical needs. Proposing solutions in one comprehensive reference made sense as the strategy, process, and system design of any performance management program needs alignment. Throughout the book, we have highlighted leading practices based on our experiences on the ground with customers. We have paid special attention to explaining common pain points experienced when deploying such a process and system. Mitigation steps to alleviate these pain points are provided as well.

The book is composed of two parts. The first part, "Performance Management: Overview and Process," focuses on the process and theory of performance management within the organization. This section provides an overview of the performance management process and key concepts for making a successful program.

The second part, "Performance Management: System Functionality and Implementation," reviews the functionality in the SAP HCM Employee Performance Management module. Configuration and development items are carefully discussed and example scenarios are reviewed.

Each chapter is dedicated to a unique topic and organized in a logical fashion:

Chapter 1 introduces the book and sets the stage for the reader on what to expect within its content.

Chapter 2 presents an overview of SAP's Employee Performance Management capability, highlighting the differences between previous functionality and new functionality. A matrix describes the functionality available in all current SAP versions (i.e., before Enterprise 4.7, Enterprise 4.7 Extension

Set 1.1 and 2.0, ECC 5.0, and ECC 6.0). Functionality is broken down into categories such as technology, configuration, process control, and reporting.

Chapter 3 provides an overview of the performance management process, including best practices on how to execute a performance management strategy within the organization. Topics include goal and objective setting, mid-year reviews, peer reviews, self-evaluation, 360-degree feedback, and final performance evaluations.

Chapter 4 focuses on corporate strategy, including the importance of developing a strategic plan for the organization. Use of pillars to enforce alignment to the corporate strategy is discussed with example scenarios to illustrate its effectiveness. This chapter also highlights the difference between goals and objectives and the process for their review and approval. Communication of the corporate strategy is also discussed as a vital part of the performance management process and as a mechanism to reinforcement the message from senior leaders.

Chapter 5 discusses the development plan and its overall importance within the performance management process. This chapter includes information on how development planning is typically integrated, what parties are involved in its creation and closure, and options for deployment.

Chapter 6 discusses the lessons we learned along the way in our various project implementations. In addition to sharing our experiences on what to expect and how to best mitigate risk, we will also supplement the discussion with concrete examples referencing real-life scenarios.

Chapter 7 starts the second part of the book, "Performance Management: System Functionality and Implementation." In this chapter, we discuss how to turn business requirements into solid system design. Basic configuration components are described, including appraisal statuses/substatuses, pushbuttons, and form design. Configuration settings are reviewed to ensure that functionality is properly activated.

Chapter 8 presents the appraisal catalog (Transaction PHAP_CATALOG) in detail. The catalog structure, including the appraisal template, criteria groups, and criteria, is explained and dissected to help you understand its full capabilities. Important concepts are highlighted such as the appraisal header, column and row access, layout appearance, and status flow.

Chapter 9 contains advanced configuration, including utilities such as quick configuration, web and print layout, configuration checks, and protocol behind transports. Configuration outside of the appraisal catalog is also covered, including basic settings (Transaction OOHAP_BASIC). Important concepts such as workflow and value lists are examined as well.

Chapter 10 offers a thorough review of the Business Add-Ins (BAdIs) available within the performance management system. These user exits provide customers the extensibility they are looking for. Broken out by area, each standard-delivered BAdI is described with the out-of-the-box implementations and popular custom uses as well.

Chapter 11 reviews the portal-related configuration needed to implement performance management in the SAP NetWeaver Portal. A review of the BSP-based iViews and the MbO Status Overview provides a glimpse at what the end users will see from the portal. Each participant in the process — appraisee, appraiser, part appraiser, and further participant — is discussed.

Chapter 12 covers the operational side of the deployment: administrative and reporting needs. Whether it be preparing documents or changing appraisal statuses, Transaction PHAP_ADMIN is explained in detail with its varied uses. Business Intelligence is also discussed.

Chapter 13 discusses security authorizations in SAP, including the new R/3 authorization object P_HAP_DOC. Structural authorization and its impact on performance management is covered as well.

Chapter 14 presents the technical link between pay and performance. This chapter discusses the out-of-the-box performance management and compensation integration within SAP. We'll walk through both the configuration at the appraisal level and in compensation management (eligibility and guidelines) via the Implementation Guide (IMG).

The **Appendices** of the book provide helpful reference information, including important performance management R/3 transaction codes, relevant PD (Personnel Development) objects and infotype tables, BAdIs, and additional resources on where to find more information.

We hope you find this book informative and easy-to-read. We anticipate providing you with new perspectives, practical anecdotes, and "food for thought" as you embark on improving your performance management program.

Sincerely, **Christos Kotsakis** & **Jeremy Masters**

New York, NY
November 2007

Acknowledgments

This project draws inspiration from the efforts and support of many individuals. Without these folks, this book would not have been possible.

We are indebted to Vinny Stabile, Senior Vice President of People at JetBlue Airways. Vinny has been an inspiration and role model for leadership, showing us how to engage an entire organization with the values and commitment to create an energetic, passionate, and honest work environment we have seen in very few companies. His wisdom has reshaped the very way we view the Human Resources function.

Our work has also benefited immensely from the influence of a wide variety of colleagues. We would particularly like to thank Venkat Challa for his support in delivering some of the most complex projects we have faced in our careers. His ability to focus on complex problems and deliver comprehensive solutions has helped us improve our ability to shape solutions in ways that have delighted our clients.

This project would not have been possible without the help, guidance, and support from the folks at Galileo Press. We would especially like to thank Jenifer Niles who has made this book possible and has encouraged us to get the words onto the printed page. Without her, this book would not exist.

Finally, we are very grateful to our families, who supported us during the writing of this book and love us beyond anything we can put into words.

PART I
Performance Management:
Overview and Process

This part of the book focuses on the process and theory of performance management within the organization. It also provides an overview of the performance management process and key concepts for making a successful program.

In today's fast-paced and competitive work environment, achieving business priorities is a crucial part of a company's viability within the marketplace. Establishing a mechanism to track company goals and employee objectives increases the organization's ability to execute a corporate-wide strategy. A book devoted to SAP Performance Management will help HR practitioners gain a better understanding of performance management within SAP. Details on how to implement the Performance Management module will assist in its successful delivery.

1   Introduction

Managing talent within the organization is one of the most important initiatives for the Human Resources function today. Fostering a work environment that emanates productivity, innovation, and efficiency has long been the charge of senior leaders. Without capable and skilled employees, an organization will never achieve its business plans no matter how innovative the product or exciting the service.

So, how are organizations faring with developing and grooming their talent? How well are companies achieving their business priorities? Are strategic initiatives being met or even tracked? How closely do companies carry out these imperatives by living the core values of the organization? Are any patterns detectable? Although some companies are very good at "staying the course" and achieving their targeted results, most organizations can do a lot better at defining a strategy and executing it. Companies now realize that their most important asset is human capital. Without talented and dedicated employees, organizations will surely fail in achieving results.

This book was written to aid in the implementation of SAP HR performance management and assist SAP HR practitioners who may be new to performance management. In writing the book, we attempt to enhance your understanding of how performance management can improve and develop employees, help the organization achieve its strategic business plans, and establish a dynamic work environment that fosters innovation and thought leadership.

Besides the strategic and process discussion mentioned previously, we also cover the implementation of the *Objective Setting and Appraisals (OSA)* module within SAP.

1.1 Target Audience

This book is designed for both HR and IT professionals interested in learning more about SAP's Performance Management capability available in the latest releases. Those benefiting most from the book will fall into two main categories:

- HR and IT professionals who are not familiar with the performance management process or SAP's solution.
- HR and IT professionals who are familiar with the performance management process but do not know what SAP's latest Performance Management solution can offer.

Regardless of your level of expertise in the performance management process, you will find the discussion in Chapter 6 to be informative. These lessons learned draw from experiences we have encountered during engagements at various clients implementing this very same functionality.

Project managers and other project team members can benefit from this book as well. For example, your security resource may want to read Chapter 13 on authorizations in performance management. Chapter 11 speaks to the integration with the SAP NetWeaver Portal and is helpful for a portal resource to read.

1.2 Book Layout

The book is comprised of two parts. The first part focuses on process and strategy. Those new to performance management will find these chapters of particular interest. Topics such as cascading goals, objective setting, and development planning are covered. Lessons learned from project work are also discussed.

The second part of the book is a practical guide to its implementation. Configuration, development, and security are covered in detail. Both project implementation activities as well as more operational processes (such as administrative tasks and reporting) are discussed.

1.3   Product Releases

This book is based on the ERP2005 system; this is sometimes referred to as Enterprise Central Component 6.0 (ECC 6.0). However, because many clients have not upgraded yet (at the time of this publishing), we wanted to be sure that the book made mention of functionality available starting from Enterprise 4.7 Extension Set 1.1 (including ECC 5.0). Although most screenshots in this book were taken on an ECC 6.0 system, many are still relevant for the earlier releases.

Customers on Enterprise 4.7 Extension Set 1.10 and Enterprise 4.7 Extension Set 2.00 will also benefit from knowing the limitations of their own versions. Knowing what functionality is available in the latest releases is important for those considering an upgrade in the near future. A common question we hear from clients is "What do I get if I upgrade?" To answer this question (quite directly), we have been careful to distinguish functionality that is (or is not) available in each of the releases. Chapter 8 and Chapter 9 on configuration and Chapter 10 on Business Add-Ins (BAdIs) have many references to product releases and function availability.

1.4   Summary

In the pages that follow, we have put together a comprehensive guide on SAP's Performance Management solution. We will first provide an overview of performance management within the SAP HCM solution. Knowing the background and value proposition behind SAP's solution will enable you to get started on the right foot. We hope you enjoy the book!

SAP's recent focus on talent management has received an overwhelmingly positive response from its customers. The new performance management offering Objective Setting and Appraisals (OSA) now affords the flexibility and integration that many companies have been looking for. This chapter provides an overview of the Performance Management module and explores its evolution within the SAP HCM suite.

2 Overview of SAP's Performance Management Solution

Today, employee performance management is one of the foundational components within SAP's talent management strategy. SAP's focus on strategic HCM (Human Capital Management) processes, such as performance and compensation management, succession planning, and eRecruitment has been driven by a strong market need. Customers are now seeking solutions that can track and boost performance improvement throughout their enterprise. SAP's latest Performance Management solution *Objective Setting and Appraisals (OSA)* provides its customers with just that. The flexibility and extensibility available within the new module provides companies with the tools they need to implement an end-to-end performance management process that leverages their SAP HR investment.

2.1 Background and Value Proposition

For years, many clients recorded performance management results using Word and Excel document templates. Organizations that needed robust functionality purchased third-party applications or built custom in-house solutions that were made available on the company's intranet. Others had no formal process because performance was either not measured or not measured consistently.

SAP's first Performance Management module, *Appraisal Systems*, was met with lukewarm response from SAP clients. This was, in part, due to the fact that not many clients had the SAP Portal (or any web-based application) for employee and manager self service and, therefore, instituting a secure, online process was difficult, if not impossible, for many organizations. The initial solution did not conform to the concept of management by objectives (MBO). The notion of management by objectives based on strategic company goals did not materialize until the recent Objective Setting and Appraisals (OSA) module was released. In Appraisal Systems, performance was evaluated more as an afterthought than as a continuous cycle throughout the year. Although linkages were established to the Compensation Management module, integration with other modules was not as strong as it is with the new functionality.

The new OSA functionality has become very popular with SAP clients. Clients are excited about the new functionality and integration capabilities. SAP identified several advantages with OSA that enhance the value proposition. Implementing SAP's newest Performance Management solution provides clients with the following advantages:

▶ Helps to communicate the enterprise strategy

▶ Helps to translate enterprise strategy, area, and department goals into individual employee objectives

▶ Enables line managers to be flexible and focused when setting objectives with their employees

▶ Supports flexible and future-oriented performance planning

▶ Provides comprehensive comparison options as a basis for pay based on fair performance.

Communicating the corporate strategy is one of the most important themes woven into SAP's overall performance management offering. Goal alignment from the very top of the organization to rank-and-file employees is of paramount importance. Employees should set individual performance objectives against corporate and department goals based on the strategic plan of the organization. These concepts are discussed in detail in Chapter 3.

Figure 2.1 shows SAP's depiction of cascading goals. Strategic goals, delivered within the Strategic Enterprise Management (SEM) solution, are shown cascading to organizational goals at the employee level. Employees, using appraisal forms within the OSA module align their personal objectives to these goals.

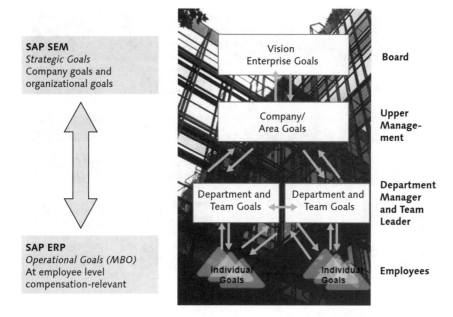

SAP SEM
Strategic Goals
Company goals and
organizational goals

SAP ERP
Operational Goals (MBO)
At employee level
compensation-relevant

Vision
Enterprise Goals — Board

Company/
Area Goals — Upper Management

Department and Team Goals ←→ Department and Team Goals — Department Manager and Team Leader

Individual Goals — Individual Goals — Employees

Figure 2.1 SAP Depiction of Cascading Goals: From Strategic Goals at the Top of the Organization to Operational Goals at the Employee Level

2.2 Performance Management Within the Larger Context

The performance management process is part of a larger Talent Management application suite. SAP has adopted several high-level themes to describe how companies need to engage and groom talent within the organization:

- Pay for Performance
- Educate and Develop
- Identify and Grow
- Attract and Acquire

These themes are integrated and contribute to each other. Figure 2.2 illustrates how interdependent these areas are with one another.

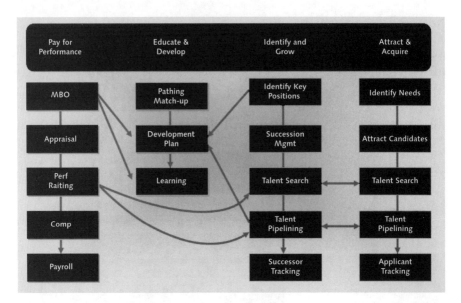

Figure 2.2 Performance Management within the larger Talent Management Strategy and the Linkages within the Solution

With Pay for Performance, employee performance and behaviors can be quantified with a rating that is then made available to compensation management. This rating will then be used as one input for compensation payout (e.g., merit, bonus, and so on).

The Educate and Develop theme speaks to identifying areas where the employee needs development. This area includes creating and monitoring their development plan as well as identifying and attending the training needed to close the development need.

Succession planning is the key focus within the Identify and Grow theme. Identifying key positions and high potentials, tracking readiness for these high potentials, and grooming future leaders are the primary activities.

Recruitment practices are integral for the Attract and Acquire theme. Sourcing and selecting the right candidates both inside and outside the organization is one of most powerful functions for HR to deliver effectively.

Without execution of these themes, a holistic approach to talent management cannot be achieved.

2.3   Integration

SAP has always touted its integration capabilities. The Performance Management module has many touch points with other modules within the HCM suite. Figure 2.3 illustrates this integration. Customers on the latest ERP release (ECC 6.0) will be in the best position to leverage the efficiencies of an integrated system.

Figure 2.3 Integration Components Within SAP's Performance Management Solution

The following components have integration points with the Performance Management module. Some components, such as Organizational Management and Personnel Administration are prerequisites, whereas others, such as Compensation Management and Personnel Development, are not required but are frequently integrated by customers.

2.3.1   Personnel Administration

Basic employee data, such as name and personnel number, are needed for the performance management application. This module is a prerequisite.

2.3.2 Organizational Management

Organizational Management information, such as the employee's "chief" manager and organizational unit, is integral to the appraisal document, especially its header (discussed in Chapter 8). Several standard programs are also based on the employee's organizational assignment within the organizational structure.

2.3.3 Compensation Management

Integration with Compensation Management is common due to the popularity of performance-based payout. A pay for performance philosophy is now widespread among companies and can easily be executed using the linkages between performance and compensation management.

2.3.4 Personnel Development

Integration with qualifications and development plans components of the Personnel Development module can be achieved without too much effort and set up. Qualifications, such as competencies, that an employee is developing can be easily included in a performance management document. Qualifications and development plans can even default into the appraisal based on position and/or job assignment within Organization Management.

2.3.5 Learning Solution (LSO)

Integration with the Learning Solution (LSO) is also available. Classroom and online training classes can be included within an employee's overall performance improvement plan for the year.

2.3.6 Business Intelligence (BI)

Data extractors exist for the standard queries available within SAP NetWeaver Business Intelligence (BI) functionality. Many clients expect to implement BI in the coming years. There is a lot of excitement around providing key stakeholders from executives to line managers with analytics available within a data warehousing solution.

2.3.7 Strategic Enterprise Management (SEM)

Integration with Strategic Enterprise Management (SEM) is an option for those customers who want to directly link corporate goals to individual performance objectives.

2.4 Functionality Matrix

SAP has recently experienced a big transition within its performance management offering. In the matrix that follows in Table 2.1, SAP's performance management functionality is reviewed in detail. The matrix breaks down functionality and the versions that support it. The following versions are covered:

▶ Appraisal System (available as of version 4.5B)

▶ Performance Management in EE 1.10 (available as of version Enterprise Extension Set 1.10)

▶ Performance Management in EE 2.00 (available as of version Enterprise Extension Set 2.00)

▶ Performance Management in ERP 2004 (available as of version ECC 5.0)

▶ Performance Management in ERP 2005 (available as of version ECC 6.0)

Functionality Overview	Appraisal System	Performance Management in EE 1.10	Performance Management in EE 2.00	Performance Management in ERP 2004	Performance Management in ERP 2005
General					
Technology	R/3 4.6C ITS	R/3 4.7 Enterprise 1.10 Web (BSP)	R/3 4.7 Enterprise 2.00 Web (BSP)	R/3 ECC 5.0 Web (BSP)	R/3 Web ECC 6.0 (BSP and WebDynpro)
Greatest flexibility due to the existence of BAdIs	Not Applicable	43 Definitions/ 56 Implementations	51 Definitions/ 93 Implementations	52 Definitions/ 110 Implementations	53 Definitions/ 114 Implementations
Print templates in Adobe forms					✔

Table 2.1 Functionality Overview by Version (Performance Management Before 4.7, Within Enterprise 4.7 Extension Set 1.10, Within Enterprise 4.7 Extension Set 2.00, Within ECC 5.0, and Within ECC 6.0)

Functionality Overview	Appraisal System	Performance Management in EE 1.10	Performance Management in EE 2.00	Performance Management in ERP 2004	Performance Management in ERP 2005
Availability					
Manager Self Service (MSS Portal)	✔	✔	✔	✔	✔
Employee Self Service (ESS Portal)	✔	✔	✔	✔	✔
Manager's Desktop	✔	✔	✔	✔	✔
Personnel Development Profile (Transaction: PPPM)	✔	✔	✔	✔	✔
Integration					
Organizational Management	✔	✔	✔	✔	✔
Personnel Administration	✔	✔	✔	✔	✔
Personnel Development-Qualifications	✔	✔	✔	✔	✔
Personnel Development-Development Plans				✔	✔
Compensation Management	✔	✔	✔	✔	✔
Strategic Enterprise Management (SEM)		✔	✔	✔	✔
Learning Solution (LSO)				✔	✔
Business Intelligence (BI)	✔		✔ (ver. 3.2)	✔ (ver. 3.2)	✔ (ver. 3.2)

Table 2.1 Functionality Overview by Version (Performance Management Before 4.7, Within Enterprise 4.7 Extension Set 1.10, Within Enterprise 4.7 Extension Set 2.00, Within ECC 5.0, and Within ECC 6.0) (Cont.)

Functionality Overview	Appraisal System	Performance Management in EE 1.10	Performance Management in EE 2.00	Performance Management in ERP 2004	Performance Management in ERP 2005
Configuration					
General					
Clear catalog structure (can view hierarchical structure in OSA)		✔ (categories)	✔ (categories)	✔ (categories)	✔ (categories)
Multilingual capability	✔	✔	✔	✔	✔
Delivers business content (templates, categories)		✔ (example templates)	✔ (example templates/ categories)	✔ (example templates/ categories)	✔ (example templates/ categories)
Wizard support for creating forms			✔ (standard)	✔ (standard w/BAdI to extend)	✔ (standard w/BAdI to extend)
Calibration support				✔	✔
Templates					
Offer templates based on employee attributes				✔	✔
Make Part Appraisers mandatory				✔	✔
Depict variety of templates (appraisal templates, valuation templates, and survey templates)		✔	✔	✔	✔

Table 2.1 Functionality Overview by Version (Performance Management Before 4.7, Within Enterprise 4.7 Extension Set 1.10, Within Enterprise 4.7 Extension Set 2.00, Within ECC 5.0, and Within ECC 6.0) (Cont.)

Functionality Overview	Appraisal System	Performance Management in EE 1.10	Performance Management in EE 2.00	Performance Management in ERP 2004	Performance Management in ERP 2005
Automatic numbering of criteria (items)		✔	✔	✔	✔
Any template structure depth		✔	✔	✔	✔
Unlimited number of criteria (items)		✔	✔	✔	✔
Several dimensions (pieces of information) per criterion (column)		✔ (e.g., enter weighting)	✔ (e.g., enter weighting)	✔ (e.g., enter weighting)	✔ (e.g., enter weighting)
Weighting of criteria (items)		✔	✔	✔	✔
Reusability of criteria (items)		✔	✔	✔	✔
Any evaluation option		✔	✔	✔	✔
Value description for more objective valuation		✔	✔	✔	✔
Include additional information (header data, links) and personalize templates		✔	✔	✔	✔
Dynamic cell values				✔	✔
Processing of attachments			✔	✔ (phase dependent)	✔ (phase dependent)

Table 2.1 Functionality Overview by Version (Performance Management Before 4.7, Within Enterprise 4.7 Extension Set 1.10, Within Enterprise 4.7 Extension Set 2.00, Within ECC 5.0, and Within ECC 6.0) (Cont.)

Functionality Overview	Appraisal System	Performance Management in EE 1.10	Performance Management in EE 2.00	Performance Management in ERP 2004	Performance Management in ERP 2005
Link to qualifications catalog and balanced scorecard		✔	✔	✔	✔
Link to courses in the SAP LSO				✔	✔
Link to development elements in Development Plans				✔	✔
Link to managers objective setting document and employee previous document			✔	✔	✔
Value determination across multiple documents			✔	✔	✔
Every PD-object can be a template element		✔	✔	✔	✔
Define customer-specific naming status			✔	✔	✔
Quick configuration			✔	✔	✔
Business consistency check		✔	✔	✔	✔
Offline capability					✔

Table 2.1 Functionality Overview by Version (Performance Management Before 4.7, Within Enterprise 4.7 Extension Set 1.10, Within Enterprise 4.7 Extension Set 2.00, Within ECC 5.0, and Within ECC 6.0) (Cont.)

Functionality Overview	Appraisal System	Performance Management in EE 1.10	Performance Management in EE 2.00	Performance Management in ERP 2004	Performance Management in ERP 2005
Draft notes (only viewed by author until uploaded)					✔
Comment on status change (e.g., enter reason for evaluation)					✔
Catalog Interaction					
Release templates using status management		✔	✔	✔	✔
Copy and paste		✔	✔	✔	✔
Transport connection for templates	✔ (manual)	✔ (manual)	✔ (automatic)	✔ (automatic)	✔ (automatic)
Download/upload templates			✔	✔	✔
Application					
General					
Anonymous appraisals (see negative list)	✔	✔	✔	✔	✔
Adjust user interface without the need for modifications		✔ (layout config, CSS, BSP Customer implementation)	✔ (layout config, CSS, BSP Customer implementation)	✔ (layout config, CSS, BSP Customer implementation)	✔ (layout config, CSS, BSP and WebDynpro Customer implementation)

Table 2.1 Functionality Overview by Version (Performance Management Before 4.7, Within Enterprise 4.7 Extension Set 1.10, Within Enterprise 4.7 Extension Set 2.00, Within ECC 5.0, and Within ECC 6.0) (Cont.)

Functionality Overview	Appraisal System	Performance Management in EE 1.10	Performance Management in EE 2.00	Performance Management in ERP 2004	Performance Management in ERP 2005
Template-specific print option		✔	✔	✔	✔
Document					
Define Objectives					
Standardized objectives (enterprise objectives)	(restricted)	✔	✔	✔	✔
Freely definable individual objectives	(restricted)	✔	✔	✔	✔
Enhance/add criteria (items) to the application freely		✔	✔	✔	✔
Delete criteria (items) in the application		✔	✔	✔	✔
Part appraisals possible	✔	✔ (max. 18)	✔ (max. 18)	✔ (max. 18)	✔ (max. 18)
Can define additional persons involved		✔	✔	✔	✔
Availability of roles (part appraiser, additional persons involved)		✔	✔	✔	✔
Attachments	✔	✔	✔	✔	✔
Action log		✔	✔	✔	✔

Table 2.1 Functionality Overview by Version (Performance Management Before 4.7, Within Enterprise 4.7 Extension Set 1.10, Within Enterprise 4.7 Extension Set 2.00, Within ECC 5.0, and Within ECC 6.0) (Cont.)

Functionality Overview	Appraisal System	Performance Management in EE 1.10	Performance Management in EE 2.00	Performance Management in ERP 2004	Performance Management in ERP 2005
Detailed Action log (When, who and what — deleted, added or changed objectives, entry or changes of final appraisal)					✔
Process Control					
Status administration (process support)			✔ (OSA inc. substatus)	✔ (OSA inc. substatus)	✔ (OSA inc. substatus)
Detailed administration of authorizations (template, document, and column)		✔	✔	✔	✔
Detailed administration of authorizations for row (access)					✔
Follow-up activities	✔	✔	✔	✔	✔
Create worklist	✔	✔	✔	✔	✔
Administrator can prepare several documents simultaneously		✔	✔	✔	✔ (also for several org units)

Table 2.1 Functionality Overview by Version (Performance Management Before 4.7, Within Enterprise 4.7 Extension Set 1.10, Within Enterprise 4.7 Extension Set 2.00, Within ECC 5.0, and Within ECC 6.0) (Cont.)

Functionality Overview	Appraisal System	Performance Management in EE 1.10	Performance Management in EE 2.00	Performance Management in ERP 2004	Performance Management in ERP 2005
Workflow connection	✔	✔ (using customer implementations)	✔ (standard scenarios delivered)	✔ (standard scenarios delivered)	✔ (standard scenarios delivered)
Reporting					
General					
Save versions	✔				
Template-specific and customer-specific reporting	✔	✔	✔	✔	✔
BW connection	✔		✔	✔	✔
Specific					
Ranking list		✔	✔	✔	✔
Excel download		✔	✔	✔	✔
Mass printing		✔	✔	✔	✔
Analysis tool			✔	✔	✔

Table 2.1 Functionality Overview by Version (Performance Management Before 4.7, Within Enterprise 4.7 Extension Set 1.10, Within Enterprise 4.7 Extension Set 2.00, Within ECC 5.0, and Within ECC 6.0) (Cont.)

2.5 Summary

In this chapter, you have seen how SAP's Performance Management solution has evolved over the years. The current product, Objective Setting, and Appraisals (OSA), is a robust tool capable of providing clients with the flexibility they need to effectively manage and measure employees' performance against corporate goals.

Integration is also strong. The Compensation Management and Personnel Development modules are the most commonly integrated, but customers are offered a wide variety of other options, including Business Intelligence (BI) and Strategic Enterprise Management (SEM).

In the next chapter, we take a deeper dive into the performance management process itself by covering such important topics as setting strategic goals, departmental goals, and individual objectives, conducting mid-year reviews, and completing self-evaluation and final assessments.

Performance management is a flexible process that links employees and managers in the identification and evaluation of key performance objectives, competencies, and values. In this chapter we will explore the entire process.

3   The Performance Management Process

Performance management is a flexible, process-based framework that enables managers and employees to work together to develop a set of objectives and a plan for achieving them. The process must support the partnership between employee and manager but also minimize the impact or burden the process places on the organization.

At a high level, the actors, employees, and managers cycle through the stages of planning, acting, managing, and reviewing.

Figure 3.1 shows the high-level stages of performance management. Each stage contains multiple steps that combine to make up the overall process.

Planning
- Defining goals
- Defining objectives
- Linking objectives to goals
- Gain commitment

Managing
- Tracking performance
- Coaching individuals
- Reinforce goals

Acting

Reviewing
- Evaluate results
- Feedback
- Calibrate

Figure 3.1 High-Level Stages of the Performance Management Process

The performance management process described in this chapter can be adapted to support various levels of periodic feedback and improvement through additional steps, as well as informal meetings between the employee and the manager.

Most companies implement the performance management process to support year-end reviews that ultimately drive the promotion and compensation processes. The reality is, however, that performance management can be much more than a tool to determine promotions and compensation.

The goal of the performance management process is to help employees improve their performance and effectiveness by helping them better understand what they are responsible for, how they will be measured, and how the work they are doing fits into the organization as a whole. This understanding can drive higher levels of performance and employee satisfaction (see Figure 3.2).

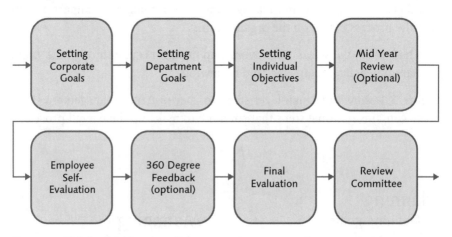

Figure 3.2 High-level Performance Management Process

3.1   Objectives of the Performance Management Process

Designing and implementing a performance management process yields many benefits. Typically, the process is designed to achieve the following objectives:

▶ Provide a process that allows employees and managers to identify key objectives and individual performance measures that align with the department and the overall organization.

▸ Provide employees and managers the framework in which to have open and honest communication about the contributions that the employee is making and achievement of their objectives.

▸ Provide managers an opportunity to help employees in areas that need improvement as well as the identification of skills that will allow the employee to perform the job more effectively.

▸ Provide the employee the ability to collaborate with the manager to develop a plan for achieving objectives and improving job performance.

3.2   Setting Corporate and Departmental Goals

The performance management process begins at the start of the year with the setting of corporate and department goals. This stage in the process constitutes the planning cycle, which will provide the foundation for an effective process.

At the start of the year, the senior leadership team will gather and define the corporate goals. These goals are presented to the organization and are used to derive the department goals.

Managers define the goals of the department and align them to the corporate goals. After the goals are defined and aligned to the corporate goals, managers can release the process to the employees. Employees and managers can then begin the process of setting their individual objectives and aligning them to the department goals and corporate goals.

This part of the process is defined in more detail in Chapter 4 "Setting the Corporate Strategy."

3.3   Setting Individual Objectives

Setting individual objectives logically starts at the beginning of the year right after the goals of the company and the department have been set. Employees can refer to these goals and draft a set of objectives that they will discuss with their manager. Employees go through the process of setting SMART (you will learn about SMART in Chapter 4) objectives along with a corresponding weight. Additionally, employees can align objectives to one or more goals set by their manager.

3.3.1 Organizing the Number and Weight of Objectives

Most companies try to limit the number of objectives that employees should set. This is not a hard and fast rule, but most believe employees should limit the number of key objectives to only those that they can effectively focus on. Companies often choose a limit of around five key objectives. Some companies choose to systematically limit the number of objectives that employees can set, whereas others provide the limit in a guideline. Additional guidelines can be imposed that predetermine one or more objectives. For example, managers should have one objective dedicated to effectively managing and developing their employees.

It is also good practice to have the sum of all weightings equal 100%. Weightings are an important tool for the manager to use in highlighting which objectives carry greater importance to the department and subsequently the company. The weightings provide the employee with clear guidance on which objectives should take priority and which objectives will have a greater impact on their year-end rating.

3.3.2 Manager Review of Objectives

After the employee has set, weighted, and aligned objectives, he sets up a meeting with his manager to discuss these objectives. This meeting between the manager and the employee is the most important event in the objective-setting process. Effective leadership comes into play here as managers can best determine whether the objectives the employee has set are realistic, whether they make effective use of the available resources, whether they align to company and departmental goals, and whether they can truly be measured.

Managers have an opportunity to shape the objectives and help the employee understand why they are important and how they will be measured. To help employees better understand how they will be evaluated, managers can help them refine the objectives and assign a weight to show which objectives are more critical to the success of the department.

Having this candid discussion with employees averts common problems that many employees face during this part of the process. All too often, employees have a fear that the objectives are not achievable, will require extraordinary effort, and are not within their control or capabilities.

In the preceding example, managers need to be sensitive to the landscape that would prevent junior consultants from achieving higher objectives. Managers need to pay close attention to the dynamics involved in these discussions and help employees gain the confidence needed to understand and agree to their objectives. High-performance cultures benefit when employees are less defensive, have greater confidence, and are more open to change.

3.4 Mid-Year Reviews

The mid-year review process is designed to formalize the review of progress against the objectives set at the beginning of the year. To maintain a performance-based culture, it's best to have informal discussions throughout the year that focus on providing employees continuous feedback and support so they can reach their objectives. Having this process take place throughout the year not only reduces the effort of the formal mid-year reviews but also positions the manager to be proactive and manage execution.

3.4.1 Changing Objectives Mid-Year

Setting objectives at the start of the year usually comes with some assumptions about business conditions, roles and responsibilities, and business priorities. Business conditions often change, and most successful companies continually adapt to meet those changes. Additionally, employees are moved within the organizations, either as a function of business need or opportunity. All these factors require a formal mid-year review to allow managers to systematically modify and/or change objectives that better align with the new performance expectations or job responsibilities.

3.4.2 Peer Reviews

Peer reviews can be a very powerful part of the review process and often lead to higher employee performance. Peer reviews are often conducted by colleagues and coworkers to offer more relevant feedback to the employee and to provide a higher degree of accuracy that allows the employee to gain a better perspective on how best to improve performance. Peer reviews also provide the manager with a wide array of information about an employee that can be used to shape the mid-year review process.

> **Note**
>
> One important fact to note about performance is that it's not only the results that matter but also how the results have been attained. Conducting peer reviews can also help managers gain a better view of how employees contribute to the overall performance of the department. Managers can then use this information to guide employees on achieving better performance and higher quality of work.

3.4.3 Preparing for the Mid-Year Review

Making the most of the mid-year review requires a fair amount of preparation on the part of the manager. The manager should review the employee's roles and responsibilities and performance expectations. Managers should also use any notes gathered from informal meetings and results from peer reviews if they are part of the process.

The manager should make an initial determination about the employee's performance against the stated objectives. Being prepared to discuss key points allows the employee to understand how he can best take actions to continue to achieve the objectives.

In the event that roles and responsibilities or business priorities have changed, managers must prepare the updated and/or new objectives as well as any targets that need to be revised. Changes in an employee's objectives should not be a surprise but do need to be communicated and clarified, especially if they are a factor in the employee's overall compensation and bonus calculation.

3.4.4 Conducting the Mid-Year Review

The mid-year review is usually conducted in a one-on-one dialogue between the manager and the employee. These meetings can vary in approach but ultimately should cover the following objectives:

- Review current progress against objectives.
- Redefine objectives and/or targets if required.
- Provide feedback based on observations and coaching that can be used to achieve objectives.
- Incorporate feedback from the peer review.
- Reinforce department goals and corporate strategy if applicable.

Depending on the mid-year process, the employee may have provided a self-evaluation that updates the status of each objective. If the process includes a self-evaluation, managers need to review the assessment that was provided and verify that the information provided contains measurable statements. Employees should be encouraged to provide statements that are measured to reflect the progress against each objective. Objectives that have not been started should be marked as not started.

3.5 Self-Evaluation

In preparation for the final evaluation, employees complete a self-evaluation that is submitted to the manager for review. The self-evaluation involves the employee conducting a self-evaluation of his job performance, skills, and attributes. The evaluation is then referenced by the manager during the manager evaluation.

The self-evaluation is also a tool that improves communication between the employee and manager. Employees commit to achieve certain objectives and follow company values during the year. The self-evaluation allows the employee to describe his contributions at any point in the process, which enables an environment of continuous feedback.

3.5.1 Self-Rating

In many instances, employees conduct the self-evaluation against the same criteria that the manager will evaluate. Employees provide narratives on how they accomplished predefined objectives and often rate themselves using the same rating scale the manager uses.

Having employees rate themselves is a good practice, and although many people think that employees will rate themselves unrealistically high, that's often not the case when objectives are clearly defined and measurable.

3.6   360-Degree Feedback

The 360-degree feedback form is often referred to as the *360*. As the name implies, peers, managers, any direct reports, and possibly clients and suppliers review the employee. Basically, the 360 provides valuable feedback from people that interact with and are closest to the employee, allowing the input to be used as a true measure of an employee's performance and to highlight areas of improvement.

3.6.1   Conducting a 360 Review

Many companies limit the use of the 360 review process to managers and senior level managers. This approach is starting to change as companies discover cost-effective ways to execute a 360 review.

In most implementations, the 360 review is initiated by the manager and sent to key individuals that are believed to be closest to the employee (see Figure 3.3). The actual number of evaluators varies by organization but should be limited to the people that have direct interactions with the employee. The feedback is generally provided anonymously and collected by the manager. Each evaluator works in parallel and is unable to see who else is conducting an evaluation nor can they see any of the comments provided.

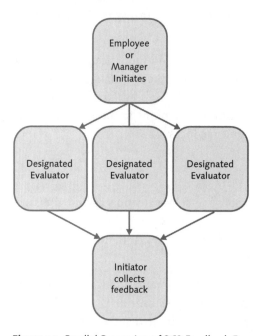

Figure 3.3 Parallel Processing of 360 Feedback Forms

After the feedback is collected from the designated evaluators, the manager can review the feedback and prepare for a dialogue with the employee in which the manager can provide the critical feedback that will help the employee's performance.

The feedback provided through this type of review is very valuable because it has a higher degree of honesty and includes targeted examples. The level of honest feedback is attributed to the approach of keeping the evaluators anonymous and having the manager initiate the 360 evaluation. The 360-degree feedback process along with the self-evaluation has many positive effects to the overall performance management process. Following are some key benefits:

▸ Helps employees improve performance and how they achieve objectives, which ultimately leads to the achievement of department and company goals

▸ Fosters an environment of continuous improvement through regular feedback

▸ Provides employees with an actionable plan for improving skills and behaviors

▸ Allows managers and employees to have a shared understanding of what needs to be improved and how the employee is contributing to the success of the organization

3.7   Final Evaluation

The performance management process concludes with the final evaluation and rating of the employee. The final evaluation provides a focal point where the manager can document performance, competencies, motivation, and any development issues. It's the key point in the year where the manager can step back and reflect on how far the employee has progressed.

3.7.1   Conducting the Year-End Review

The final evaluation is typically the conclusion of the process whereby managers review employees and provide a narrative describing how well the employee did in meeting the objectives that were set at the beginning of the year. Depending on the forms in use, managers will also evaluate the employee on corporate values and a set of competencies, each of which may contain a rating scale.

Managers are encouraged to use this review to really gauge how employees performed during the period that the evaluation covers. It is very important that managers consider how the employee achieved the objectives and whether it was in line with the corporate values.

3.7.2 Use of Self-Evaluations

One of the ways that companies choose to implement the manager evaluation form is by providing the employee self-evaluation as a reference point. This approach allows the manager to review the employee's narrative and rating. The manager then provides a narrative and rating that can be based on what the employee has substantiated.

3.8 Review Committees

Many organizations complete the process by using several review committees. These committees are usually broken out by function and are tasked to provide a consensus on the ratings that have been assigned to employees. The objective is to review employees against their peers and, in many cases, force the distributions of ratings based on the percentages set by the organization. The review process is fairly involved and needs to be organized so that all the information necessary to make decisions on an employee's rating is available.

The following information should be made available during the review committee meeting:

▸ Historical ratings and comments from previous evaluations

▸ Time in current position and position history

▸ Current development plan

Employees are compared to their peers using several different criteria, including benchmark employees at each rating. Using benchmark employees at a particular rating is very useful because it sets the accepted standard for performance at that level.

3.8.1 Use of a Facilitator

The use of a facilitator in review committee meetings is a good way to make the meetings more effective. Review committee meetings can be long depending on the number of employees being reviewed and can often require bringing other people into the meeting to validate certain information.

Primarily, representatives from the human resources or organizational development department will facilitate the meeting to allow the participants to focus on ranking the employees.

The role of the facilitator should be structured and have the following responsibilities:

1. Initiate the meeting and set the ground rules for the distribution of rankings, the rating guidelines, and the approach for evaluating employees.
2. Act as a timekeeper to allow enough time for each employee that needs to be reviewed.
3. Mediate between meeting participants and make sure the process is managed effectively.
4. Maintain consistency in ratings, especially with managers that commonly rate employees too high or too low.
5. Identify any areas that would cause the results of the meeting to be questioned, for example, managers that try to barter for ratings.

3.8.2 Results of the Review Committee

After the review committees have ended, the adjusted ratings and comments are collected and communicated to the respective managers. The ratings are usually entered into the system by the manager and audited by HR. This distributes the work and also makes sure that the manager is aware of any changes that were decided on during the review committee.

3.9 Communicating the Employee Evaluation

The last step in the process is for the manager to deliver the assessment of the employee's performance. At this stage, the manager has gathered all the necessary information and prepares to deliver the final assessment and, more importantly, the employee's final performance rating.

Managers should prepare for delivering the results by doing the following:

► Schedule a meeting with the employee, and select a private location without any distractions.
► Ask the employee to consider areas for development and possible activities that could contribute to the development plan.

> **Managers should prepare for delivering the results by doing the following:**
>
> ► Review any guidelines provided by the organizations on effectively delivering feedback.
> ► Gather past performance evaluations and other supporting documentation to respond to specific questions the employee may have.

The meeting with the employee can be fairly positive unless the manager is delivering tough messages to an employee that has not met his objectives or is a poor performer overall. These meetings tend to be very emotional because employees may feel like they should be ranked higher and/or compare themselves to others.

To maximize the effectiveness of the meeting, managers should focus on key messages, talk objectively about past performance, and use specific examples that the employee can relate to. Messages to the employee should be delivered in a positive manner and be followed by constructive ways the employee can improve his performance.

Managers should also listen to the employee and encourage feedback to better understand how the employee views the results of the evaluation.

3.9.1   Signing Off the Final Evaluation

Depending on the system, the process is completed by the manager and employee signing off the final evaluation. Systems such as SAP Performance Management enable the manager to release the evaluation to the employee for one final review where the employee can sign off and provide comments stating that he agrees with the overall evaluation.

3.10   Summary

In this chapter we reviewed the components of the performance management process. When looking at your existing process or designing a new process for your organization, it is helpful to look at each step in the process as it relates to the stages of planning, acting, managing, and reviewing. Breaking the process steps down by stages and mapping them into swim lanes will provide you with a clear view of what each actor is responsible for in the process.

It is also important to consider that not every part of the process is required. For example, your organization may not require 360 degree evaluations or extensive review committees to calibrate ratings. The components of the performance management process are flexible and can be used to design a process that suits your organization.

In the next chapter we will expand on the process of setting the corporate strategy. The corporate strategy defines the goals of the organization and effectively aligns and positions the organization to achieve and sustain success.

Managing by objectives has long been regarded as the best approach for executing the goals of a department and subsequently the company. These objectives begin at the top with the corporate strategy. In this chapter we will explore goal setting, objective setting, and how to communicate strategies effectively.

4   Setting the Corporate Strategy

Setting a corporate strategy is one of the most important enablers of a successful company. Achieving and sustaining success in today's competitive business environment requires that companies have the right business model and support it by setting strategies that effectively use the company's available resources to deliver along its business model.

Management strives to be the best in their industry by driving innovation and efficiencies in every aspect of their business, such as marketing, product development, and supply chain. To do this, management must understand its business model and have a clear understanding of what makes them different and what gives it the competitive edge over the competition, both foreign and domestic. After management has an understanding of the internal and external business landscape and has completed quantitative analysis, they can set a corporate strategy to drive toward its goals.

Before linking the corporate strategy to the performance management process, you must first understand some of the pitfalls that companies hit when setting strategies and goals. Since the emergence of *corporate strategies* in the 1960s, the term has been used so often that it has lost some of its meaning. Many corporate strategies read more like aspirations than strategies. Management makes goal statements versus setting a true corporate strategy that is based on quantitative analysis. Many managers also view the corporate strategy as a tool that is owned by senior management.

The performance management process can be used as a key link to the corporate strategy and can help solve some of the problems related to how companies drive this strategy throughout the organization. The performance management process can be used to drive a performance-based culture, but more importantly, it can drive the organization to move in the same direction.

Leaders set the company's goals in a plan that incorporates the various business verticals, communicate it with employees, and rally the company to align and achieve the goals.

Surprisingly, many companies do not do a good job creating the corporate strategy and subsequently the corporate goals. They fail to make the corporate goals understandable and applicable to the business or simply fail to communicate the strategy to the organization. Another challenge is that companies do not follow a standard process for performance management and driving corporate strategy through goals and objectives.

Without a corporate strategy and a set of corporate goals, executives and managers alike do not have a direction for which to develop and align departmental strategies that will ultimately help the company meet its goals. The effectiveness of the performance management process is reduced as employees and managers find it difficult to set meaningful goals and objectives that they can be measured by.

In this chapter, we break down the components of a corporate strategy as it relates to the performance management process, and discuss the elements that go into it and some of the difficulties companies face in reaching their goals while maintaining alignment with their corporate strategy.

4.1   Developing the Strategic Plan

A corporate strategy can tell you a lot about the company's current outlook and maturity level. Some companies are gearing toward growth, others are focused on stabilizing current operations and reducing expenses, and still others are changing direction altogether as they chart a new course for their companies.

Companies approach the process of setting the corporate strategy in different ways, but the outcome is fairly similar in that a corporate plan is created and disseminated throughout the organization. The plan most often consists of one or more goals from each business vertical, and it outlines the company's stated direction for the upcoming year. Some companies choose to create a new plan each year, whereas other more mature companies create plans that span from three to five years into the future.

Whatever the approach, the following standard guidelines should be applied.

> **The Plan:**
>
> 1. Should embody the key business verticals that will make the strategy successful
> 2. Should be clear and concise
> 3. Should take into account the corporate values
> 4. Should be understood by every employee in the organization

4.1.1 The Process for Creating the Plan

Companies take different approaches when creating the plan but in essence follow the same basic process:

- Establish a set of high-level goals for the organization.
- Cascade the goals to lower levels of the organization.
- Support the goals with specific objectives and action plans.
- Define key results and performance indicators that will be used to measure the success of the overall plan.
- Monitor the plan at all levels to track its status.

> **Note**
>
> In many larger companies, senior executives often choose to have a working session that is designed to produce a set of goals for the organization. Other companies may be managed from the top down and have a set of *drivers* sometimes referred to as *pillars*.

4.1.2 Use of Pillars to Enhance Alignment

A *driver* or *pillar* is a distinct component of a strategy that serves as a foundation. Many companies set the foundation for the strategy prior to setting goals and then map each goal to a pillar. In essence, the pillar serves as a bucket in which senior level executives can align the corporate goals.

Let's look at an example case where pillars can be very effective:

> **Scenario**
>
> A new CEO has been brought in to drive new organizational efficiencies, reduce costs, get the company back to profitability, and prepare for an initial public offering. The CEO gathers his team of high-level executives and outlines the four pillars of his plan.

Scenario (Cont.)

1. Grow Profitably
2. Fund Our Future
3. Inspire Our Customers
4. Work Together

The CEO provides high-level guidelines for each of the pillars (as shown in Table 4.1).

Grow Profitably	Increase profit margins per outlet, outsource noncore functions, create zero growth in overhead.
Fund Our Future	Restore the health of our channel. Support store operators that are unable to meet quality and key operating metrics.
Inspire Our Customers	Create products that our customers love, and drive our sales growth until we surpass the competition.
Work Together	Create an environment where people can team up to achieve excellence, and where we can encourage and develop our employees to be results oriented.

Table 4.1 High-level Guidelines for Each Pillar

The CEO then starts to work with his key senior executives to lay out the goals for each of the pillars. They tackle each of the business verticals and align goals to each pillar.

As you can see, the pillars are the foundation for the plan and can easily be communicated to the organization.

When the plan is completed, it will serve as the basis for the overall alignment of the organization. The goals contained in the plan will be used to complete the corporate strategy by allowing executives and managers to align their departmental goals to the goals contained in the plan.

4.2   Goals and Objectives

You can see from the previous section that the corporate strategy is defined in a plan that contains goals and possibly pillars. To achieve the goals, the organization needs to gain commitment and have employees and managers set objectives that align with those goals.

4.2.1 Goals versus Objectives

We need to take a moment and discuss these key elements. Goals and objectives are often confused to be one and the same. People often refer to an objective as a goal and provide a goal when an objective is required. This confusion is what makes management by objectives (MBO) difficult, and it often leads to the process of evaluating performance more subjectively than it should be.

A *goal* is simply an outcome statement that clearly defines what an organization is trying to accomplish. Goals must be at a high enough level that a set of actions can be put in place to achieve them.

An *objective* is what your actions or intentions will accomplish. It is a very specific statement that can be measured to determine how well the objective was accomplished.

Many companies label objectives as SMART. SMART is an acronym that is often used to guide you in setting a good objective. Familiarizing employees with the acronym is a great way to introduce the concept of setting objectives.

SMART stands for the following:

▶ **Specific**
Objectives need to specify what you want to achieve.

▶ **Measurable**
You should be able to measure your progress against the objective.

▶ **Achievable**
Objectives need to be achievable, something that can be attained.

▶ **Realistic**
You should have an influence on achieving the objective.

▶ **Time Based**
You need to know when the objective will be achieved or realized.

Let's set an example objective using these guidelines:

Increase sales of widgets in North America by 20% by the third quarter of 2007 by adding five distributors to our distribution channel and increasing channel incentives by 10%.

The simple objective is Specific and is both Measurable and Time Based as it outlines a detailed objective with a specific time frame in which it needs to be accomplished. What we cannot tell is whether it is Achievable or Realistic, but a manager should be able to easily determine whether enough resources or time is available as well as whether any obstacles will make this objective unrealistic.

The employee who is committing to this objective should have the capability to control the outcome and be able to source and add distributors to the channel and drive the financial plans needed to approve the increase in incentives.

Table 4.2 provides a comparison of goals versus objectives to make the differences between the two easier to understand.

Goals	Objectives
Broad in nature	Narrow and focused in nature
General intentions that outline direction	Precise and measurable
Intangible	Tangible
Often abstract	Always concrete
Cannot be validated	Can be validated

Table 4.2 Comparing Goals and Objectives

It is very important that managers and employees can differentiate between goals and objectives. This differentiation is important because you do not want very detailed objectives to be introduced in the corporate plan but rather at the individual contributor level. Having a precise objective in the corporate strategy makes it difficult to cascade that throughout the organization and does not resonate across the different verticals of the organization.

> **Note**
>
> We are not suggesting that targets cannot be set to better define a goal. For example, "increase store growth by 20% globally" is an acceptable goal. Even though the goal is somewhat measurable and can be validated, it is still broad in nature. It does not suggest how to accomplish the goal and leaves it to the various business verticals to put in place a strategy to achieve the goal.

4.3 Cascading Goals

Cascading goals is the next step in further defining the corporate strategy. The goals of the company are pushed down to the organization and adapted by each manager so that objectives can be defined and aligned. This approach positions the organization to execute against the plan.

The process of cascading goals is fairly simple in theory. The process starts with senior level management defining goals for their organization and continues with each subordinate manager creating his goals based on his manager's goals. As the goals are applied in each department, they become less broad in nature and relate specifically to what that department will do to focus on helping achieve the overall corporate goals.

This process is important because it drives the corporate strategy throughout the organization and makes it relevant to each business vertical. It also creates the foundation on which employees will base their objectives.

Although the process is simple to understand, it is fairly difficult for companies to implement. The first major challenge is getting the goals to propagate the organization in a hierarchical fashion. It is easier and more effective if managers can base their goals on those set by their manager versus having to directly interpret the overall corporate goals. Getting managers to complete goals and allowing them to cascade throughout the organization has proven to be a difficult process for several reasons. Table 4.3 lists some of the most common reasons for the ineffectiveness of this process and steps that have been taken to mitigate the problem.

Issue	Suggested Approach
Corporate goals are not available or set early enough in the process. Many companies fail to set or communicate the corporate goals early enough in the process, making it difficult for managers to set their goals.	Companies should set and communicate goals at least three weeks prior to requiring managers to start the process. Communication is the key. If the process and timelines are not communicated well, the remaining parts of the process will be negatively impacted.
Lack of communication and top-down support of the process.	This process is fairly difficult to execute without holding managers accountable. The process is effective if it is supported by senior management and encouraged at key meetings. This emphasizes the importance of the process and makes it clear to all management levels that the company is holding them accountable to complete it.

Table 4.3 Most Common Reasons Cascading Goals are Not Effective

Issue	Suggested Approach
Lack of monitoring for the process.	Monitoring which organizations have not complied and presenting that information in a scorecard is one of the best ways to make this process effective. Dramatic improvements are made when managers know they are being measured, and senior managers are held accountable against their individual scorecard.
Lack of training.	It is one thing to get the process completed and yet another to get quality results. Managers struggle with structuring goals for their organization and following the guidelines. It is essential to provide some training either online or in small classrooms. Training the managers to use the process and define goals contributes to the overall success of the planning process.
Difficult to use application and tools.	Many performance management applications are not intuitive and often have a complex set of statuses that the user needs to understand. Simplification needs to be a guiding principle and the availability of an overall process view that the users can refer to when they have questions about the process and timeline.

Table 4.3 Most Common Reasons Cascading Goals are Not Effective (Cont.)

Refining the goals as they are adapted at each level of the organization is fundamental to getting the alignment and commitment from managers and employees. As employees set objectives, they can align to relevant goals that provide a clearer picture of how they fit into the organization and the definition of success within their respective department.

4.3.1 Alternative Approaches to Setting and Cascading Goals

Organizations can vary in structure and function, which requires a special process for setting and disseminating goals. It is very important to recognize parts of the organization, especially when they are larger in size and perform the same function, which results in most people having the same goals.

One example can be found in a call center where most of the employees share the same goals in handling calls and customer satisfaction levels. In this case, it may be preferable to have all the goals and possibly the objectives pre-assigned and communicated rather than having each employee enter them individually.

Some organizations also define a required goal and objective. An example of this is an organization that predefines that all managers have one objective dedicated to the management of employees in their department. This type of objective is usually distributed as a boilerplate, and managers can modify it as needed. The intent of these predetermined objectives is to standardize the evaluation process and ensure that the values of the organization are demonstrated by requiring a specific objective as a measurement of success.

4.4   Becoming Tactical Through Objective Setting

After the goals of the organization are in place, employees and managers can begin to set their individual objectives. These objectives embody the commitment to the organization, describe what the employee will do to achieve the department and company goals, and describe how the employee will do it.

This part of the planning process is the most critical as it puts the goals of the organization into very specific objectives that will be monitored throughout the remainder of the year. Failure to achieve these objectives often comes with a penalty to the organization and thus impacts the overall performance.

The process for setting the objectives starts with the employee and ends with the common understanding between employee and manager of what the objectives are, when they should be accomplished, and how much weight each carries.

4.4.1   Setting Individual Objectives

This process can begin with the employee drafting his objectives prior to or while meeting with his manager and finally both parties agreeing on these objectives prior to entering them into a system (see Figure 4.1). Managers often prefer to handle this process in different ways according to their management style, corporate culture, and work environment. Most organizations provide a guideline but leave it to the manager to determine what works for their department.

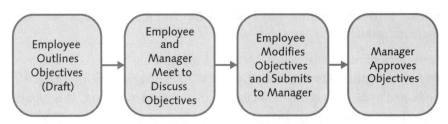

Figure 4.1 High-Level Process for Setting and Confirming Individual Objectives

The key step in the process is to make sure that meaningful dialog happens between the employee and the manager. It is essential that the employee understands and agrees to the objectives as well as the weightings that have been assigned. Both parties need to leave the meeting with a common understanding and a commitment to one another as well as the organization that they will achieve the objectives.

Managers must drive the meeting to accomplish the following objectives:

▸ Establish the objectives the employee is measured on.

▸ Identify the key responsibilities the employee will have during this evaluation period.

▸ Align the objectives to the department goals, the corporate goals, or both.

▸ Determine what development gaps exist that will prevent the employee from achieving the objectives.

▸ Identify key skills that will be needed to successfully achieve the objectives.

▸ Weight the objectives according to complexity and importance to the organization.

4.4.2 Submitting the Objectives for Approval

After the manager and the employee have concluded the meeting to review objectives, the employee goes back and modifies the objectives based on his understanding from the meeting.

The employee can take this time to internalize what was discussed and formulate a plan for achieving the objectives.

After all the details of the objectives are complete, the employee can enter the objectives into the system. The employee then submits the objectives to the manager, in essence, signing off on the commitment that they have made to the department and the company that they will achieve the objectives.

4.4.3 Reviewing and Approving the Objectives

The manager is the final approver on the individual objectives that an employee has set. The manager then reviews the objectives that have been submitted by the employee and confirms that the required objectives, guidance, and weightings are correct.

After the objectives have been reviewed and approved, they are officially on record and represent the commitment that the employee and the manager have made to the organization. The employee is committing to achieve the stated objectives, and the manager is committing to support and develop the employee to ensure that the objectives are achieved.

Once the objectives are approved, the planning phase of the performance management process is complete. The remainder of the process is dedicated to monitoring and managing the execution of the objectives and desired results.

4.5 Communicating Strategy

Communication is the key to the successful adoption of the strategy. Employees and managers alike cannot commit to a plan that they have not heard about or are unclear about the details.

Although leaders attempt to communicate by setting the goals and priorities, they fail to understand that the words and phrases that make up the goals may have little meaning to employees. To be effective, leaders at various levels must communicate the strategy at various points in the planning phase by translating goals into actions and priorities.

4.5.1 Components of the Communication

Essentially, managers must provide a high-level overview of the strategy and what the company is willing to trade off to achieve the overall objectives. Many managers fail to outline what takes precedence, resulting in ambiguity and ineffectiveness when tough decisions need to be made. Employees will commit to a plan that is not fully defined as long as they can hear clear messages about what the company wants to achieve and what it is willing to give up to do it.

Employees also need to understand who is going to be accountable for the overall success of the plan and why this plan is being put into place.

Most important, the communication has to serve as the foundation for action. Employees will be able to act if they understand the message and have a macro-level view of the direction with clear directives.

4.5.2 Effective Communication Techniques

One of the most effective techniques for communicating a strategy is to focus on a few of the key messages that are clearly linked to the success of the organization. Employees can clearly understand the message and how the subject matter relates to the success of the organization.

When delivering the communication, leaders need to actively listen for any obstacles that could cause the strategy to fail as well as any potential misunderstandings.

Leaders should translate the key messages into something meaningful to the employee by focusing on actions and priorities versus a broad goal that can be misinterpreted.

4.5.3 Reinforcing the Strategy

Reinforcing the strategy through various methods encourages employees to remain committed. Employees are more likely to stay engaged and remember the strategy if the key messages are repeated and made relevant.

Leaders are more effective if they can continue to deliver consistent messages repeatedly through various channels. Repeated delivery of key messages allows the employee to commit them to memory and reinforces the importance of the strategy.

Use of channels such as corporate portals and official communications greatly influence how messages are interpreted and allow leaders to gain a wider acceptance.

4.6 Summary

In this chapter we have expanded the process of defining the corporate strategy as it relates to the performance management process. Each company will approach the definition of the corporate goals differently, making it difficult to automate, however the outcome should be the same with the plan (strategy) and goals being set and communicated throughout the organization.

Without a documented plan, the organization will not be aligned to common goals and will most likely set objectives that will not contribute to the company's success.

We have also defined goals and objectives and how to use them effectively to measure employee performance. Many organizations use these terms interchangeably or simply rely on defining a set of objectives. Both approaches can be effective as long as employees set SMART objectives.

Companies need to move beyond human resources and toward human capital. People are assets that must be valued, measured, and developed. A key to retaining employees is to provide solid development plans for them. In this chapter we will explore Development Planning, and the use of Skills and Competency Models.

5 Development Planning

Developing employees is a key component of performance management and contributes to the success of your organization. People are the most valuable asset in an organization, and managing their development is a strategic way to increase employee performance and help employees gain the key skills and knowledge they need to execute their key objectives.

The individual development plan focuses on the growth of the employee and is constructed to manage the development of new knowledge, skills, and improved behaviors. Executing the development plan should result in the improvement of the employees' job performance and their ability to execute against the objectives they have set.

5.1 Individual Development Plans

Individual development plans focus on the importance of personal growth by defining what areas the individual employee must improve and allowing both the manager and employee to monitor and manage the execution of the development plan.

5.1.1 What Is an Individual Development Plan?

The individual development plan provides a planning process that captures both professional development and career aspirations. The plan is typically in the form of an online tool that employees must complete and submit to their manager. The development plan helps employees understand what skills they want to develop or improve, how they intend to develop the skills, and in what timeframe.

5.1.2 Purpose and Benefits of Individual Development Plans

The purpose of conducting the development planning process is to aid in aligning the employee training and development with the goals and objectives of the organization. We have stated in this chapter that employees are the most important assets, and therefore developing employees is the key to achieving the goals of the department as well as achieving and sustaining a competitive advantage.

Additionally, managers working with employees develop a better understanding of their employees' goals, strengths, and areas that need development. The process also positions employees to take personal responsibility for their career development, and managers to assist and guide employees in acquiring or enhancing the skills and knowledge they need to achieve their goals.

5.1.3 Roles and Responsibilities

The development planning process is a collaborative one whereby employees and managers work together to complete the development plan. After the development plan is completed, employees are responsible for their development and related training needed to acquire new skills or enhance existing skills and knowledge.

Employees play a major role in the development process and are mainly responsible for the following objectives:

► Conduct an assessment of their current level of competency versus the competency required to effectively perform their job.

► Identify future career goals and the required development needed to achieve the career goals.

► Review how their development is progressing based on their development plan and stated goals.

Managers support the employee in the development process and are responsible for the following objectives:

► Conduct employee assessments to understand the strengths of their team and the development needs based on the requirements of the organization.

► Align employee's career goals and development to the goals and objectives of the department.

▸ Provide employees with regular coaching and guidance to achieve career goals and obtain new skills or improve existing skills.

▸ Monitor the progress that employees are making against the development plan.

5.2 Components of an Individual Development Plan

Development plans can vary from one organization to another. Some organizations require that the employee maintain the development plan, whereas others make the process optional and leave it to the employee and manager to decide if a development plan is needed. Although development plans differ from one organization to another, they attempt to capture the following information:

▸ The career goals that the employee wants to accomplish

▸ The skills and knowledge the employee wants to learn in support of their career goals

▸ How the employee is going to acquire the skills and knowledge

▸ The resources that the employee will require to achieve the goals

▸ The date that the employee will begin to work on achieving the goal and target date for completion

The forms usually contain the employee profile with name, current position, position history, and previous year's appraisal ratings. This additional information provides the manager with a complete snapshot of the employee and allows the manager to better understand the employee's development needs.

5.2.1 Sections of the Development Plan

Typically, development plans are broken out in sections. The following list represents commonly used sections in development plans:

▸ The goals section allows the employee to input short-, medium-, and long-term career goals.

▸ The skills and knowledge section allows the employee to input the skills he needs to develop and the knowledge he needs to acquire.

▶ The approach section allows the employee to list the actions and steps that he will take to execute the development plan.

▶ The resources and opportunities section allows the employee to specify what opportunities he needs to develop his career as well as the resources that he requires.

Due to the importance of the development plan to the organization, it is fairly typical to have employees and managers sign the development plan to signify that they both agree to commit to the development objectives listed in the plan.

5.3   Development Planning Process

The individual development planning process is a collaborative process that is executed in an iterative approach. Employees and managers must maintain constant communication for the process to be effective (see Figure 5.1).

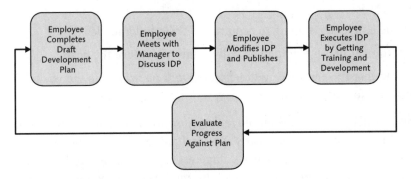

Figure 5.1 Individual Development Plan Process

5.3.1   Completing the Draft Development Plan

Employees begin the process by drafting the development plan. It is essential that the employees assess their development needs and career aspirations prior to meeting with their manager. To facilitate the creation of the development plan, employees should ask themselves the following questions:

▶ What are my career goals and aspirations?

▶ What skills do I need to develop?

▶ What direction is my department going in, and what skills do I need to achieve my objectives?

▶ What areas do I need to improve, and how do I go about it?

Managers should also participate in this step of the process by reviewing each of their employees and understanding their strengths and weaknesses. They should align the development for each employee with the goals of the department and take into consideration the next position the employee will progress to.

5.3.2 Employee and Manager Review

After the draft plan is completed, the manager and employee can set up a meeting to discuss the development plan. The manager can start by reviewing the draft that the employee has prepared and focusing on the key elements.

The first area of focus should be the goals of the employee. Depending on the form that is used, employees are usually prompted to address goals in the short-term (within the next year), mid-term (within one to two years), and long-term (within two to three years). The employees goals are important to the overall development plan and help the manager better understand how the employee views his professional career.

The second area of focus should be the skills and knowledge the employee has highlighted for development. The skills should align with the objectives that the employee has set, the goals of the department, and the job requirements. Employees should have the necessary skills and knowledge that is required for their job and should develop the skills needed for the future position.

The third and last areas are the resources needed to achieve the goals as well as the next steps. Managers should pay close attention to the resources the employee is requesting and make sure they are realistic. Additionally, the next steps, which usually outline opportunities and learning that needs to take place, should be realistic and within budget. Employees may specify training that is outside the budget of the department, making it difficult to develop the needed skills. Managers need to coordinate what is possible based on budget and department needs.

5.3.3 Prepare the Development Plan

At the conclusion of the meeting with their manager, employees can use the input from the discussion with their manager to complete the development plan and submit it for sign-off.

Employees need to be encouraged to think through the development planning process and recognize that achieving their career goals and development is their responsibility.

5.3.4 Execute the Development Plan

The completed development plan provides the employees a framework with which they can begin to develop the skills that have been identified. Employees can view the development plan in conjunction with the objectives they have set and identify how to approach their development.

Attending training classes is the most common approach for obtaining new skills and knowledge; however, many development plans are oriented toward opportunity. Employees seek to learn how to lead others or understand different parts of the business. This development is much harder to achieve because it relies on the availability of opportunities that might not present themselves. This is precisely the point where the employee and the manager need to collaborate to create the opportunities that the employee needs for development.

5.3.5 Evaluate Progress of the Development Plan

Managers must take an active part in monitoring progress against the development plan. As stated before, managers play a key role in the development of employees. This is *one* of the most important, if not *the* most important, goals of the manager.

Managers need to set up periodic reviews with the employee to track the progress. In these review meetings, managers can coach the employee on how to develop the skills and discuss what areas still need improvement. This is especially the case when it involves leading others or taking on a new area of the business. Employees may get overwhelmed with the effort needed to achieve new skills and may not realize that the lack of performance can have a direct impact on the performance of the department.

Development plans can also be refined based on these meetings, and employees and managers should maintain a record of how they are progressing.

5.4 Using Skills and Competency Models

The use of skills and competency models is starting to gain popularity mainly because of the capability of human resource information systems such as SAP HR. These systems make it possible to maintain detailed skills and competency models that describe the competencies needed to do a particular job.

5.4.1 Competency Catalog

Skills and competencies are usually compiled into a catalog and put into logical groupings that make it easier to locate and identify the area that they relate to.

The catalog is usually structured in a hierarchy with each level comprising a category and containing skills and competencies. The catalog is made available to HR professionals and exposed to employees through the performance management process.

5.4.2 Structure of a Competency Model

A skills and competency model is structured around the main organizational entities such as job, position, and person.

At a high level, *jobs* provide a generic description and high-level skills and competencies that are required. The *position* is a more detailed instance of the job and contains additional skills and competencies that refine what the job does. Each of these assignments carries a rating on the minimum required to hold the position or the job.

> **Example**
>
> An example of this is a software development job. The job titled "Software Engineer" has competencies such as communication, problem solving, and so on. The position titled "Java Developer" has additional competencies and specific skills such as Java Language, Java Patterns, and so on.

The employee, on the other hand, is assigned a set of skills and competencies and a rating depicting how well he has mastered the respective skills and competencies.

Figure 5.2 shows the relationships between skills and competencies and the respective entity. These relationships can evolve over time, but the general requirements should stay constant.

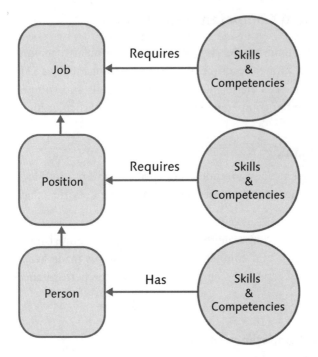

Figure 5.2 Relationships Between Skills and Competencies, and Job, Position, and Person

5.4.3 Using Skills and Competency Models

After a skill and competency model is in place, it becomes a powerful tool enabling the manager to run reports that show how qualified an employee is to hold his current or future position.

The process compares the skills and the competencies that an employee has with the minimum required by the job and positions and highlights the areas the employee needs to develop.

Matching the gaps in skills and competencies gives the employee and manager the ability to structure the development plan and create opportunities that help the employee develop his career and performance in his job.

5.5 Summary

In this chapter we learned how training and developing individuals is an essential part of achieving the goals of the department and subsequently the company. Every day that an employee comes to work is an opportunity for new skill development and professional improvement.

Development plans can be initiated at any point in the year, and managers should make it mandatory for employees to complete a development plan as part of the normal course of doing business.

Additionally, development plans can be used to assist employees in reinforcing existing, or acquiring new skills, that will ultimately increase the employee's ability to achieve their objectives and overall performance.

In the next chapter we will cover the lessons learned from various projects in which the Performance Management module was implemented, either independently or as part of a larger SAP HR implementation.

If you approach things the way you have always approached them, you will always end up with the same results. But if you learn from your experiences and apply what you learn to your own projects, you can end up with much better results. In this chapter we will explore some real-world lessons learned from a variety of implementations.

6   Lessons Learned

This chapter presents a summary of the lessons learned from various projects that have implemented the Performance Management module either independently or as part of a larger SAP HR implementation. We have selected lessons learned that have applied across more than one implementation. Although not all project circumstances are the same, we can draw many parallels from one engagement to the next.

The lessons learned are organized by topic, including the following topics:

- Performance Management Process, including goal setting, objective setting
- Development Planning
- Change Management
- System Implementation

This should not be seen as a comprehensive list of "gotchas." The lessons learned should be understood and related in the context of your own implementation. Depending on your organization's size, culture, and global reach, some lessons learned will mean more to you than others.

6.1   Performance Management Process

Performance management has been around for more than five decades with the process evolving over the years. Companies choose to implement the process differently, but many of the core concepts and approaches remain the same. An effective performance management process relies on more than the implementation of a system; rather, it needs a holistic mix of a rich system implementation, simple processes, communication, and accountability at all levels.

6.1.1 Overall Performance Management Process

In this section we outline some key factors to consider when implementing a performance management process.

Implement a process (automated or manual) to handle changes in organizational assignments.

Performance management is a long-running process that usually spans the calendar or fiscal year and is dependent on the relationship between manager and employee as well as employee and job. In the normal course of business, employees change managers, jobs, or both, which requires them to change objectives and development plan priorities. Additionally, new employees are hired into the company, requiring them to set objectives.

Typically, performance management forms are not available for input unless the process is open for a particular cycle. This makes sense for employees that have signed off on their objectives but creates an exception for employees that are hired into the company.

It is recommended to have an automated or manual process that is triggered by changes in manager, position, or employment status. The trigger can set the form to a particular status that gives the employee access to make the necessary changes.

Create a scorecard for managers to track progress and compliance across their organization.

The performance management process requires a high degree of compliance to be effective. Holding employees and managers accountable at all levels is the best way to achieve compliance. Senior leadership must enforce the message that everyone is accountable. HR may want to provide an application that serves as a scorecard showing compliance levels for each part of the process.

We have found that managers take action more rapidly when they can quickly see where they are in the process. Web-based applications, such as a portal or Business Intelligence (BI) solution, can give managers views at-a-glance. Additionally, the scorecard relieves HR from having to perform administrative follow-up on the process, such as tracking down who has not completed forms or running compliance reports.

Keep the process and forms simple.

Often, the process gets overcomplicated during the blueprinting phase of the project, making it difficult to implement and subsequently not easy to use by participants in the process. You should be able to explain the process in a clear and concise manner. If your mapped out processes continue to cross swim lanes, you may have overcomplicated the process.

Teach employees and managers how to give and receive feedback.

The system has little influence on the overall success of performance management if the culture is not conducive to giving and receiving feedback. Although it sounds like a fairytale that such a culture can exist, we have been shocked with departments that are closed and avoid constructive feedback.

The system and processes cannot enforce an open behavior. This is a key area where management and HR can be engaged to change the culture so that it encourages feedback. HR should also provide ample information and education on how best to share feedback. The material should be separated and directly related to employees and managers because they play different roles when providing feedback.

From a legal perspective, it is also important that managers are assessing their direct reports on the right criteria. Feedback such as "Tom is a great resource, despite his young age" and "Barbara is just like 'one of the guys'" is not appropriate in a performance evaluation and, if taken the wrong way, can lead to a lawsuit. It is smart, then, to provide reminders to managers on what is business appropriate and what is not within a review.

6.1.2   Goal Setting

This is a key part of the performance management process that starts at the top.

Goal Setting should start at the top of the organization.

Goals need to cascade from the very top of the organization. Individual objectives cannot link to a corporate strategy if corporate and department goals have not been cascaded.

The senior leaders of your organization must be engaged to create their department goals. The strategic vision of the company must be made apparent to line managers and rank-in-file employees. Without cascaded goals, the vision will not be executed successfully.

Associate goals to a "pillar."

Goals are frequently associated to a pillar. A *pillar* is a theme that describes and drives the corporate strategy.

Example pillars include:
1. Grow Profitably
2. Put Our Customers First
3. Become a Marketplace Leader
4. Develop Our Employees

Typically, pillars are assigned when the goals are created. Companies commonly change or tweak their pillars from year to year as business changes. However, these themes should be general enough so that a core set does not change. Most companies are fine with three or four pillars to support their strategic goals.

6.1.3 Objective Setting

Objective setting is an effective tool for evaluating performance.

Automate the pre-population of objectives and generate forms.

In many organizations, subsets of employees do the same job and are required to self-evaluate against a predefined set of objectives. Examples include call center employees, sales representatives, administrative assistants, and aircraft pilots. These jobs are very different, but the employees are all measured the same at the end of the year.

An effective way to address jobs that are ultimately measured the same is to automate the process and use a template set of objectives. Representatives from HR can create a set of predetermined objectives and assign them to employees that hold a specific job. This process eliminates the need for these large groups of employees to set objectives that have already been determined by HR or senior management. Using an automated approach reduces the overall effort by eliminating the creation step and requires that employees be responsible for only completing the self-assessment later in the cycle.

Using this approach should not remove the need for employees and managers to meet and discuss the objectives. We have seen this approach limit those discussions because everyone is expected to already understand the objectives. We recommend that the meetings continue to be scheduled and that HR reinforces the need for these meetings to occur.

Automate objective setting forms for employees for the given period.

The manual creation of objective setting forms is generally a simple task requiring the employee to select the period he will be evaluated on and the manager that will conduct the evaluation. Although the process is simple, we have found that automating the generation of forms streamlines the process, provides for a better user experience, and reduces room for error.

The practice can be further streamlined by sending an email to the employee when the form is generated to inform the employee that the process has started with related information and a link to access the form. Form automation at the outset of the process has become popular due to its savings in cost and time.

6.1.4 Mid-Year Review

Mid-year reviews are an important way to confirm that employees and managers understand their objectives and to evaluate performance.

Make the mid-year review a formal process that does not require ratings.

The mid-year review should be a formal process but should not focus on rating the employee. The mid-year review could be a time when both the employee and manager meet informally to discuss the employee's progress against the objectives. Objectives can be refined and comments entered, but assigning ratings at this point in the process is typically not recommended. Managers should focus on coaching and monitoring the employee while continuing to encourage him to achieve the objectives.

The mid-year review is also an opportunity to review the development plan or create one if it has not been developed yet. Managers can identify whether the employee needs to develop additional skills to perform his job function successfully. It is also a good opportunity to review the training plan. External and internal training courses may have been cancelled or postponed, or the employee or manager may want to change the training for something more pertinent to their current job duties.

6.1.5 Self-Assessment

The self-assessment part of the process is important in helping employees learn to evaluate themselves objectively based on their defined goals and objectives.

Allow the employee to evaluate himself on the self-assessment without requiring a self-rating.

Allowing employees to self-rate themselves can potentially cause unnecessary friction between the employee and the manager. Self-evaluations should allow the employee to reflect on how he achieved or fell short on achieving objectives. Asking the employees to rate themselves places an extra burden on the process as the conversation could easily turn into a numbers discussion instead of a performance discussion.

6.1.6 Final Evaluation

Performing the final process is the culminating point of the entire process, and it is essential that it be conducted according to the implementation plan.

Enforce the final evaluation process to ensure it is conducted in a fair and open manner.

We cannot stress enough how important it is to make sure the final evaluation process is conducted in a fair and open manner, especially if the performance management process is being introduced to the organization for the first time. When trying to implement a performance-based culture, expect many complaints from managers who feel like they have been forced to use the process and employees who feel like they are subjected to being ranked unfairly.

The process needs to be enforced at every level, and review committees should be created to calibrate ratings. These review committees should be facilitated by HR or a third party. Close attention should be given to any type of deals that managers have made to support certain employees. HR must make sure that the process is fair and that messages back to employees are given with clear reasons and in support of the rating that was given.

6.2   Development Planning

Forms needed to complete the development plan should not be complex forms that employees and managers need to spend time filling out; rather the form should be simple and allow the employee to focus on the key areas they want to develop.

The development plan form should be its own document

Although development planning and objective setting can happen at the same time, we recommend not combining the forms. Some companies choose to combine the development plan and objective setting/performance appraisal on the same form, which causes unnecessary complexity in the implementation and makes the process more difficult.

The development plan and objective setting process may not share the same lifecycle, and having them on different forms enables employees and managers to initiate a development plan at any point in the year. Development objectives can be revisited and honed depending on shifting business priorities or employee job changes.

6.3   Change Management

Change management is often overlooked when implementing a new system. However, change management is an essential part of performance management projects because the process affects every employee in the organization and requires a high rate of adoption for the process to be completed successfully.

6.3.1   Adoption and Compliance

Ensuring that everyone learns and understands the process is essential to its effectiveness.

Conduct usability labs as early as possible with a representative set of users

This process is definitely not one of the most popular ones, and employees tend to leave setting objectives, self-evaluations, and mid-year reviews until the last minute. The result is that managers have to complete a large amount of evaluations at once and usually in a short time.

Having the best user experience possible and an intuitive flow for accessing the forms helps both employees and managers complete the process with less effort and frustration.

During the realization phase of the project, find a point where the forms are working as expected (or close to as expected), and create a user group that can test the application. Have individual sessions where you provide the users with a scenario, and ask them to complete that part of the process. Do not provide them with any instruction on how to complete the appraisal document, but do observe where they get stuck. When users are at a dead end and can no longer navigate, ask them to explain what does not make sense on the screen and what they would expect in order to continue.

After all the users have completed the usability lab, collect the results, and isolate the common issues. It is best to address these issues before rolling out the process to get the maximum acceptance and adoption of the new solution.

6.3.2 Communication

Effective communication is very important to the successful implementation of your performance management process.

Limit the number of automated emails that are generated from the system.

Automated communications can sound like a great idea during blueprinting, but we advise that email automation be kept to a minimum. Emails work well to kick off the process but can become overwhelming if they are used to notify employees and managers of every change in the state of the form.

At the end of the blueprinting phase, it is important to review the various notifications and communications that employees and managers will receive to make sure they will not be overwhelmed. Look at alternatives such as portal work items or manage notification in bulk centrally from HR.

6.3.3 Stakeholder Management

Stakeholders are a valuable part of the performance review process, but it is critical that they be managed well.

Form a steering committee to review project progress and resolve project-level issues.

A steering committee should be formed during the project to review project status and advise on any outstanding issues.

Typically, the committee is comprised of senior level management and other key stakeholders of the process. The project sponsor or his representative is usually on the committee as well.

A steering committee also can exist after go-live by advising on more operational issues or future enhancements and projects.

Review any changes in forms or process with affected business units and functions.

Nothing should be done in a vacuum, especially when it impacts the entire organization. Redesigning forms should prompt the review from other areas in the company that may have dependencies or comments about how the form will impact their areas.

We have seen organizations complete the blueprint and delay the project because they could not get the required sign-offs when other functions did not agree with the redesigned form.

Additionally, we believe that the learning and development (L&D) organization should at a minimum review the process and the forms. A better approach is to have an L&D team member directly assigned to the project, especially if the development planning process is being revisited or changed.

Understand the dynamics of different business units and functions within the organization before setting process timelines.

During the blueprint phase, it is not valid to assume that a process timeline will be applicable to everyone in the organization. You must consider that different parts of the organization become resource constrained at different times in the year. The burden of another process at a critical time of the year will surely end up with poor adoption and compliance.

Depending on the industry or business, you may need to design a flexible process that can be open at different times of the year. You can further simplify the system implementation by communicating a set of dates and keeping the system open for a longer period of time.

You could keep the process for objective setting open for four weeks in the system but communicate the deadlines that include the first three weeks to part of the organization and extend it another week for the business unit that requires extra time.

6.4 System Implementation

Performance management systems can be fairly complex to implement. The system must effectively manage the process and secure sensitive information from unauthorized users. Additionally the usability of the application will be very important to the overall acceptance and adoption within the organization.

6.4.1 Security

One of the first steps during implementation is establishing security controls.

Put controls in place to safeguard information during implementation as well as in production.

Do not underestimate the effort of defining and managing security during the implementation. Depending on your requirements, you may need to convert evaluations and ratings from previous years. This data is highly sensitive and should not be used during development or testing. Use only sample data when testing, and assign specific users access when you need to load the data during the cutover.

Limit the number of HR users that have access to the data after the system is in production. Only key HR users should be able to see evaluations and ratings along with the employee and the manager. Managers should only see evaluations and ratings for employees within their span of control.

6.4.2 Access to Forms and Navigation

Allowing users access to forms using an easy navigation system is critical to the success of the process.

Allow for as much real estate as possible for form display.

Depending on your portal configuration, the page that contains a form may have other elements such as menus and/or iViews constraining real estate. When positioning a form in the portal, it should occupy as much of the screen real estate as possible to support adding more reviewers and objectives.

Try to avoid popping up the form as a new screen (pop-up window) because of issues with the browser pop-up blocking and poor user experience. Warning and error messages should be presented in an area that is visible to the end user.

Test your portal solution and appraisal forms with multiple browsers.

With the SAP portal supporting more and more browsers and the trend to allow employees access from home, it becomes critical to test the various browsers during the QA phase of the project.

We have seen many companies set the standard to Internet Explorer 6.x and at the same time communicate that the portal is available over the Internet and can be used from home. This approach helped many users get access to key applications such as benefits enrollment, performance management, and so on but caused the IT department many issues when other browsers such as Firefox were used.

Manage session timeouts to prevent the loss of data.

Evaluation forms can take a fair amount of time to complete as employees consider how to complete the form and may also use an outside editor such as word to write objectives and self-evaluations.

Most implementations implement a timeout when a session is inactive. A common issue that occurs is that the system appears to be inactive as the employee is typing large sections of text causing the system to timeout the session. The employee discovers that the session has timed out as they attempt to commit the changes they have made and subsequently lose all the data they have input into the form. This is very frustrating for users and does not reflect well on the system.

We recommend increasing the session timeout settings or implementing an enhancement that periodically pings the system to prevent it from timing out while the user is working with a form.

6.5   Summary

As we have seen in this chapter, lessons learned in SAP implementations are invaluable to delivering a usable solution with a high rate of adoption. We encourage you to use these lessons and connect with other companies that have implemented the SAP Performance Management solution to gain a better understanding of how you can improve your process and/or system implementation.

From a system implementation perspective, the main objective when implementing performance management is to increase usability, adoption, and compliance. Using lessons learned to avoid issues or implement best practices will ease the transition from a paper based solution or legacy system to your new performance management system.

This chapter concludes Part I of this book. Part I provided you with core concepts in performance management as well as strategic thoughts on how to integrate talent management into your overall strategy effectively. In the chapters of Part II, we will discuss how to turn your business requirements into a solid design, providing you with the information and tools you need to build an efficient process.

PART II
Performance Management:
System Functionality and Implementation

This part of the book reviews the functionality in the SAP HCM Employee Performance Management module. Configuration and development items are also carefully discussed and example scenarios are reviewed.

Implementation of performance management can be a challenge due to the multitude of components involved, including R/3 configuration, Business Add-Ins (BAdIs), and portal integration. This chapter explains how you can maximize the build of your performance management solution by conducting effective blueprint requirement sessions.

7 Laying the Groundwork for Configuration

The systems specialist or business personnel responsible for the configuration of performance management may initially be surprised to find that most of the module's configuration is performed inside one Transaction PHAP_CATALOG. Despite this fact, the Performance Management module configuration is one of the trickiest within the HR module because:

► It requires heavy integration with Personnel Administration and Organizational Management, so having a seasoned HR resource who is knowledgeable of core HR functionality and key data elements is instrumental in understanding the total performance management picture, its capabilities, and its limitations.

► Much of the process will be web-based for most clients, which requires that you have a resource with at least a working knowledge of the SAP NetWeaver Portal. Having a stable portal platform is one of the critical success factors in a performance management implementation.

► Technical knowledge and a solid grasp of the standard Business Add-Ins (BAdIs) is an important part of understanding the extensibility of the tool. Without a clear understanding of these components, configuration of the Performance Management module can be a daunting task.

In Part I you learned the core concepts in performance management along with strategic thoughts on how to integrate talent management into your overall strategy effectively. Beginning with this chapter, we enter into Part II where we will discuss how to turn your business requirements into a solid design. We will also provide you with the information and tools you need to build an efficient process.

7.1 Turning Requirements into Design

Knowing the fundamentals of the SAP Performance Management solution will help shape the design of the "to-be" process. By understanding core concepts inherent within the module, business requirement gathering can be more effective because you can architect a process that both satisfies business needs and stays close to the SAP standard functionality. In the sections that follow, we discuss how to conduct blueprint meetings more effectively.

7.1.1 Conducting Blueprint Sessions

There are several components to a good design of your performance management system. First and foremost is a solid knowledge of the flow of the process. Without a firm understanding of how the process changes hands from start to finish, designing the status flow, pushbuttons, workflow notifications, and other important system activities would be extremely challenging.

As with other projects, much of an implementation's success depends on a solid blueprint. The blueprint holds the design of the new application based on the requirements of the business. You should expect a blueprint to last between six to eight weeks, depending on how many forms are involved, the complexity of each form, and the extent of process reengineering undertaken. The first few weeks of your blueprint should be spent understanding the current or "as-is" process, design, and pain points. Targeting process inefficiencies will go a long way in achieving a successful future, or "to-be" process.

After the as-is processes are firmly understood, the project team should delve into the "to-be" design, which typically covers the following topics:

- To-be process, including the following:
  - Appraisal creation (manual versus automated)
  - Status flow (defines the process exchanges)
  - Part appraiser functionality (if needed)
  - Appraisal maintenance
  - Workflow/notification requirements
- Form design
- Portal integration
- Security

▶ Reporting

▶ Change management impacts, including communications, stakeholder management, and training

When these meetings are completed, it is best to conduct follow-up sessions with the business personnel to confirm that the requirements gathered up to that point are in line with their vision. A playback session should be conducted for the business in which the project team "plays back" the to-be processes.

Tip

Process flows, demos, and screenshots are often used to conduct *storyboards* during these playback sessions. Storyboards provide a pictorial diagram representing how the process will exist in the new world.

Process and system gaps are reviewed and options are presented during the playback session. By the end of the meeting (or meetings, there could be many), the goal is that business personnel will feel that their future state vision has been clearly articulated by the project team. After formal sign-off is secured, the project team can begin the development or build phase of the project.

The following sections highlight information regarding specific areas of the blueprinting. From form design to workflow notification, each design element should be considered with the larger process in mind. Expect that some assumptions and requirements going into the blueprinting may change by the end of your workshops. Compared with other areas in SAP HR, Performance Management is one of those modules where innovation in its design is encouraged and often required. SAP provides many customer enhancements via BAdIs (described in detail in later chapters) where innovative design can be implemented.

7.1.2   Statuses

Form statuses in performance management drive the process. *Statuses*, along with so-called "pushbuttons," allow end users to move the appraisal document along in the overall process. These *pushbuttons* provide the mechanism to change statuses and trigger workflow notifications (from version 4.7, Extension Set 2.0). For example, a user selecting a pushbutton called **Review Objectives** could move the appraisal from status **In Planning** (status 2) to **In Review** (status 3).

SAP provides the statuses listed in Table 7.1. You cannot change these statuses; only rename them if required.

Status	Status Name
1	In Preparation
2	In Planning
3	In Review
4	In Process
5	Complete
6	Approved
7	Closed Approved
8	Rejected
9	Closed Rejected

Table 7.1 Standard Statuses Provided by SAP

Depending on your unique process requirements, you may decide to use these statuses in a different manner than SAP intended. However, we will first review how each status was intended to be used out-of-the-box by SAP. Each status is described with popular uses referenced. The status discussion described here assumes you are implementing an objective setting appraisal. Other types of performance management forms, such as year-end evaluations and 360s (feedback provided by peers, coworkers, and so on in addition to the manager), may differ in the use of a particular status (or may skip a status altogether) depending on the requirements of the process.

The *In Preparation* status (status 1) is used for process initiation. The header of the document (described in detail in the next chapter) is created during this phase. This header, which holds important information such as appraisee, appraiser, and validity dates, can be prepopulated based on customer-defined rules. During the preparation stage, this information can be overridden by an administrator or end user (presumably the appraiser), but, in most cases, the appraisal header is created via a system process.

After the document is prepared, the *In Planning* status (status 2) is reached. In typical objective-setting scenarios, this phase is where the employee or manager sets individual objectives. Appraisees and appraisers enter objectives depending on your process. For most implementations, end users see their appraisal for the first time in this status.

During the *In Review* status (status 3), objectives are formally reviewed by appraisers. Typically, an appraiser reviews objectives for accuracy and completeness (ensuring they are SMART, for example). Reviews can be conducted at several levels of the reporting hierarchy and by dotted or dual-lined managers, if required. Reviews can also be done throughout the appraisal period if, for example, mid-year reviews are a part of the process.

At evaluation time, managers (or administrators) will set the appraisal document's status to *In Process* (status 4). During this stage, assessments (by the appraiser and typically a self-evaluation by the appraisee) are performed. Also at this time, part appraisal documents (if used) are sent to the appropriate part appraiser to record their own assessment of the appraisee's performance. Part appraisers, an important concept in this solution, are discussed in detail in later chapters.

After assessments are finalized, the document can be set to *Complete* (status 5). If you do not activate a formal approval process for your appraisal, this is the last status in your process. Note that final performance ratings can only be read by the Compensation module when the document reaches this final status (if no approval was activated). Compensation management integration is described in detail in Chapter 14.

If you decide to activate the approval functionality in the configuration, four more statuses become available:

▸ Approved (status 6)
▸ Closed Approved (status 7)
▸ Rejected (status 8)
▸ Closed Rejected (status 9)

Depending on the complexity of your business process flow, these statuses are available to assist in gaining the appropriate use of approvals by the necessary decision makers. They are by no means mandatory and are sometimes skipped to reduce the complexity of the assessment process timeline.

7.1.3 Substatuses

Substatuses are an important part of innovating the appraisal process. Configurable substatuses have become available as of Enterprise 4.7 Extension Set 2.0. As discussed, you cannot add additional statues, but you can add additional substatuses to your template. The addition of substatuses allows you to expand and enrich your process by providing more structured ways of tracking the process from start to finish.

> **Example**
>
> A custom substatus called *Mid-Year Review* could be configured within the In Review status to delineate a stage within the process for conducting mid-year performance reviews.

Of course, adding additional statuses increases the complexity of your form, but these additions are usually value added.

One substatus comes standard in the system: *Part Appraisal In Process* (substatus 1), which is valid during the In Process status. This is regarded as a special substatus and has certain characteristics that will be discussed in detail in later chapters. To seek feedback from dual- and dotted-line managers, you can use this part appraisal functionality. If you decide that you will not be using part appraisal functionality, it is important that you do not delete this substatus. This substatus is part of the standard SAP configuration and should not be removed because you may want to leverage the functionality in other processes or forms.

7.1.4 Pushbuttons

Pushbuttons allow the user to drive the appraisal to different statuses and substatuses, thereby enabling the process to smoothly flow from beginning to end. You can restrict authorization to pushbuttons for certain users. Adding pushbuttons to forms is common practice, especially if you have created additional custom substatuses. Configurable pushbuttons have become available as of Enterprise 4.7 Extension Set 2.0. Pushbuttons are discussed in depth in the next chapter.

7.1.5 Workflow Notification

Understanding workflow notification requirements is an important part of the process because it is essential in keeping the process moving forward.

Alerting managers and employees about deadlines and action items is paramount to any successful performance management process.

The standard workflow scenarios provided by SAP are basic work item notifications. This means that a work item appears in the portal (and the backend SAP Inbox) when triggered via a pushbutton on the form.

> **Tip**
>
> For some companies, email "notifications" sent to corporate email (e.g., Outlook, Lotus Notes, etc.) are preferable (or are needed in addition to) work item notifications sent to the portal inbox. This can be achieved by development efforts with a skilled SAP Workflow resource

Workflow notifications are discussed in detail in later chapters.

7.1.6   Form Design

Form design is one of the most important aspects of the overall process design. The layout and overall form construction is an opportunity to arrange content in the right fashion with priority focused on what is of primary importance.

As with any other user interface, remember not to overwhelm users with clutter. From usability studies conducted over several years, a short and succinct form has been found more beneficial in terms of usability and overall impact than a longer and more verbose document. It is good idea to secure separate sign-offs from the business owner(s) on the form's design (in addition to the overall process). This way, your performance management stakeholders will know exactly what their end product will look like.

In some cases, it may make sense to implement a customer-defined user interface (UI). If the proper resources are available during implementation and for support after go-live, customizing a frontend provides a way to overhaul the look-and-feel of the form. Some clients feel compelled to redesign the frontend of the form, whereas others seem complacent with the standard form's appearance. If a redesign of the form is requested (typically implemented using Business Server Pages [BSP] technology), you need to ensure that the usability and appearance of the form are well understood by the time blueprinting is completed. Look-and-feel changes during the build and testing project phases can have a significant impact on the go-live date.

7.2 Basic Configuration Settings for Performance Management

This section reviews the preliminary procedures necessary to ensure that you have correctly set up your SAP environment for performance management usage. It is important to ensure that these first steps are completed before moving into the appraisal catalog. The appraisal catalog, discussed in the next chapter in detail, is the main vehicle for template configuration.

7.2.1 Activation Switch for the HR Extension Set

Ensure that you have activated the HR extension set. Whether your system is versioned 4.7, 5.0, or 6.0, it is important to double-check that the actual extension set configuration switch is turned on for Human Resources. Without doing this, menu options and configuration activities for performance management will not be available to you. To check this, go to the IMG (Transaction **SPRO**), and check the IMG activity **Activation Switch for SAP R/3 Enterprise Extension Set**. Confirm that the EA-HR **Human Capital Management** checkbox is enabled, as shown in Figure 7.1.

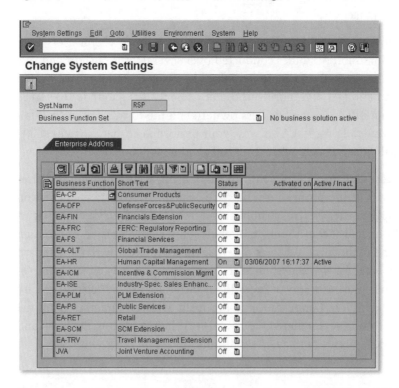

Figure 7.1 Activation Switch EA-HR (HR Extension Set) Turned on Within an ECC 6.0 System

Additionally, you may want to ask your Basis team to verify the activation log via Transaction SCPR20PR. BCSet (Business Configuration Set) EA-HR-AKH (**Enterprise HR Switch for IMG**) displays the results of the activation as shown in Figure 7.2.

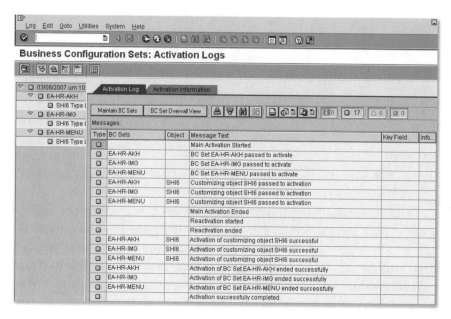

Figure 7.2 Activation Log Results for BC Set EA-HR-AKH Within Transaction SCPR20PR

Note

Reference SAP Note 855959 for more information on how to check the activation log after running Transaction SCPR20PR.

7.2.2 Activation of New Personnel Appraisals

Another important configuration switch is available in system Table T77S0. This table is where the general settings are made to determine if the system should be using the old or new appraisal functionality, both in the personnel appraisals and business event (i.e., training) modules. Based on the value entered in this table, none, some, or all of the new functionality will be activated. To access this table, you can either go to the IMG (Transaction SPRO) and access **Personnel Management • Personnel Development • Objective Setting and Appraisals • Edit Basic Settings**, or you can directly access the table via Transaction OOHAP_SETTINGS_PA.

In Table 7.2, each value and its description are listed.

Value of Semantic Abbreviation	Description of Value
(blank)	Retain old appraisal system for both personnel appraisals and business event appraisals (i.e., no performance management functionality will be used).
X	Replace personnel appraisals with new performance management functionality but retain business event appraisals.
T	Replace business event appraisals with performance management functionality but retain personnel appraisals with old functionality.
A	Replace both personnel appraisals and business event appraisals with new performance management functionality.

Table 7.2 Table Setting Options in Table T77SO for Group HAP00 Semantic Abbreviation REPLA

If you are implementing performance management for the first time, value A is most likely your selection. Choosing A as the value lets you activate the new performance management functionality in both the Personnel Appraisals (Performance Management module) and the Business Event (Training/LSO) module. Choosing a value of X activates the new Performance Management module in the Personnel Appraisals module but retains the old functionality in the Training module. This is pertinent if you have used Business Event management in the past and wanted to keep the old appraisal functionality active. Figure 7.3 shows an example of settings for group HAP00 semantic abbreviation REPLA in Table T77SO.

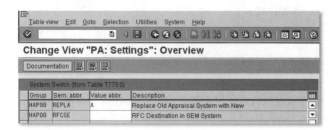

Figure 7.3 View of Table T77SO for Group HAP00, Semantic Abbreviation REPLA

7.3 Summary: Ready, Set, Configure!

With these constructs in mind, it is easier for you to achieve a more cohesive design for your performance management process. Following the suggestions noted earlier can help you prepare for your upcoming performance configuration activities. The chapter that follows delves into the appraisal catalog (Transaction PHAP_CATALOG). In this chapter, we will review the major configuration areas within the performance management application. Get ready to design your new performance management application!

The Appraisal Catalog provides customers with a robust platform on which to configure appraisal forms. This chapter reviews the vital configuration inherent within the Appraisal Catalog, including background information about its structure and a thorough description of the basic setup.

8 Configuring Appraisals in the Appraisal Catalog

The Appraisal Template Catalog is the main repository for performance management configuration. You access the catalog via Transaction PHAP_CATALOG. This one transaction houses all appraisal templates configured for use within your performance management processes. The templates that you construct here form the basis of the forms your end users view on the SAP NetWeaver Portal. Beginning with the creation of the category structure through to releasing your template, the information discussed in this chapter gives you the basics for building your appraisal templates.

8.1 Catalog Structure: The Category Group and Category

At a high level, the Appraisal Template Catalog is organized by category groups, categories, and then templates. Organized in a hierarchy, these elements form the basis of appraisal configuration. The elements of the appraisal form, including criteria groups, criteria, qualifications, and so on, are also configured in the hierarchy. We discuss each item in this section and highlight important configuration points along the way.

8.1.1 Category Groups

Category groups are the topmost node of the hierarchy, followed by categories, and then the appraisal templates. Each appraisal rolls up to only one category group, and each category group has an associated ID. The *category group ID* is an eight-digit number defined in the configuration. Out-of-the-box, SAP delivers category groups 00000001 for Personnel Appraisals, 00000010 for the Learning Solution, and 00000100 for eRecruiting. The system automatically creates these category groups the first time you access the Appraisal Catalog via Transaction PHAP_CATALOG.

> **Tip**
>
> Transaction PHAP_CATALOG displays forms in all categories (Personnel Appraisal, Learning Solution, and eRecruiting) versus Transaction PHAP_CATALOG_PA, which only displays forms within the Personnel Appraisal category.

You should not change the IDs of these groups. This is because these IDs come standard out-of-the-box and are reserved specifically for each functional area. Figure 8.1 shows a custom form (entitled **Personal Performance Plan**) under the **Personnel Appraisals** category group.

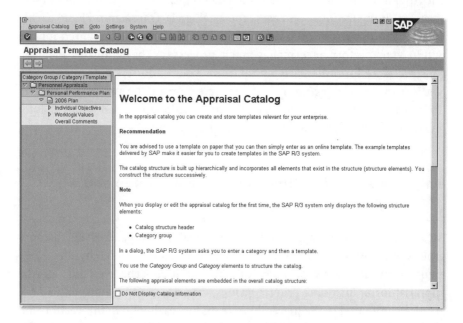

Figure 8.1 Appraisal Template Catalog via Transaction PHAP_CATALOG

Category groups store two main elements within the configuration: object types and status flow. (For those using Enterprise 4.7 Extension Set 1.1, the **Status Flow** tab is not available, as the status and substatus components are not configurable in the system.) The object type and status are configured here for the lower-level elements (namely categories and templates) to gain access to them. For example, a status that is not made available at the category group level will not be accessible to any subordinate category or template.

The first step in category group configuration is identifying the allowed *object types*. Object types are those Personnel Development (PD) object types you want to make available to the form. This step identifies to the system that these objects are permissible during performance management processes as "participants" or "actors."

Figure 8.2 shows the **Personnel Appraisals** category group with the **P (Person**) object as the only allowed object type. Other object types that may make sense here are User (US), Customer (KU), and Business Partner (BP), if any of them are to be included within your process.

> **Note**
>
> After you have added an object type to a category group and used it in one of your templates, it cannot be removed.

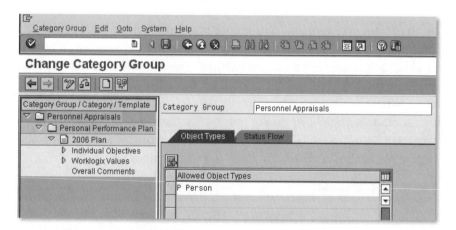

Figure 8.2 Object Types Tab for Configuration of the Category Group

The second element of configuration for category groups is the **status flow**. The **Status Flow** tab defines what statuses, users, and workflows are available during the process. These three subelements are configured on the respective tabs entitled **Status, Person Authorized**, and **Event** (see Figure 8.3).

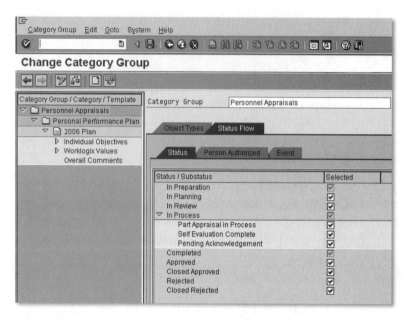

Figure 8.3 Statuses Available, Identified at the Category Group Level

On the **Status** tab, appraisal statuses are made available to your underlying configuration when the appropriate checkbox under the **Selected** column is checked. For most customers, selecting all statuses at the category group level is typical as it allows for maximum flexibility when designing your forms in later years. For example, if you decide in the future to roll out a performance management approval process, statuses 6-9 (**Approved**, **Closed Approved**, **Rejected**, and **Closed Rejected**) will be available to your templates despite not having implemented them in your previous processes.

> **Note**
>
> You cannot remove the **In Preparation** (status 1), **In Process** (status 4), and **Completed** (status 5) statuses because SAP makes these required for objective setting forms.

On the **Person Authorized** tab (see Figure 8.4), you define which users will have access to change statuses during the process. Later in the configuration, you will see how to authorize certain users to change statuses via defined pushbuttons. For most implementations, you will want to have at least the **Appraiser** and **Appraisee** in the **Selected** list. Also, if you will be allowing feedback from other parties (either because you are implementing a 360-degree feedback process, or because it is a part of your normal appraisal process), you should include the **Part Appraiser** as well.

Figure 8.4 Person Authorized Tab, Within the Status Flow Tab

Finally, on the **Event** tab, you define which workflow events (i.e., workflow notifications) can be made available within your processes. Figure 8.5 shows all events being selected, meaning that all workflow notifications will be made available for all templates within that category group. Each workflow event corresponds to a standard delivered SAP workflow. Be aware that these workflow notifications are work items and not emails. If emails are desired in addition to (or in lieu of) work items, customizations will need to be made to the workflow.

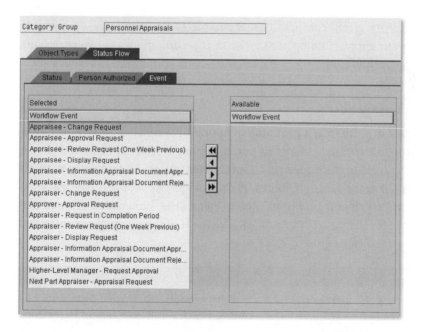

Figure 8.5 Workflow Notifications Made Available on the Events Tab, Within the Status Flow Tab

Configuration of the category groups can also be viewed in a tabular format via Transaction OOHAP_CAT_GROUP (see Figure 8.6). This transaction provides a different view of the category group and category configuration stored in the T77HAP* tables. Although most configuration is typically performed via the Appraisal Catalog, you can use this transaction to configure if you want to view the configuration from a different perspective. You should, however, execute your configuration procedures in Transaction PHAP_CAT-ALOG.

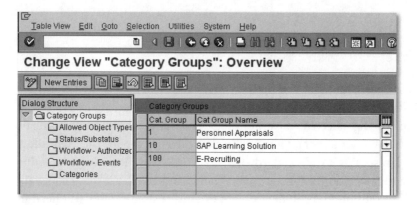

Figure 8.6 Transaction OOHAP_CAT_GROUP

After category group configuration is complete, you must create a category to hold your appraisal template(s). The next section discusses categories and category configuration.

8.1.2 Categories

A category is more than a grouping of appraisal templates. As with the category group, a *category* stores important configuration information that it makes available to the underlying appraisal templates. All templates within a category share the same attributes. A category stores six main configuration elements: Participants, Columns, Roles, Value Lists, Enhancements, and Status Flow. Like the category group, each element of the category is configured on its own tab (see Figure 8.7).

> **Note**
>
> In Enterprise 4.7 Extension Set 1.1, the **Enhancements** tab is called **Exits**, and the **Status Flow** tab does not exist. In Extension Set 1.1, substatuses cannot be created or integrated into the process.

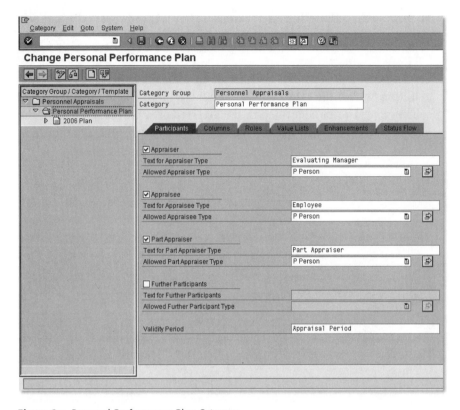

Figure 8.7 Personal Performance Plan Category

Configuration of a category is very similar to the category group. In fact, the **Status Flow** tab is configured in exactly the same manner for the category as it is for the category group. Each tab is discussed here in detail:

▶ **Participants**

The **Participants** tab identifies the actors who can be involved in your appraisal process (for all appraisal templates under that category). In addition to identifying the participants of the process (part appraiser, further participant, etc.), this tab enables you to provide category-specific labels. For example, you might want to replace the term Appraiser with Evaluating Manager, replace Appraisee with Employee, and replace Validity Period with Appraisal Period. Also, you must identify which objects are "allowed" for each participant. In most implementations, object type P (for person, or employee) is used for the selected participants. If you decide to include more than one allowed object type per participant, use the multiple selection box to the right of the object type to insert additional objects. In Enterprise 4.7 Extension Set 1.1, only user (US) and person (P) are allowed.

▶ **Columns**

The **Columns** tab identifies which columns are available to the appraisal templates within the category (see Figure 8.8). Both standard and custom columns need to be identified in the **Selected** area on the left side of the screen. We will discuss custom columns in the next chapter. Columns that are not identified here will not be available at the template level.

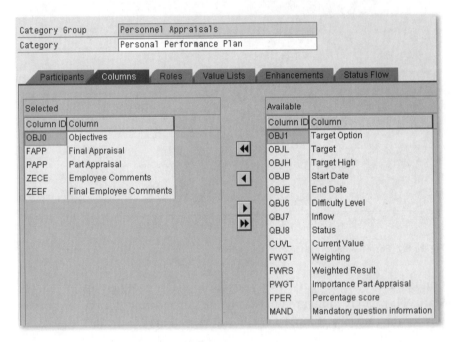

Figure 8.8 Columns Selected at the Category Level

▶ **Roles**

Another important concept that permeates throughout the performance management functionality is that of the role. A *role* allows authorization checks to be performed at the template, criteria group, or criteria level. Roles are most important for those processes using the Part Appraisal functionality, as it allows you to prohibit certain users from editing appraisal elements in part appraisal documents. By not assigning a role to a particular criterion, all users with that role will be unable to edit that line item during the part evaluation. The **Roles** tab is where you identify which roles you want to be available for the underlying templates. Figure 8.9 shows the **Manager** and **Self** (i.e., Employee) role selected.

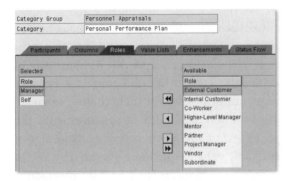

Figure 8.9 Roles at the Category Level

▶ **Value Lists**

Value lists are an important part of many performance management processes because they store scale information such as performance ratings, dates, and business event types/development plan statuses. In most implementations, you will have a rating scale used within your template to record a final performance rating for an employee. Figure 8.10 shows a "quality" performance rating scale selected as the only value list available within the category. Most categories (and templates) will have at least one quality or quantity scale because section ratings and overall form appraisal ratings are typically based on a list or selection of values. Configuration of value lists, including differences between quality and quantity scales, is discussed in detail in the next chapter.

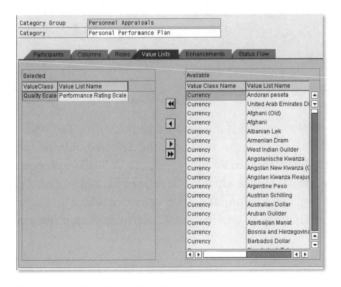

Figure 8.10 Value Lists at the Category Level

▶ **Enhancements**

Customer-implemented user exits are identified on the **Enhancements** tab (see Figure 8.11). (Again, note that *enhancements* are referred to as *exits* in Enterprise 4.7 Extension Set 1.1). Enhancements provide a robust way of including customer-specific business logic inside the appraisal. Because SAP cannot predict the various business rules for their clients, enhancements are an important part of the solution. Without enhancements, the appraisal would be very rigid. Expect to implement several enhancements, anywhere from five to fifteen. These enhancements are provided by SAP as "standard" hooks where customers can institute their own business logic.

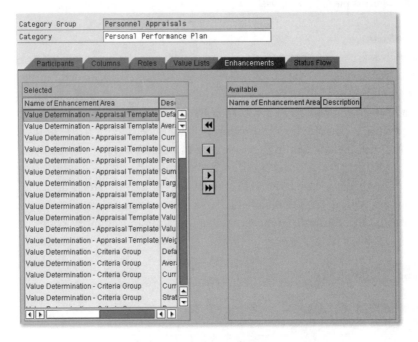

Figure 8.11 Enhancements at the Category Level

▶ Enhancements are implemented via Business Add-Ins (BAdIs). The BAdIs that are used in the template need to be on the **Selected** side of the **Enhancements** tab to be referenced within a template. A BAdI implementation shows on the **Available** side when the developer has completed and activated the BAdI implementation, and after you have added it to the enhancement area in Transaction OOHAP_BASIC. Chapter 10 describes in detail the available BAdIs and how to implement and integrate them into your appraisal template.

▸ **Status Flow**

The last tab at the category level, **Status Flow**, operates exactly like the **Status Flow** tab at the category group level. At the category level, you can be more specific about which statuses, users, and workflows you want to make available for your templates within that category. Figure 8.12 shows the **Status Flow** tab with all statuses checked, which means any template under this category will be able to use any status, including the substatus **Part Appraisal In Process** (but not the custom substatus **Self-Evaluation Complete** or **Pending Acknowledgment**). You will learn how to create custom substatuses in the next chapter.

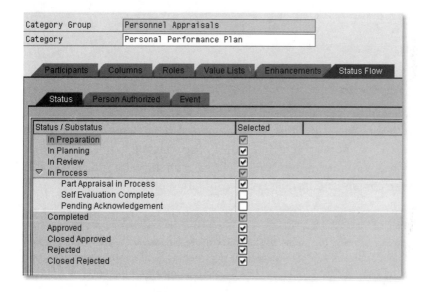

Figure 8.12 Status Flow at the Category Level

Like Transaction OOHAP_CAT_GROUP for category groups, category configuration can also be viewed outside the catalog in a tabular format using Transaction OOHAP_CATEGORY. This Transaction, seen in Figure 8.13, provides a different view of the category configuration stored in the T77HAP* tables. Again, as with category groups, you should not perform your configuration activities here. PHAP_CATALOG is the proper area to perform your template configuration.

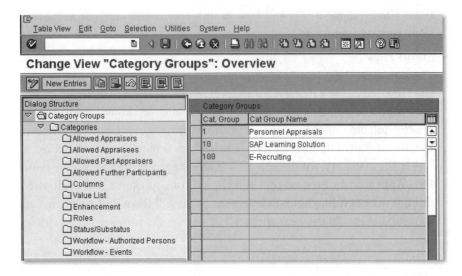

Figure 8.13 Transaction OOHAP_CATEGORY

8.1.3 Templates

Most of the configuration is performed on the appraisal form at the appraisal template level. You can think of an appraisal document or form as an instance of your appraisal template. After your template is released to your production environment, employees will have an appraisal document that inherits the content and business rules configured on this template.

Tip

Although you can use the same appraisal template from year to year, you should create a new appraisal template each year. Not only will requirements most likely change, but also reporting will be easier if unique templates are used.

The next section discusses appraisal configuration in detail.

8.2 The Appraisal Template

Much of your efforts during the realization (or build) phase of the project will be on finalizing configuration elements at the appraisal template level. As with the category group and category, the appraisal template is represented in the catalog hierarchy in Transaction PHAP_CATALOG. Depending on your version of SAP, you will have up to eight tabs to configure (Enterprise 4.7 Extension Set 1.1 does not have the **Status Flow** tab). The components of the template are described in detail in the following sections.

8.2.1 Description

The **Description** tab allows you to maintain an explanation of the template. This is often where the appraisal's overall purpose is and/or where the form directions are stated. Two types of descriptions are available in the **Description** dropdown list: **Standard** and **Web Layout**. The text saved in the Standard description is used when the form is printed (via the standard Adobe PDF functionality). The text saved in the Web Layout option is used when the form is displayed on the SAP NetWeaver Portal. HTML tags are supported in the Web Layout description, which is useful if you want to use bold, underline, or italics on some text in the form. If the Web Layout is not identified, the unformatted text from the Standard description is used on the portal.

The **Description** tab also comes with a full set of editing tools (see Figure 8.14). Commands such as **Copy**, **Cut**, **Paste**, **Undo**, and **Redo** are available. You can also import and export verbiage saved in text files (file extension .txt). Be careful if you copy and paste from Microsoft Word because hidden characters (such as carriage returns) sometimes appear on the printed form as asterisks, quotes, or strange symbols.

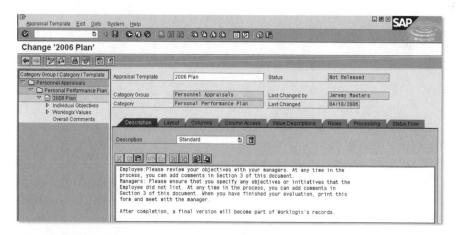

Figure 8.14 Template Description Tab

Description information is stored in Table HRP1002 and cannot be easily accessed other than from the Appraisal Catalog. You should only make updates to the descriptions via Transaction PHAP_CATALOG. SAP did not intend for appraisal verbiage to be editing in anything but the Appraisal Catalog editor.

8.2.2 Layout

The **Layout** tab controls some important form appearance features, including the numbering of the form and its header. Layout controls both the output of the web form as well as the printed documented. Layout control is template-wide, meaning that the properties are universally inherited throughout the form. Figure 8.15 shows the **Numbering** and **Header** sections of the **Layout** tab.

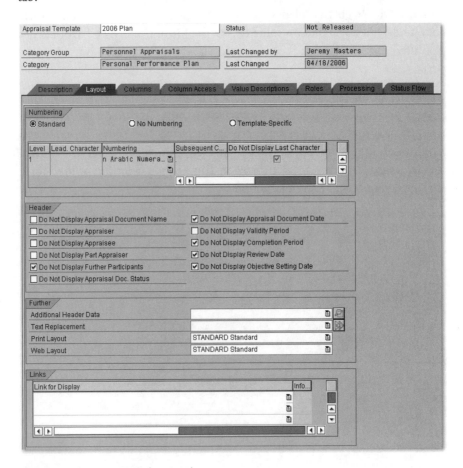

Figure 8.15 Layout at Template Level

The numbering system of your appraisal document can either be standard, template-specific, or have none (via the **No Numbering** option). You can make template-specific changes based on requirements, but most customers are content with the standard numbering or with no numbering at all.

The header of an appraisal is the topmost portion of the form. The appraisal header holds key information such as the appraiser name, appraisee name, appraisal status, and the validity period of the document. All or some of this information can be suppressed from the end user, if desired. For example, if you decide not to use the Part Appraisal functionality, you can elect to hide the **Part Appraisal** section in the **Header** by selecting the checkbox **Do Not Display Part Appraiser**.

The lower-half of the **Layout** tab houses miscellaneous layout configuration options. In the **Further section**, four dropdown options provide you with the ability to change the following layout-related configurations:

- **Additional Header Data**
  This option allows master data information, such as the appraisee's position title and organizational unit, to appear on the form. SAP delivers enhancement PERSONNEL_HEADER_DATA, which returns the appraisee's organizational unit, personnel area, personnel subarea, employee group, and employee subgroup. The BAdI used, HRHAP00_ADD_HEADER, is discussed further in Chapter 10.

- **Text Replacement**
  This option allows a dynamic replacement of special characters (e.g., the expression "&1") with the actual names of appraisal participants. SAP delivers enhancement APPRAISER_AND_APPRAISEE, which substitutes the expression "&1" and "&2" with the name of the appraiser and appraisee, respectively. The BAdI used, HRHAP00_TEXT_SUBST, is discussed further in Chapter 10.

- **Print Layout**
  This option allows an alternative to the standard PDF (Smartform or Adobe Form) used for printing the form. It calls BAdI HRHAP00_SMART-FORMS.

- **Web Layout**
  This option allows an alternative to the standard BSP application HAP_DOC-UMENT. It calls BAdI HRHAP00_BSP_TMPL.

- At the bottom of the Layout tab, there is a Links section. Configuring a link here allows end users to click on a pushbutton in the form to view

additional information or perform an action (typically by launching another window). SAP provides several standard links, including the ability
to have the appraisee and appraiser view the appraisee's existing qualifications. For a list of the standard links provided by SAP, refer to Chapter
10 on available BAdI implementations within BAdI HRHAP00_LINK.

▸ Layout information is stored in table HRP5021. This information should
only be changed via the Appraisal Catalog.

8.2.3 Columns

The **Columns** tab is one of the most important within the catalog because it
controls much of the form's appearance. The tab is composed of four sections: **Column**, **Objective Setting**, **Web Settings**, and **Dynamic Setting** (see
Figure 8.16).

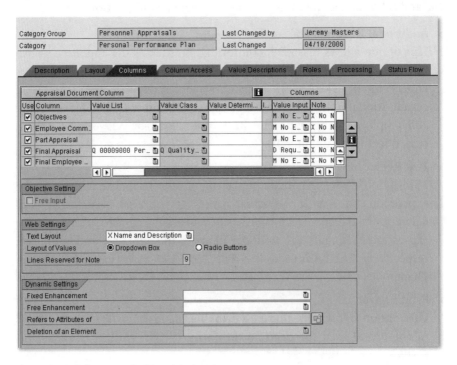

Figure 8.16 Columns at the Template Level

Depending on the element (template, criteria group, and criteria), the column table will be configured differently. As with other areas at the template
level, the columns in the form need to be made available to the underlying
form elements (criteria group and criteria). Most column configuration will

be performed at the criteria group and criteria level. See the next section on column configuration for details.

The **Web Settings** section controls the output of certain element-level configuration, such as text layout, value layout, and notes. The text layout dropdown has three options: **Name, Description,** and **Name and Description.** If **Name** is chosen, the row element for the template renders the name of the form but not the verbiage placed on the **Description** tab. If **Description** is selected, only the description (and not the name) is shown on the form. With the final option, both the name and description are displayed.

The **Layout of Values** radio button provides the ability to determine whether the value list for that row is shown as radio buttons or as a dropdown box. The **Lines Reserved for Note** option allows you to specify how many lines are shown on the form. SAP allows up to nine lines per row (e.g., what is shown initially on the appraisal), but there is no restriction on how much feedback can be captured within the document.

Dynamic Settings, such as **Fixed Enhancement** and **Free Enhancement,** are more pertinent at the criteria group level. This configuration is discussed in the next chapter.

Column information is stored in table **HRP5022.** This information should only be changed via the Appraisal Catalog.

8.2.4   Column Access

Column access provides the ability to grant access to columns based on the participant type and relevant status. Each column (listed as a row on the **Column Access** tab) is associated with a column owner (see Figure 8.17). As shown in Figure 8.17, the **Column Owner** can either be the **AE Appraisee, AR Appraiser, AA Appraiser and Appraisee, OT Further Participant,** or **PA Part Appraiser.** By default, the **Part Appraisal** column can only have the **PA Part Appraiser** as its owner, and therefore it is disabled (grayed out) by the system.

The actual columns of the table within the tab are dependent on the statuses of your process. Exactly two columns appear for each status: the first column (the one on the left) defines the access for the column's owner. The second column (the one on the right) defines the access for all others involved in the process. For example, you might define that for the **Objectives** column, the **Column Owner** should be **AA Appraisee and Appraiser.** Furthermore, the appraisee and appraiser should have change access in the Planning and Review statuses but display access for the remainder of the process. Figure 8.17 shows this configuration on the first line of the **Column Access** table entitled **Objectives**.

Access levels are typically defined as **X Change, Display (blank)**, and **H Hide**, but you can have more complicated access levels. For example, there is an option **Change for Appraiser, Display for Others (V)** access level, which is available in the **Other** column for each status. This option is especially attractive if you have the appraisee as owner, but you want the appraiser (and not a higher-level manger) to be able to change the appraisal element in that column.

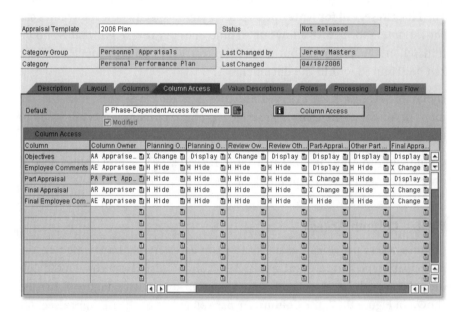

Figure 8.17 Column Access at the Template Level

- ► Several standard configurations are available for column access as well. SAP delivers such configuration defaults as **Phase-Dependent Access for Owner**, **Free Access for All**, and **Maintenance for Owner, Visibility for All**. On your template, you should select the access level that most resembles your requirements and then modify them as necessary. After you have made modifications from the default, the **Modified** checkbox is checked automatically to indicate that you have altered a standard configuration.

- ► Column access information is stored in Table HRP5023. This information should only be changed using the Appraisal Catalog.

8.2.5 Value Descriptions

Value descriptions explain the meaning behind the scales or value lists in your form. A scale or value list enables evaluators to rate an appraisee on their performance. This might be for objectives met or performance achieved during the year. The **Value Descriptions** tab is only populated if you have identified a value list at that particular element level. In Figure 8.18, a value list is shown with five value IDs (0000-0004). Clicking on the box to the left of the value ID populates its description (shown in the box to the right). You can override the standard description by unchecking the **Default Value** checkbox. This is useful if the descriptions differ from one part of the form to another. However, value list descriptions are typically universal throughout the appraisal.

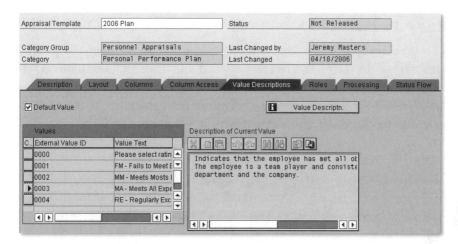

Figure 8.18 Value Descriptions at the Template Level

8.2.6 Roles

Roles allow you to differentiate users so you can allow restrictions on who can evaluate the appraisee during part appraisal evaluations. You may not want to permit certain part appraisers from evaluating a particular objective or value assessment, for example. A part appraiser who is a colleague may only be asked to evaluate an appraisee on teamwork, whereas the appraisee's manager (also a part appraiser) is responsible for giving a full assessment.

▸ Only the roles selected at the category level will be available for selection at the template level. In Figure 8.19, both roles — **Manager** and **Self** — are selected, meaning that this element (template) can be accessible for users identified as Manager and Self (i.e., the employee).

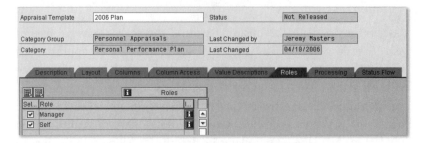

Figure 8.19 Roles Permitted at the Appraisal Template Level

▸ Role information is stored in Table HRP5024. This information should only be changed via the Appraisal Catalog.

8.2.7 Processing

The **Processing** tab (see Figure 8.20) is critical for defining the general attributes of the template. The tab is divided into three sections: **General Settings**, **Part-Appraisal Settings**, and **Follow-Up Processing**. The **Processing** tab is relevant at the form level and does not exist elsewhere within the catalog. Settings here affect all elements within your appraisal form.

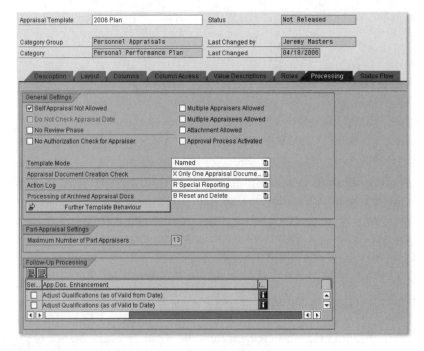

Figure 8.20 Processing Tab at the Template Level

General Settings

In the **General Settings** section, there are several important indicators to configure. You should review and understand what each of these mean and determine whether any would have an impact on your implementation.

▸ To begin, the **Self Appraisal Not Allowed** checkbox is self-explanatory. If your template has this checked, a user cannot be both the appraiser and appraisee of the same document. In an objective setting scenario, this selection is checked.

▸ The **Do Not Check Appraisal Date** checkbox allows you to determine whether or not the system checks the appraisal date against the validity date of the document. Please note that this checkbox will be disabled if you have specified not to use the appraisal document date on the **Layout** tab of your template.

▸ The **No Review Phase** option is important if your process does not require any objective setting or mid-year review. If this selection is marked, the **In Review** status (status 3) is not available for inclusion within the template. This disables (grays out) the **In Review** status in the **Status Flow** tab (discussed in the next section).

▸ The **No Authorization Check for Appraiser** checkbox is an important security option that allows you to specify whether an authorization check should be made to determine whether or not the user has access to the appraiser (i.e., the appraiser's personnel number) of the document. This indicator is of particular value if you have implemented structural authorizations. For example, if you have used the popular RH_GET_MANAGER_ ASSIGNMENT function module within an authorization profile that you have granted to all managers, the managers in your organization will be unable to view their own appraisal unless this indicator is set. This is because the structural profile has excluded the user's own manager from their overall profile. To sidestep this authorization, ensure that the **No Authorization Check for Appraiser** checkbox is selected.

▸ The next two settings, **Multiple Appraisers Allowed** and **Multiple Appraisees Allowed**, are straightforward. Most objective setting appraisal documents only have one appraiser and only one appraisee. Even in situations where an employee has moved from one part of the organization to another within the evaluation period and feedback is required from both sending and receiving managers, it is more common to have only one appraiser and seek part appraisal feedback from the other. In most business scenarios, the receiving manager (i.e., the current manager) is better positioned as the appraiser and should be responsible for soliciting feedback from the receiving manager.

> **Tip**
>
> If multiple appraisers are allowed within your process, they will share access to all columns based on Column Access configuration. Be careful because this means that one appraiser could change or delete feedback provided by another appraiser.

▸ Some customers require their forms to accept attachments. The **Attachment Allowed** checkbox selection provides this ability on the appraisal form. When active, an **Attachments** button appears on the form, allowing the user to browse the computer for an attachment (accepted file formats include .doc, .xls, and .pdf). Note that you must have the Generic Object Services functionality active in your system. To enable this, you will need to verify that group GENER, semantic abbreviation OBJSV, is set to 1 in table **T77S0**.

▸ Depending on the business requirements, a formal approval process may be required. When the **Approval Process Activated** option is selected, statuses six through nine are enabled in your template. This means that once the document is Completed (i.e. placed in status 5), statuses **Approved** (status 6), **Closed Approved** (status 7), **Rejected** (status 8), and **Closed Rejected** (status 9) become available within your process.

▸ The next four dropdown selections available on the **Processing** tab collect key requirements for form processing. **Template Mode** allows you to perform anonymous appraisals. If the **Anonymous with Registration** option is selected, an administrator must register participants as appraisers for anonymous feedback. The administrator enters participants in a separate table so they are not associated with the actual appraisal document. If the **Anonymous without Registration** option is selected, any user may participate in the appraisal — no administrator work is required. For objective setting appraisals, you will want to select the **Named** option; which explicitly identifies the names of those participants involved in the appraisal document.

▸ The **Appraisal Document Creation Check** option allows you to identify whether more than one appraisal form for an appraisee can be created in a given timeframe. The **Only One Appraisal Document** option permits only one form to be created per appraisee, whereas the **Only One**

Appraisal Document Without Appraiser Check option holds the same restriction but does not validate the appraiser. The last option, **Unlimited Appraisal Documents**, allows you to create an indefinite amount of documents regardless of the validity period.

> **Tip**
>
> The option **Unlimited Appraisal Documents** under the **Appraisal Document Creation Check** is most often useful in a development environment as restricting the number of appraisal documents per appraisee can be cumbersome while performing your unit testing.

► The first option, **Only One Appraisal Document**, is probably your best bet for most objective setting scenarios.

► You also set audit logs to be active in the configuration via the **Action Log** selection on the **Processing** tab. Up to and including version ECC 5.0, the **Action Log** has three options: **Special Reporting**, **Can Be Displayed for All Appraisals**, and **Not Activated**. The **Special Reporting** option allows the action log to record appraisal-level changes only. Information logged includes changes to and views of the appraisal document as well as status updates, but not data such as changes to ratings or deletion and modification of objectives (see Figure 8.21). The log can be viewed via Transaction **SLG1** (Analyze Application Log) by selecting object HRHAP00 (Appraisal Systems), subobject DOCUMENT (Appraisal Document: Action Log). Typically, only an administrator has access to these logs. If this information is made available to online users of the form, the **Action Log** configuration option **Can Be Displayed for All Appraisals** should be selected. Doing so adds the **Action Log** button to the form, which gives users the ability to view the log for themselves in a separate pop-up box. As an alternative, you can also implement BAdI HRHAP00_ACTION_LOG to extend the type of information stored in the log.

► As of version ECC 6.0, the Action Log is significantly enhanced with the inclusion of two new options: **Detailed, Can Be Displayed for All Appraisals**, and **Detailed Special Reporting**. They both return detailed audit information, including changes to all values and appraisal elements. You may want to consult with your audit department to understand which appraisal information should be audited. This new capability provides a more thorough manner of tracking changes to performance management documents.

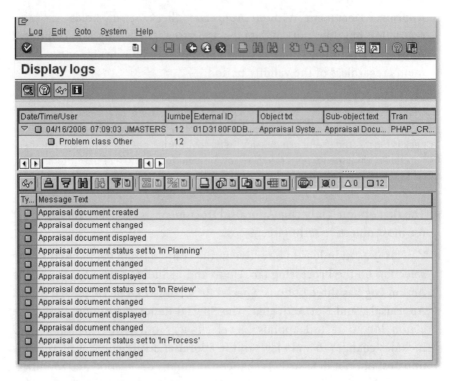

Figure 8.21 Output of Application Log (Transaction SLG1) for Object HRHAP00 (Appraisal Systems)

▶ The last dropdown option within the **Processing** tab, entitled **Processing of Archived Appraisal Documents**, is integral for appraisals in the status Complete (status 5). This selection determines if an appraisal document can be reset (i.e., placed back into a previous status) or deleted. Most customers, seeking maximum flexibility in their process, choose the **Reset and Delete** option.

▶ In the last area of **General Settings**, a button entitled **Further Template Behavior** is available. Clicking on this button opens the dialog box for **Further Template Enhancements** (see Figure 8.22). Several important template-level enhancements reside in this dialog box. For example, column access, header changes, pushbutton access, and business check logic are implemented through BAdI implementations, which are identified here. Chapter 10 discusses these BAdIs in detail.

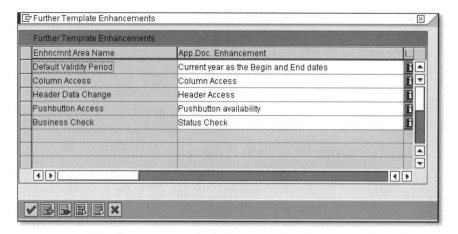

Further Template Enhancements		
Enhncmnt Area Name	App.Doc. Enhancement	I...
Default Validity Period	Current year as the Begin and End dates	ℹ
Column Access	Column Access	ℹ
Header Data Change	Header Access	ℹ
Pushbutton Access	Pushbutton availability	ℹ
Business Check	Status Check	ℹ

Figure 8.22 Further Template Enhancements Dialog Box Within the Processing tab

Part-Appraiser Settings

The second section of the **Processing** tab, **Part-Appraiser Settings**, enables you to configure a maximum number of part appraisers. For 360-degree appraisals, no maximum exists for the number of part appraisers allowed. However, for an objective setting appraisal, the maximum number of part appraisers allowed is 20 minus the number of other columns in the template, divided by the number of part appraiser columns. The number of part appraiser columns can either be one or two, depending on whether you include the **Part Appraiser Importance (PWGT)** column with the **Part Appraiser (PAPP)** column. In most objective setting scenarios, you will not need more than one or two part appraisers.

Follow-up Processing

The third and final section of the **Processing** tab stores information on the **Follow-up Processing** functionality. Follow-up processing is relevant only if you have included qualifications within your appraisal. Appraisees' qualifications that are rated within their appraisal document can be updated automatically after the appraisal is set to the Complete status. There are four standard options here:

▶ **Adjust Qualifications (as of Valid from Date)**
This option creates (or adjusts, if one exists) qualification(s) effective from the start date of the appraisal.

▶ **Adjust Qualifications (as of Valid to Date)**
This option creates (or adjusts, if one exists) qualification(s) effective from the end date of the appraisal.

▶ **Adjust Qualifications with Notes (Valid from Date)**
This option creates (or adjusts, if one exists) qualification(s) effective from the start date of the appraisal *and* records the appraisal feedback for that qualification into the qualification's notes field.

▶ **Adjust Qualifications with Notes (Valid to Date)**
This option creates (or adjusts, if one exists) qualification(s) effective from the end date of the appraisal *and* records the appraisal feedback for that qualification into the qualification's notes field.

Processing information is stored in Table HRP5025. This information should only be changed via the Appraisal Catalog.

8.2.8 Status Flow

Status flow is one of the most important parts of the template configuration, because it controls the overall flow of the process. In the status flow, you control which users can select which pushbuttons to move the appraisal document to a particular status. Configuration of status movement, pushbutton authorization, and workflow notifications are all controlled here.

The **Status Flow** tab is divided into two sections. On the left, a status hierarchy is shown with all available statuses for that template. If you are implementing an objective setting appraisal, the **In Preparation, In Process,** and **Completed** statuses are enabled automatically because they are required by the system. Depending on the complexity of your business process, you may or may not use all statuses. For most objective setting appraisals, you will employ most standard statuses, including **In Planning**.

> **Tip**
>
> As a best practice, try to streamline your process to involve the fewest number of statuses and substatuses. A simple, intuitive process is what most customers strive for at the outset of a design, but few end up attaining that goal when all is said and done.

On the right side of the **Status Flow** tab, details for the available pushbuttons for each tab can be viewed by double-clicking on the status name within the hierarchy on the left. Information such as pushbutton name, pushbutton authorization, target status/substatus, and workflow event are configurable in this section.

> **Note**
>
> You cannot create custom statuses, but you can create a custom substatus (the exception being those using Enterprise 4.7 Extension Set 1.1). Custom substatuses make the application very extensible and are discussed in the next chapter.

As mentioned earlier, the pushbutton information on the right is valuable for identifying which participant can move the appraisal process forward and when they move forward (or back) in the process. You can define several pushbuttons per status depending on the requirements of your process flow. The numbers on the top-right of the right-hand section indicate the number of pushbuttons for that status as well as which number pushbutton you are currently editing. Use the right- and left arrows to scroll though the pushbuttons available per status.

The **Outbound Status** and **Outbound Substatus** are always display only because they identify the status/substatus you are currently editing. You perform pushbutton configuration within the **Status Flow: Options** box. The dropdown values for pushbuttons, person authorized, and status/substatus are configured in Transaction OOHAP_BASIC (as discussed in the next chapter). For each outgoing status and substatus combination, you can specify one or more pushbuttons. Every pushbutton has a target status and substatus that drives the document's new status after being clicked by the user. Only participants identified in the **Person Authorized** dropdown selection are permitted to click the pushbutton. The **Next Status** selection determines how the status changes are implemented. The **Saved and Leave Appraisal Document** option changes the document status when the user clicks on the pushbutton and then immediately exits the document, whereas the **Saved and Change to Display Mode** option changes the document status but moves the document to a display mode in the new status.

As of ECC 6.0, an additional **Create Note** dropdown is available on the **Status Flow** tab. This option (not pictured in Figure 8.23), allows you to request comments from a user when the user changes a particular status. For example, you could make it mandatory for all managers to provide final comments when rejecting a document. This robust functionality can provide for a cleaner audit trail for document tracking.

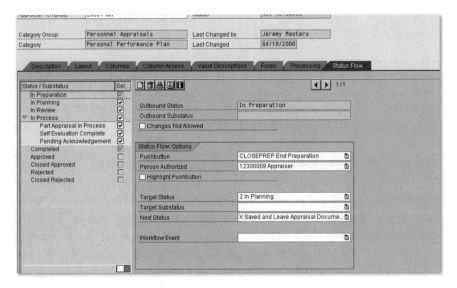

Figure 8.23 Status Flow at the Template Level

At first, you may encounter errors when attempting to release your form due to status flow restrictions. This is very common and can be quite frustrating if you do not know all the system restrictions. Table 8.1 provides you with a list of all possible outbound statuses and target statuses you should take into consideration when editing the status flow of your appraisal form.

Outbound Status	Target Status	Comments
In Preparation	In Preparation	
	In Planning	If Objective Setting Agreement is defined
	In Process	Only if Final Appraisal or Part Appraisal is defined
In Planning	In Preparation	Only if Objective Setting Agreement is defined
	In Planning	
	In Review	If Review Phase is defined
	In Process	If Final Appraisal or Part Appraisal is defined
	Completed	Only if no Part Appraisal/Final Appraisal is defined) or higher status

Table 8.1 Outbound Status and Target Status Restrictions

Outbound Status	Target Status	Comments
In Review	In Review	
	In Process	
	Completed or higher	Only if no Part Appraisal/Final Appraisal is defined
In Process	In Preparation	Only if no Objective Setting Phase is defined
	In Process	
	Completed or higher status	
	Part Appraisal Completed	
Completed	In Planning	Only if Objective Setting Agreement (and no Final Appraisal or Part Appraisal) and no Review Phase is defined
	In Review	Only if Objective Setting Agreement (and no Final Appraisal or Part Appraisal) and Review Phase is defined
	In Process	Only if Final Appraisal or Part Appraisal is defined
	Approved	
	Rejected	
	Closed Approved	
	Closed Rejected	
Approved	Closed Approved	
	Rejected	
	Closed Rejected	
Closed Approved	No status change allowed	
Rejected	In Planning	Only if Objective Setting Agreement (and no Final Appraisal or Part Appraisal) and no Review Phase is defined
	In Review	Only if Objective Setting Agreement (and no Final Appraisal or Part Appraisal) and review phase is defined

Table 8.1 Outbound Status and Target Status Restrictions (Cont.)

Outbound Status	Target Status	Comments
	In Process	If Final Appraisal or Part Appraisal is defined
	Approved	
	Closed Approved	
	Closed Rejected	
Closed Rejected	No status change allowed	

Table 8.1 Outbound Status and Target Status Restrictions (Cont.)

Status flow information is stored in Table HRP5026. This information should only be changed via the Appraisal Catalog.

The **Processing** tab is the last configurable item within the template catalog at the appraisal level. Further configuration is performed on the individual elements of the appraisal. The sections that follow discuss how to configure the remaining two appraisal elements: criteria groups and criteria.

8.3   Criteria Group and Criteria Configuration

After an appraisal template is defined, criteria groups and criteria can be created. Criteria groups and criteria are the building blocks of the appraisal. They form the structure of the document, providing the platform for objective definition and feedback by evaluators. If you think of the appraisal as a grid, each row represents either a criteria group or criteria defined in the template (with the exception of the topmost row, which is the template element itself).

From a system perspective, criteria groups are stored as VB objects, whereas criteria are stored as VC objects in the database. Both VB and VC elements can exist directly off the template (VA object). Both criteria groups and criteria can be *end nodes* within a document, meaning either a VB or a VC element can provide closure to a section of the form. The following section highlights the important tab elements that comprise both criteria groups and criteria.

8.3.1   Description

The description of a criteria group or criteria is depicted on the **Description** tab of that element. This tab behaves in the same exact manner as described earlier for the template level.

8.3.2   Columns

Column configuration at the criteria group/criteria level is crucial to the process because it defines key columns available as well as user input requirements. As discussed earlier, it is important that you have already made columns available at the category and template level. You will need to do this on the **Columns** tab so that columns are available to criteria groups and criteria (see Figure 8.24).

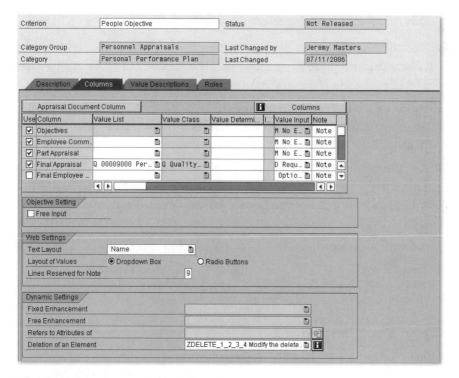

Figure 8.24 Criteria Group Column Configuration

To use a particular column for an element (i.e., a row), you must select the checkbox in the **Use** column next to the appropriate appraisal column (e.g., **Objectives**, **Final Appraisal**). This allows the column to appear for that particular element. For each appraisal column (listed as a row in the configuration table), the following columns are available: **Value List, Value Class, Value Determination, Information, Value Input**, and **Note**. When a value list is assigned to a column, it pulls in the respective value class. If you pull in information onto either the value list or note of a particular cell within your appraisal, you can use the Value Determination functionality. If a value determination is specified, a blue icon appears in the **Information** column to its right. This contains information on the value determination BAdI selected. Value determination BAdIs are discussed in detail in Chapter 10.

The last two columns on the **Columns** tab are **Value Input** and **Note**. You indicate whether a value for a particular criteria group or criteria is required, optional, or not relevant in the **Value Input** column. For example, self-assessment ratings may be optional in your template for an appraisee, but a final performance rating may be required for the appraiser.

Finally, the **Note** column specifies the following:

▶ **Note Display (D)**
A note that may have been added to this objective cannot be changed. An objective is added from the Balanced Scorecard, for example.

▶ **Note Can No Longer Be Displayed (H)**
Every participant can read but not change a note written by another participant. A field for entering a note is available for every participant.

▶ **Required entry (M)**
Each (part) appraiser must enter a mandatory text in the note field before the appraisal document can be saved (this is available as of ECC 5.0).

▶ **No Note (X)**
No note is displayed.

▶ **Note (blank)**
The note can be changed by all participants.

8.3.3 Value Descriptions

Value descriptions are handled in the same manner as the template. As at the appraisal level, you can override value descriptions at the criteria group and criteria level.

8.3.4 Roles

Roles at the criteria group and criteria level operate in the same fashion as described in the template configuration. As mentioned earlier, roles play an important part within the part appraisal process because they allow you to filter which roles should provide feedback for which row elements (e.g., criteria groups, criteria, templates).

8.3.5 Element Access

Element access is a new feature available as of ECC 6.0. Integrating element-level access to your form is a great feature because it determines row availability per participant. Row access extensibility is now enhanced by controlling certain users (e.g., part appraisers) from providing feedback on particularly sensitive form elements. For example, if you had an objective setting appraisal composed of both objectives and corporate values, you could restrict part appraisers (e.g., a project manager or prior manager) from viewing/evaluating the corporate values section. This way, the part appraiser can only provide feedback on how the appraisee met his objectives.

The system provides four configurable options to configure element access security:

▶ **Change**
  The participant can change the element in the corresponding phase.

▶ **Display**
  The participant can display the element in the corresponding phase.

▶ **Hide Values**
  The participant can see the element but not the values entered for the element, such as weighting or final rating.

▶ **Hide**
  The participant cannot see the element, and the entire row is hidden.

8.4 Summary

As you have seen, the Appraisal Catalog provides a robust mechanism to configure appraisal templates. Mastering Transaction PHAP_CHANGE will make your configuration activities go a lot smoother. In the next chapter, you will delve into some advanced techniques you can use when configuring the form. It is important to know which shortcuts you can take and which you should avoid. Let's take a closer look at the configuration and get our hands dirty!

In this chapter we will take a deeper look at some of the more advanced areas of the configuration. By the chapter's end, you will see how to further customize the performance management application through its extensible framework.

9 Advanced Configuration Techniques

In Chapter 8, we reviewed the basics of the Appraisal Catalog. We will now discuss some additional functionality that will assist you in mastering the catalog as well as some advanced configuration. Understanding everything offered from the catalog and its extensible components will go a long way in speeding up the build and deployment of your form. We will first discuss some advanced components of the Appraisal Catalog and then later delve into some enhanced customizing such as the creation of custom columns, pushbuttons, substatuses, and value lists.

9.1 Advanced Concepts Within the Appraisal Catalog

In addition to configuring the template's tabs, criteria groups, and criteria, there are other important features of the catalog. Several options are available by selecting a button on the application toolbar or by right-clicking on the template itself (in the hierarchy). Each is discussed in detail with appropriate examples to demonstrate its importance to the overall form configuration.

9.1.1 Understanding Template Statuses

The status of the appraisal template should not be confused with the status of the appraisal form. Form appraisal statuses, such as In Planning, In Review, and In Process are process-related statuses and have nothing to do with template status. A template status can be Not Released, Released, or Archived.

A template with a status of Not Released means it is not available for productive use. A template remains as Not Released during configuration because you can only edit the template configuration when it is in this status. Templates in your development system should only be the templates labeled as Not Released; whereas those in your quality assurance and production systems should never be Not Released.

After you are ready to use the form, change its status to Released. Only at this time can you create appraisal documents in the system. Once released, you cannot change the form unless you reset the status to Not Released. To do this, first double-click on the appraisal template in PHAP_CATALOG. Either select **Appraisal Template • Status • Cancel Release**, or right-click on the template and select **Status • Cancel Release**.

Note that after you have released the template and created appraisal documents for the template, you cannot unrelease the template in that environment. If you need to modify the template while it is in production, those changes must be done in the development environment and propagated up the landscape via a transport.

An important aspect of releasing a template is that it is hierarchical: If you release a parent element, all subelements are also released. This means that if the top-level appraisal template is released, all dependent children (such as criteria groups and criteria) of that template are released as well. This is especially important if you are reusing elements between appraisals. We discuss unused elements in detail later in the chapter.

An appraisal template's status is set to Archived when it is no longer used but needs to be retained for historical purposes. Archiving a template makes it unavailable for productive use but allows you to continue to use it for reporting purposes. Typically, templates are archived after the appraisal process is complete, thus making it unavailable to end users but still available for reporting.

9.1.2 Sorting and Weighting

The Sorting and Weighting function is available by right-clicking on the template or by selecting the option on the application toolbar. This allows you to sort your appraisal elements (criteria group, criteria, etc.) and appropriately weight sections of the appraisal.

Sorting is needed because newly created appraisal elements are always first displayed below the last element of the section. Numerically sorting your appraisal elements can be done efficiently at both the appraisal and criteria group levels. Sorting at the criterion level cannot be done because it does not make sense.

If a weighting is to be associated with a particular section of the appraisal (at the criteria group level, for example), you can specify this in the **Element Weighting** column. The standard weighing is 1.00. In Figure 9.1, the value 1.00 is given to the **Individual Objectives** and **Worklogix Values** sections. A value of 1.00 for both sections indicates that each of those sections is weighted equally at 50%. You can, however, change the weighting. For example, values of .75 and .25 would indicate a 75% and 25% weighting distribution between the two sections.

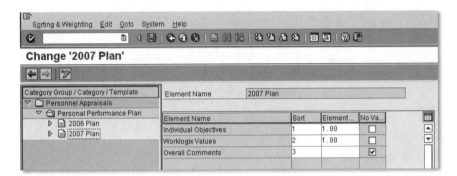

Figure 9.1 Sorting and Weighting View at the Appraisal Level

The **No Value** box indicates that the section is not valuated, meaning that it will not be included in an overall calculation. Because that section is not valuated, you are not permitted to store an element weighting if this box is checked.

9.1.3 Translating the Appraisal

For many global implementations, the ability to translate the appraisal verbiage in different languages is paramount to a successful rollout. An appraisal template that is used globally can be translated into 41 different languages that are supported by SAP, including English, Spanish, German, French, Japanese, and Chinese. All languages in table T002 are supported.

Both element descriptions and value descriptions can be translated on the appraisal template. To translate, select the element (appraisal, criteria group, etc.) you want to translate, and select the source language by either clicking on the **Translate** button in the application toolbar, or by right-clicking on the element and selecting the **Translation** option. You are first asked for the target language (see Figure 9.2). After identifying the target language, a dual-paned screen appears where you can view the source (i.e., the original) and the target language (see Figure 9.3). Here you can translate content within your appraisal document.

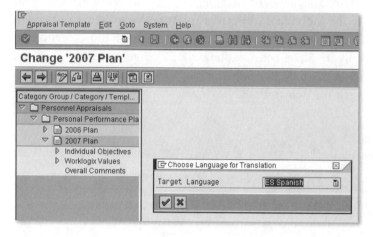

Figure 9.2 Pop Up for Target Language

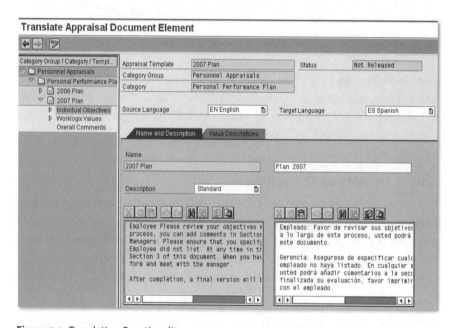

Figure 9.3 Translation Functionality

9.1.4 Copying and Pasting Appraisal Elements

Being able to copy and paste appraisal elements will significantly speed up configuration time. By default, new elements are created when you copy and paste them. An option for **Copy & Paste** (see Figure 9.4) exists in the user settings of the Appraisal Catalog (which can be accessed in Transaction PHAP_ CATALOG, by choosing **Settings • User Settings**). Selections include **Copy All Elements**, **Reuse Structure**, and **Decide Using Dialog.**

▸ In most cases, you should stick to the default option **Copy All Elements**, as this copies appraisal elements and pastes them as new elements.

▸ The **Reuse Structure** option allows you to paste the same element structure into another part of the form or into another form entirely.

▸ The last option, **Decide Using Dialog**, gives you the option each time to either copy or reuse the element IDs when you paste. Note that this user setting is not available in Extension Set 1.1; all elements that are copied are automatically pasted as new elements.

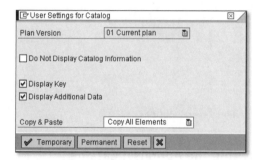

Figure 9.4 User Settings Including Copy & Paste Behavior

9.1.5 Using the Quick Configuration Option

The **Quick Configuration** option, available as of Extension Set 2.0, is a fast way to view all appraisal elements and their associated value lists, value determinations, value inputs, and notes. The option, which conveniently lists all elements (template, criteria group, criteria, etc.) with their respective column configuration, is available when you right-click on a template. Access to this option is available by simply right-clicking on the appraisal template (see Figure 9.5)

> **Example**
>
> Using the **Quick Configuration** option, you can mass replace value lists, for example. You may have decided to change a value list in the configuration and need to update all appropriate elements with this new value list. Using the Quick Configuration functionality is a convenient way to universally replace this value list throughout your template.

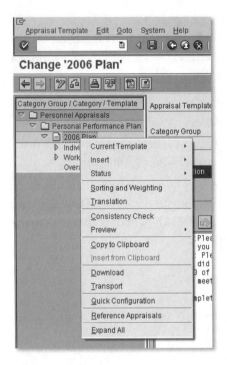

Figure 9.5 Right-clicking the Template Provides Several Options

9.1.6 Previewing the Form Within the Appraisal Catalog

You can preview both the web and print versions of your form from the Appraisal Catalog by right-clicking on the template and selecting **Preview • Print Setup**, or **Web Layout**, whichever is appropriate Alternatively, the **Print** and **Web Layout** buttons are available on the application toolbar when you double-click on an appraisal template.

Figure 9.6 shows the **Print Layout** preview. The form is launched in an Adobe Acrobat PDF file. As a side note, you should verify compatibility of your Acrobat software. This is very important if employees can access the Portal (and forms) from home via their own computers that may or may not have the latest version of Acrobat Reader.

Note

Although you can view the elements of the form and their relative position, you cannot simulate the appraisal process during the **Web Layout** preview option. The catalog renders the complete header and all available columns and rows regardless of the status and column access to give the configuration analyst a holistic view of what has been configured in the system and is not meant to replace how the form will appear throughout the process.

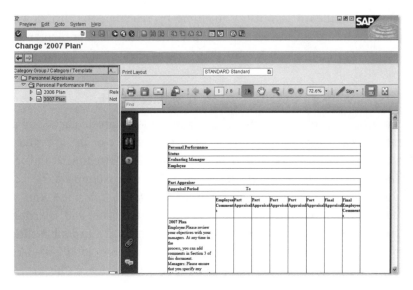

Figure 9.6 Print Layout Preview

The Web Layout is shown in Figure 9.7. As with the print layout, you should consider web browser versions when deploying on an external portal or globally, where employees can use various versions (Acrobat Reader 6.0, 7.0, 8.0, etc.) and products (Internet Explorer, Firefox, Opera, etc.).

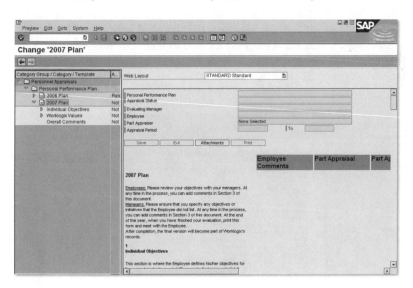

Figure 9.7 Web Layout Preview

If you have identified alternate print or web layouts in your configuration (identified on the **Layout** tab), they will show up during preview. You can also review the standard layouts at any time by selecting the dropdown menu at the top-center of the screen. SAP provides a standard implementation of both the print and web layouts that you can always refer back to.

9.1.7 Performing a Consistency and Template Check

Before releasing a template, you should perform both a template check and a consistency check. The *template check* verifies the stability of the appraisal, whereas the *consistency check* does a full validation of the template and its underlying elements (criteria group, criteria, etc.). To perform template checks, Transaction PHAP_CATALOG is used. There are two ways to select the type of check you want. The first way is by right-clicking the template, and selecting either **Template Check** or **Consistency Check**. The second way is to double-click the template, click the **Check** button on the application toolbar, and then select the check option you need (either **Template Check** or **Consistency Check**).

When the results of the consistency check are returned, they are accompanied by a green square (information), yellow triangle (warning), or red circle (error), as shown in Figure 9.8. If your template has even one red circle, you will not be able to release it.

Note

Green and yellow indicators will not prohibit you from releasing your template in a productive environment but should be reviewed for good measure. A typical yellow message might indicate that you have defined a description for an element but did not indicate that this description is to be visible. These types of warnings are informational and can be ignored if desired.

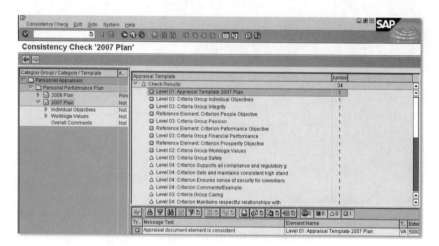

Figure 9.8 Output from the Consistency Check

9.1.8 Unused Elements

During the course of your configuration, it is common to make mistakes. Sometimes you will have extraneous appraisal elements in your catalog, either made by mistake or orphaned because you eventually decided not to use them in your template. From time-to-time, it is a good idea to review these unused elements and delete them from the catalog. To view the unused elements in your Appraisal Catalog, perform the following: when you *first* enter Transaction PHAP_CATALOG, select **Appraisal Catalog • Unused Elements**. The **Unused Elements** screen shown in Figure 9.9 appears. Here you can view and delete any unused elements that you do not need. To delete an element, simply select the appropriate row (or rows), and click on the trash can icon on the application toolbar.

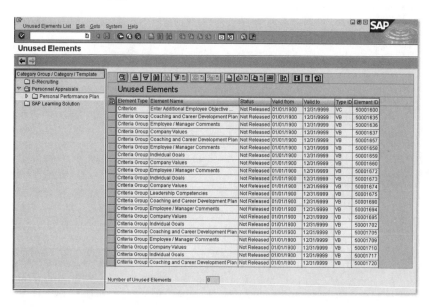

Figure 9.9 Unused Appraisal Elements

9.1.9 Verifying Your Configuration

After configuration is complete, it is a good idea to ensure that all customizing tables are consistent. SAP provides the RHHAP_CUSTOMIZING_CHECK program to perform these validation checks for you. You can run this check via Transaction PHAP_ADMIN by choosing **Utilities • Check Customizing**. Alternately, you can run this program directly via Transaction SA38 or Transaction SE38 if you have access. The purpose of this program is to verify the consistency of the following customizing Tables: T777E, T777I, T777Z, T778A, T778O, T77AD, T77HAP, T77HAP_COL, T77HAP_C_GRP, T77HAP_

EX, T77HAP_EX_AR, T77HAP_ROLE, T77HAP_VALUE_CLS, T77MWBFCD, T77MWBFCH, T77PP_PART, T77PR_V_H_P, and T77S0. An example output of this validation program can be seen in Figure 9.10.

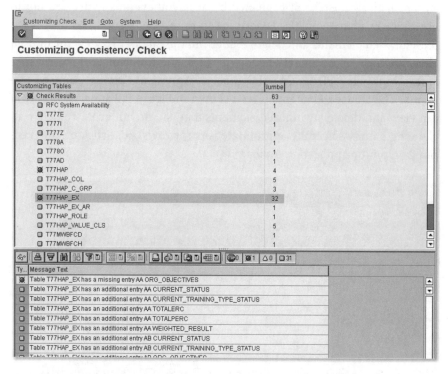

Figure 9.10 Example Output of Report RHHAP_CUSTOMIZING_CHECK

> **Tip**
>
> Often, missing configuration table entries can be discovered with the program RHHAP_CUSTOMIZING_CHECK, so keep this in mind after you complete the initial configuration and whenever you need to troubleshoot your work.

9.1.10 Moving Changes Through the System Landscape

One of the most challenging customizing activities is propagating the appraisal template through the landscape. Moving the appraisal from your development system through quality assurance and onto production can be difficult if you are not familiar with the tools available. Two options are available to move changes through your system landscape:

► You can opt to use the upload/download utility.

► You can save your changes in a transport.

You should save changes in a transport because it affords greater traceability and audit tracking. All changes are made in your development environment and can be transported into your QA and production environments, as with all of the configuration in SAP ERP.

After saving your changes in the Appraisal Catalog, you will not be prompted to save to a transport unless the transport switch in T77S0 (Group: TRSP, semantic abbreviation: CORR) is active (indicated by an "X" in the configuration). In most implementations, this transport switch is not active. Thus, you need to manually assign your template changes to a transport by right-clicking on the template and selecting **Transport**. By assigning the template to the transport, you are also assigning all underlying elements of the appraisal, including criteria group and criteria configuration. You are also permitted (and it is recommended) to transport the category in this same fashion.

Note

For those on Extension Set 1.1, the transport functionality in Transaction PHAP_ CATALOG is not available. To transport your changes, you must use program RHMOVE30 (Manually Transport Link). Read through the program's documentation thoroughly before attempting to save your appraisal changes to a transport.

Although downloading and uploading your templates is not the recommended way of promoting changes up the landscape, it is important for backup purposes. You should get in the habit of downloading template versions when you have reached milestones in your configuration. You can store the downloaded files on your PC or on a shared network at work, just in case you need to revert back to a previous version. You can download appraisal templates and categories but not category groups. SAP recommends that customers use the standard category groups. Appraisal templates are stored with an *.xsc* file extension, whereas categories are stored with a *.yhm* file extension.

To upload a category, right-click on the category group that you want to attach the category to, and select the **Upload Category** option. To upload a template, right-click on the category that you want to attach the template to, and select the **Upload Template** option. After the upload, you should immediately conduct a consistency check. When uploading and downloading between clients and systems, you may encounter a conflict with the configuration or development. Most of the time, this is due to missing or different configuration or BAdIs that are in one system but not the other. If you receive warnings or hard errors, you should research and resolve these problems first before moving on.

9.2   Customizing Appraisal Settings via OOHAP_BASIC

You have seen how Transaction PHAP_CATALOG is the backbone of performance management configuration. Although the bulk of your configuration is performed there, another Transaction, OOHAP_BASIC, provides enhanced customizing to extend the capabilities of the appraisal platform. Using Transaction OOHAP_BASIC, you can perform such activities as creating custom columns, creating custom pushbuttons, and adding new workflows that can be made available to your appraisal templates. This transaction is integral to the extensibility of the performance management application.

> **Note**
>
> In Extension Set 1.1, some of the customizing described in the following sections is not available. Those on Extension Set 1.1, for example, are somewhat limited with changing the flow of the process because substatus and pushbutton customization is not possible.

9.2.1   Custom Columns

Out-of-the-box, SAP comes with more than 15 standard columns. Standard columns, such as Objectives (**OBJ0**), Weighting (**FWGT**), Part Appraisal (**PAPP**), and Final Appraisal (**FAPP**), are fundamental to many customers' forms. As discussed in the previous chapter, columns provide a mechanism to collect appraisal information in a structured and secure manner (via the **Column Access** tab). However, there are times when additional customer-specific columns may be necessary. For example, if your performance management process has a mid-year review period, adding additional columns to collect mid-process feedback may be desired.

As with other configuration specific to a customer, the custom column IDs you create should begin with the letter Z, letter Y, or number 9 to stay within the customer namespace. After adding a column entry in Transaction OOHAP_BASIC, the column will not be immediately available in the template. After the custom configuration is performed, it will be seen at the category level under the **Available** section of the **Columns** tab. You need to make it available to the underlying templates by moving the column to the **Selected** area on the left side. To move the items from the **Available** section to the **Selected** section, select the **Column ID** in the **Available** section, and press the left arrow button. This moves the selected items to the **Selected** area. In Figure 9.11, two newly created custom columns (**ZECE** and **ZEEF**) are depicted in the **Available** section. These two columns are not available to the appraisal template until they are moved to the **Selected** area on the left side.

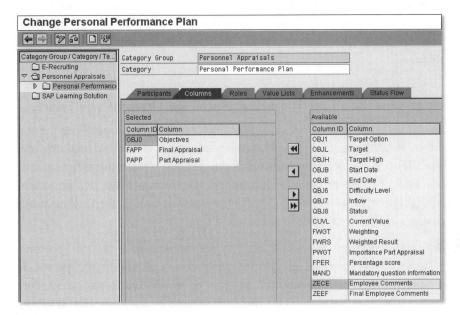

Figure 9.11 Custom Columns Employee Comments and Final Employee Comments in the Columns tab's Available Section

9.2.2 Custom Substatuses and Custom Pushbuttons

The use of custom substatuses coupled with custom pushbuttons is one of the most important enhancements to affect the flow of the process. The standard nine statuses described in Chapter 7 provide customers with the ability to support a typical process flow. However, in more complex process scenarios, additional substatuses may be needed on top of this baseline. Custom substatuses provide a tremendous amount of flexibility because custom pushbuttons can be created to move your process along to completion. Although custom statuses are *not* allowed, custom substatuses can exists beneath any status. Substatuses must be made available at the category group first as well as the category to make them available at the template level.

9.2.3 Custom Roles

Creating custom roles is less common but still possible. Roles are important for those processes using the Part Appraisal functionality because they allow you to prohibit certain users from editing appraisal elements in part appraisal documents. Standard roles include Self (**MYSELF**), Manager (**MANAGER**), and Higher-Level Manager (**HIGHER_MANAGER**). A custom role, such as Delegate or HR Manager, could be configured and developed to accommodate your specific requirements. These roles are all standard filter values of BAdI HRHAP00_SELECTION and discussed in greater depth in the next chapter.

9.2.4 Enhancing the Workflow: Authorized Persons and Events

As of Extension Set 2.0, SAP has the robust capability of controlling the status flow of the appraisal process by configuring authorized persons and workflow events. Both were introduced to provide a mechanism for enhancing the flow of the process. Understanding the basics of these two important configuration areas will help identify the controls needed for making status changes and notifications.

Authorized persons, listed in Table 9.1, permit users to access pushbuttons. Whether for a standard or custom pushbutton, an authorized person is required behind each pushbutton to indicate which end user(s) can execute that button. If you do not want to restrict access to a pushbutton, selecting the **All** option allows you to grant pushbutton access to all users of the form.

Authorized Person	Rule	Function Module
Appraiser	12300009	HRHAP_DOC_WF_ACTOR_APPRAISER
Appraisee	12300010	HRHAP_DOC_WF_ACTOR_APPRAISEE
Part Appraiser	12300011	HRHAP_DOC_WF_ACTOR_PART_APPER
Further Participants	12300012	HRHAP_DOC_WF_ACTOR_OTHERS
Higher-Level Manager (from Appraisee)	12300020	HRHAP_DOC_WF_ACTOR_HIGHER_MGR
All	N/A	N/A (no restriction to the pushbutton)

Table 9.1 Standard Authorized Persons (i.e., Workflow Rules)

It may become necessary to create a custom authorized person. A custom authorized person is needed if you want to grant pushbutton access to users other than those listed in Table 9.1. An example of a custom authorized person is for a delegate. If Delegate functionality has been established within your performance management process, you may need to add the delegate as an available authorized person. A new workflow rule needs to be created. Authorized persons are actual workflow rules.

A workflow resource can view workflow rules via Transaction PFAC. At this point, a function module is associated to the rule that provides the necessary role resolution. For example, function module HRHAP_DOC_WF_ACTOR_APPRAI-SEE resolves to the appraisee of the document. A workflow developer should not have a problem creating a custom rule. After the workflow resource has created the custom rule, you need to add it in Transaction OOHAP_BASIC in the **Workflow-Authorized Persons** folder (see Figure 9.12). All custom rules should fall under the customer namespace, beginning with the number 9.

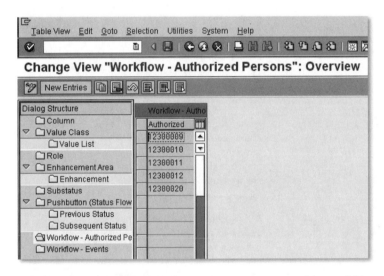

Figure 9.12 The Standard Workflow — Authorized Persons Folder Available in Transaction OOHAP_BASIC

Another use for authorized persons (workflow rules) is to support workflow events. A *workflow event* is a fancy phrase for a notification. A workflow notification provides a way to alert an actor (i.e., authorized person) within the process concerning next steps. For example, after an appraisee completes the objectives, a notification may need to be sent to the appraiser indicating that a review of those objectives is needed. This work item may be launched when the appraisee clicks "Send to Manager" for Review pushbutton for example. Immediately after this pushbutton is selected, a workflow notification is sent to the appraiser. All standard notifications (see Table 9.2) are triggered by pushbuttons.

Workflow Event	Description	Workflow Template ID
INFO_APPRAISEE_CHANGE	A work item request to change the appraisal is sent to the appraisee. The form is displayed in change mode.	12300114
INFO_APPRAISEE_CHANGE_APPROVE	A work item request to approve the appraisal is sent to the appraisee. The form is displayed in change mode.	12300116
INFO_APPRAISEE_CHANGE_REVIEW	A work item notification is sent to the appraisee one week before the review date recorded in the appraisee's appraisal document.	12300126
INFO_APPRAISEE_DISPLAY	A work item notification is sent to the appraisee stating that the document can be displayed. The form is displayed in display mode, so that no changes are possible, and no buttons for status changes are available.	12300113
INFO_APPRAISEE_DISPL_APPROVED	A work item notification is sent to the appraisee stating that the appraisal has been approved. The form is displayed in display mode, so that no changes are possible and no buttons for status changes are available.	12300120
INFO_APPRAISEE_DISPL_REJECTED	A work item notification is sent to the appraisee stating that the appraisal has been rejected. The document is displayed in display mode, so that no changes are possible and no buttons for status changes are available.	12300121
INFO_APPRAISER_CHANGE	A work item request to change the document is sent to the appraiser. The form is displayed in change mode.	12300110
INFO_APPRAISER_CHANGE_APPROVE	A work item request to approve the appraisal is sent to the appraiser. The form is displayed in change mode.	12300115
INFO_APPRAISER_CHANGE_EXE_PER	A work item notification is sent to the appraiser stating that a document needs to be completed in the time frame determined by the completion period.	12300127

Table 9.2 Standard Performance Management Workflows

Workflow Event	Description	Workflow Template ID
INFO_APPRAISER_CHANGE_REVIEW	A work item notification is sent to the appraiser one week before the review date recorded in the appraisee's appraisal.	12300125
INFO_APPRAISER_DISPLAY	A work item notification is sent to the appraiser stating that the appraisal can be displayed. The form is displayed in display mode, so that no changes are possible and no buttons for status changes are available.	12300109
INFO_APPRAISER_DISPL_APPROVED	A work item notification is sent to the appraiser stating that the appraisal has been approved. The form is displayed in display mode, so that no changes are possible and no buttons for status changes are available.	12300117
INFO_APPRAISER_DISPL_REJECTED	A work item notification is sent to the appraiser stating that the appraisal has been rejected. The form is displayed in display mode, so that no changes are possible and no buttons for status changes are available.	12300119
INFO_HIGHER_MANAGER_APPROVE	A work item request to approve the appraisal is sent to the manager's manager who is determined as the next higher chief position in the organizational structure from the appraisee. The form is displayed in change mode.	12300122
INFO_NEXT_PART_APPER_CHANGE	A work item request to assess the employee is sent to the next part appraiser. The part appraisal is displayed in change mode.	12300124

Table 9.2 Standard Performance Management Workflows (Cont.)

Tip

An article by Dr. Martina Schuh and Maurice Hagen from SAP AG entitled "Workflow-Enable Your Performance Management" is an excellent resource to learn more about statuses, substatuses, and workflow notifications within performance management. The article was published in the April 2004 issue of *HR Expert* magazine.

Custom notifications can be created and integrated into your appraisal process. If you decide to customize a workflow, it is strongly advised that you first copy a standard workflow that is closest to the one you are creating and then tweak that workflow as necessary. All workflow events are based on business object APPR_DOC. After your workflow resource has created the custom workflow, be sure to add an entry in Table SWFDVEVTY1 through Transaction SWETYPV. As with the standard workflow events, the Receiver Call should be set as **Function Module**, whereas the Receiver Function Module should be SWW_WI_CREATE_VIA_EVENT_IBF. Be sure to enable the **Linkage Activated** checkbox when you are ready to test the workflow. This event linkage can also be updated via Transaction PHAP_ADMIN by choosing **Utilities • Event Linkage (Workflow)**.

More information on workflow can be learned from Alan Rickayzen's book, *Practical Workflow for SAP: Effective Business Processes Using SAP's Web-Flow Engine* (Galileo Press/SAP PRESS; 2002).

All workflow events needed in your appraisal templates are stored in Transaction OOHAP_BASIC (see Figure 9.13). Any custom workflow that you create must be saved within this configuration before attaching it within the appraisal template on the **Status** tab.

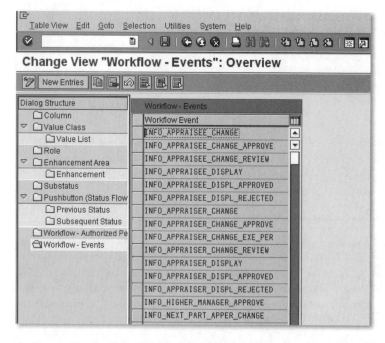

Figure 9.13 Standard Workflow Events Available in Transaction OOHAP_BASIC

Note that these notifications are supported within the Universal Worklist (UWL), which is another name for the inbox on the SAP NetWeaver Portal. It is important not to confuse notifications with corporate emails. Out-of-the-box, these workflow events do *not* send emails to Outlook, Lotus Notes, or other corporate email systems. However, if sending email is a business requirement, you can modify the workflow to do this or discuss the possibilities with a workflow resource to automate email updates based on standard work item notifications via program RSWUWFML2 Sending Notifications for Work Items.

Whether using standard or custom workflow events, these items need to be associated to a pushbutton. Whenever a user clicks on that pushbutton, the workflow event is triggered. The linkage between the pushbutton and workflow event is performed on the **Status Flow** tab within the appraisal template (see Figure 9.14).

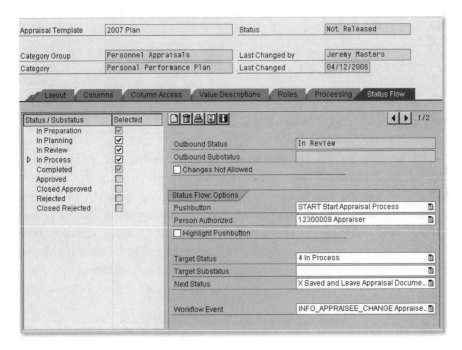

Figure 9.14 Workflow Event INFO_APPRAISEE_CHANGE Available on the Status Flow Tab

Like substatuses, workflow rules and events must be made available at the category group level and the category level to access them at the template level.

9.3 Custom Value Lists

The last section of this chapter discusses creating custom value lists (also called *scales*). After defining value lists and their importance within the overall process, we will step through an example of creating a custom value list together.

9.3.1 Value List Configuration

Value list configuration is paramount within the context of performance management. Value lists enable you to include a dropdown box or set of radio buttons containing values within the appraisal form. An example value list for a performance management rating scale is shown in Table 9.3.

Rating	Rating Description
4	Significantly Exceeds Expectations
3	Exceeds Expectations
2	Meets All Expectations
1	Fails to Meet Expectations
N/A	Not Applicable

Table 9.3 Sample Value List for a Performance Rating

To configure a value list, you need access to Transaction OOHAP_VALUE_TYPE. The transaction renders a tree structure in the left side panel, with the folders **Value List**, **Values**, and **Value description** forming the hierarchy (see Figure 9.15). If you have worked with the Qualification Catalog in the past, value lists should look familiar to you. This is because qualification proficiencies are a type of value list. For those implementing competency- and skill-based appraisals, value lists are fundamental to the integration of the two modules.

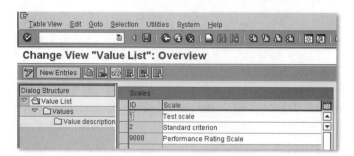

Figure 9.15 Performance Management Value Lists

When creating a value list, you are first asked whether it should be a quality scale, quantity scale, or a nonsequential quality scale (see Figure 9.16). Performance ratings are typically stored as quality scales. (Table 9.3 is a good example of a quality scale.) Quantity scales are used more for weighting, as you can specify a minimum, maximum, and interval increments. For example, your weighting scale might range from 0% to 100% in 5% increments. A nonsequential quality scale may skip an integer. For example, an example nonsequential quality scale may include ratings 1, 3, 5.

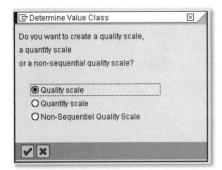

Figure 9.16 Value Class Prompt When Creating a Value List

After creating a value list, you need to specify the elements for that list. For a quality scale like the one shown in Figure 9.17, the ID value represents a scale element. For example, value **FM — Fails to Meet Expectations** is coded by the system as value ID 1, whereas the value **MA — Meets All Expectations** is coded as value ID 3. The numeric component behind the value IDs is very important if your form runs any calculations, either averaging or summation. The Compensation Management module can use any calculated ratings during compensation planning time for decision making.

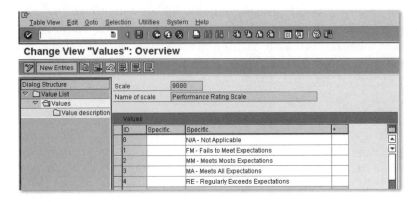

Figure 9.17 Values Within Scale (or Value List), Performance Rating Scale

An optional value description can also be configured to explain each value in more detail. As shown in Figure 9.18, several lines can be concatenated sequentially to provide this information to the end user. On the appraisal form in the portal, an **Info** link appears beside the value list that contains this description. If no descriptions are maintained, no hyperlinks will appear in the appraisal form.

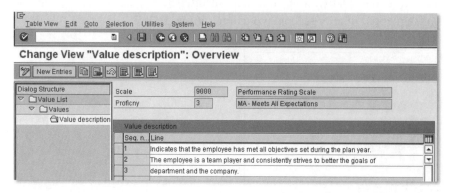

Figure 9.18 Example Value Description

After creating and configuring the value list, it must be made available at the category level before it can be made available to the template.

9.4   Summary

In this chapter, we reviewed advanced configuration techniques that will assist you in delivering a robust form to support your performance management process. From the complex areas within the Appraisal Catalog to the extensibility afforded by Transaction OOHAP_BASIC, you have seen how knowledge of these areas can provide significant process improvements. The next chapter reviews one of the most important concepts SAP Performance Management: enhancements through Business Add-Ins (BAdIs). These customizations provide substantive means to deliver an end-to-end solution that will exceed expectations.

Business Add-Ins (BAdIs) provide a robust way of enhancing your performance management system by allowing you to implement customer-specific rules according to business requirements. SAP provides many standard implementations that you can leverage, or you can create your own, which we will explore in this chapter.

10 Performance Management BAdIs

One of the most robust aspects of the Performance Management module is the abundance of BAdIs and BAdI implementations available. *BAdIs* (Business Add-Ins) are user exits available for SAP customers to implement. BAdIs provide a way of enhancing the system to meet your unique business requirements. Put another way, BAdIs and their implementations provide "the hook" needed for organizations to implement unique changes to their system.

It is important to note that a BAdI is programmed, not configured, so you need an ABAP (Advanced Business Application Programming)-knowledgeable resource to assist you in enhancing an existing BAdI implementation or creating a new implementation. After a BAdI enhancement is created by a developer, a configuration specialist must make this BAdI enhancement "available" to the template before inclusion to the form. We will cover these steps in detail in this chapter.

10.1 BAdI Areas

SAP delivers seven BAdI areas. BAdI areas are nothing more than a logical way to group the BAdIs available in the Performance Management module. The standard BAdI areas include the following:

▸ Template: Definition and Behavior
▸ Catalog
▸ Appraisal Enhancement
▸ Reporting

▸ Administrator

▸ Add-On Application

▸ Further BAdIs

Each BAdI area can be viewed using program RHHAP_BADI_OVERVIEW. You can run this program directly from either Transaction SE38 or SA38. You can also reach this program from Transaction PHAP_ADMIN by choosing **Utilities • BAdI Overview** (see Figure 10.1). All BAdIs in the Performance Management module begin with the prefix HRHAP00.

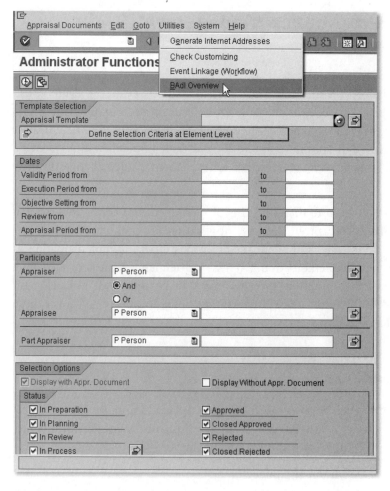

Figure 10.1 BAdI Overview Menu Option from Transaction PHAP_ADMIN

In the following sections, we cover each BAdI area, the BAdIs they contain, and the available BAdI implementations.

10.2 BAdI Area: Template Definition and Behavior

The Definition and Behavior area (see Figure 10.2) contains BAdIs that affect the operation of the appraisal form. Many of these user exits make the form dynamic and extensible. Whether the form is defaulting in data from the Personnel Administration or Organization Management modules, these BAdIs help make the solution more robust and user-intuitive.

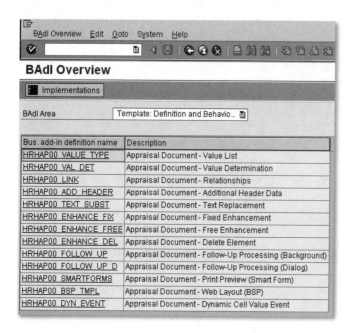

Figure 10.2 BAdI Area Template: Definition and Behavior within the BAdI Overview Screen

Each BAdI definition within BAdI Area Template: Definition and Behavior is discussed next. In some cases, a cursory explanation is given for those BAdIs that are not frequently used. In all cases, the standard implementations are discussed with their release availability.

Tip

Throughout the chapter, the availability of each BAdI implementation is discussed based on SAP release version (e.g., 4.7, ECC 5.0, etc.). It should be noted that:

▸ Any BAdI implementation available as of Enterprise Extension 4.7 Set 1.1 is also available in Enterprise Extension 4.7 Set 2.0, ECC 5.0, and ECC 6.0.

▸ Any BAdI implementation available as of Enterprise Extension 4.7 Set 2.0 is also available in ECC 5.0 and ECC 6.0.

▸ Any BAdI implementation available as of ECC 5.0 is also available in ECC 6.0.

10.2.1 HRHAP00_VALUE_TYPE (Appraisal Document — Value List)

BAdI `HRHAP00_VALUE_TYPE` enables you to create customer-specific value types that form the basis for value lists. SAP delivers many standard value types, including those to support value lists for quantity and quality scales. These scales are bound by certain rules (e.g., a quality scale must not have any gaps). Although not common, you may decide to create your own value lists to support your own requirements. For more details about value lists and their use within the system, see Chapter 9.

Table 10.1 lists the standard implementations for BAdI `HRHAP00_VALUE_TYPE` and their release availability.

Enhancement Name	BAdI Implementation	BAdI Implementation Description	Availability
D	HRHAP00_VALUE_TYPE_D	Date	As of Enterprise 4.7 Extension Set 1.1
E	HRHAP00_VALUE_TYPE_D	Status of Development Plan Item	As of ECC 5.0
M	HRHAP00_VALUE_TYPE_M	Quantity Scale	As Enterprise 4.7 of Extension Set 1.1
N	HRHAP00_VALUE_TYPE_N	Irregular Quality Scale	As of Enterprise 4.7 Extension Set 1.1
O	HRHAP00_VALUE_TYPE_O	Options	As of Enterprise 4.7 Extension Set 1.1
Q	HRHAP00_VALUE_TYPE_Q	Quality Scales	As of Enterprise 4.7 Extension Set 1.1
S	HRHAP00_VALUE_TYPE_S	Numeric Value	As of Enterprise 4.7 Extension Set 1.1
T	HRHAP00_VALUE_TYPE_T	Status of Business Event Types	As of ECC 5.0
C	HRHAP_VALUE_TYPE_C	Currency (TCURC)	As of ECC 5.0
U	HRHAP_VALUE_TYPE_CU	Unit of Measurement (T006)	As of ECC 5.0

Table 10.1 Standard BAdI Implementations for HRHAP00_VALUE_TYPE and Their Release Availability

After you have created your custom value type, you can configure your new value list in Transaction OOHAP_VALUE_TYPE. You can then associate your new value list with a particular column on the **Columns** tab. This BAdI is available as of Extension 4.7 Set 1.1.

10.2.2 HRHAP00_VAL_DET (Appraisal Document — Value Determination)

Value determination is a very powerful part of the Performance Management solution because it enables system defaulting and calculation. You can use value determination, for example, to default in the current status of a qualification or the current status of a business event such as a training course. Performing complex calculations on-the-fly is also an important capability with this BAdI.

Table 10.2 lists the standard implementations for BAdI HRHAP00_VAL_DET and their release availability.

Enhancement Name	BAdI Implementation	BAdI Implementation Description	Availability
ALTWEIGHT	HRHAP00_VAL_DET_012	Value Determination — Default Value	As of Enterprise 4.7 Extension Set 2.0
AVERAGE	HRHAP00_VAL_DET_001	Value Determination — Average (Weighted)	As of Enterprise 4.7 Extension Set 1.1
CURRENT_ PROFICIENCY	HRHAP00_VAL_DET_006	Value Determination — Current Proficiency	As of Enterprise 4.7 Extension Set 1.1
CURRENT_ STATUS	HRHAP00_VAL_DET_013	Value Determination — Status of Development Plan Item	As of ECC 5.0
CURRENT_ TRAINING_ TYPE_STATUS	HRHAP00_VAL_DET_014	Value Determination — Status of Business Event Type	As of ECC 5.0
NOTE_INIT	HRHAP00_VAL_DET_008	Value Determination — Note Pre-assignment	As of Enterprise 4.7 Extension Set 2.0
ORG_OBJEC- TIVES	HRHAP00_VAL_DET_005	Value Determination — Strategic Objectives	As of Enterprise 4.7 Extension Set 1.1

Table 10.2 Standard BAdI implementations for HRHAP00_VALUE_DET and Their Release Availability

Enhancement Name	BAdI Implementation	BAdI Implementation Description	Availability
PERCENTAGE	HRHAP00_VAL_DET_003	Value Determination — Percentage (Weighted)	As of Enterprise 4.7 Extension Set 1.1
PERFORMANCE_ MATRIX	HRHAP00_VAL_DET_004	Value Determination — Performance Overview	As of Enterprise 4.7 Extension Set 1.1
SUM_UP_ APPRAISAL_ RESULTS	HRHAP00_VAL_DET_011	Value Determination — Summary of Other Appraisal Documents	As of Enterprise 4.7 Extension Set 2.0
TARGET_ ACTUAL_ COMPARISON	HRHAP00_VAL_DET_009	Value Determination -Targ/Act.Comp. in % with Overfulfillment	As of Enterprise 4.7 Extension Set 2.0
TARGET_ ACTUAL_ COMPARISON_2	HRHAP00_VAL_DET_010	Value Determination — Targ/Act.Comp. in % w/o Overfulfillment	As of Enterprise 4.7 Extension Set 2.0
TOTAL	HRHAP00_VAL_DET_002	Value Determination — Total (Weighted)	As of Enterprise 4.7 Extension Set 1.1
WEIGHTED_ RESULT	HRHAP00_VAL_DET_007	Value Determination — Weighted Result (=FWGT * FAPP)	As of Enterprise 4.7 Extension Set 1.1

Table 10.2 Standard BAdI implementations for HRHAP00_VALUE_DET and Their Release Availability (Cont.)

To include this enhancement in your template, select the value determination of the value list for the appropriate column at the template (VA), criteria group (VB), or criterion (VC) level. This BAdI is available as of Extension 4.7 Set 1.1.

10.2.3 HRHAP00_LINK (Appraisal Document — Relationships)

The HRHAP00_LINK BAdI allows you to include buttons in your appraisal document that link out to more information. You can define up to three additional buttons in your template by selecting the suitable entry on the **Layout** tab in the **Links** section.

Table 10.3 lists the standard implementations for BAdI HRHAP00_LINK and their release availability.

Enhancement Name	BAdI Implementation	BAdI Implementation Description	Availability
DISPLAY_ DOCUMENTS_ SUM_UP_CALC	HRHAP00_LINK_005	Link — Display Documents in Validity Period	As of Enterprise 4.7 Extension Set 2.0
DISPLAY_IND_ DEVELOPMENT	HRHAP00_LINK_006	Link — Display Individual Development	As of ECC 5.0
DISPLAY_ MANAGER_ APPRAISAL	HRHAP00_LINK_004	Link — Manager's Document	As of Enterprise 4.7 Extension Set 2.0
DISPLAY_ PREVIOUS_ APPRAISAL	HRHAP00_LINK_003	Relationship — Display Last Document	As of Enterprise 4.7 Extension Set 2.0
DISPLAY_QUAL- IFICATIONS	HRHAP00_LINK_002	Link — Display Qualifications	As of Enterprise 4.7Extension Set 1.1
DISPLAY_ SCORECARD	HRHAP00_LINK_001	Link — Display Scorecard	As of Enterprise 4.7 Extension Set 1.1

Table 10.3 Standard BAdI Implementations for HRHAP00_LINK and Their Release Availability

To include this enhancement in your template, select the appropriate filter for **Link for Display** found on the **Layout** tab in the **Links** section. This BAdI is available as of Extension 4.7 Set 1.1.

10.2.4 HRHAP00_ADD_HEADER (Appraisal Document — Additional Header Data)

The HRHAP00_ADD_HEADER BAdI allows you to include additional information in the header of the appraisal. Any master data, such as the employee's cost center ID or position title, can be rendered on the appraisal document's header via this customer exit. The standard implementation, HRHAP00_ADD_ HEADER_1, includes the following data: Organizational Unit Text, Personnel Areas Text, Personnel Subarea Text, Employee Group, and Employee Subgroup.

If you want to change this additional header data, you should copy this standard implementation into your own customer namespace and modify accordingly. To include this in your template, select the appropriate filter for **Additional Header Data** found on the **Layout** tab in the **Further** section. This BAdI is available as of Extension 4.7 Set 1.1.

10.2.5 HRHAP00_TEXT_SUBST (Appraisal Document — Text Replacement)

For those customers who want to personalize an appraisal by dynamically naming the appraiser, appraisee, or part appraisers within the document, they can use the BAdI HRHAP00_TEXT_SUBST, which allows you to substitute a variable (such as &1 or &2) with actual names of the appraiser or appraisee. To include this enhancement in your template, select the appropriate filter for **Text Replacement** found on the **Layout** tab in the **Further** section. This BAdI is available as of Extension 4.7 Set 1.1.

10.2.6 HRHAP00_ENHANCE_FIX (Appraisal Document — Fixed Enhancement)

One of the more robust user exits available in the solution is BAdI HRHAP00_ENHANCE_FIX, which provides integration with several HR components, including the Qualification Catalog, Development Plans, and the Learning Solution (LSO).

Table 10.4 lists the standard implementations for BAdI HRHAP00_ENHANCE_FIX and their release availability.

Enhancement Name	BAdI Implementation	BAdI Implementation Description	Availability
ADD_BOOKED_ TRAININGS	HRHAP00_ENHANCE_FIX5	Fixed Enhancement — Add Booked Courses	As of Enterprise 4.7 Extension Set 2.0
ADD_IND_ DEVELOPMENT	HRHAP00_ENHANCE_FIX3	Fixed Enhancement — Add Development Plan Items	As of Enterprise 4.7 Extension Set 2.0
ADD_MAND_ TRAINING	HRHAP00_ENHANCE_FIX4	Fixed Enhancement — Add Required Business Event Types	As of Enterprise 4.7 Extension Set 2.0
ADD_REQUIRE- MENTS	HRHAP00_ENHANCE_FIX1	Fixed Enhancement — Add Position Requirements	As of Enterprise 4.7 ExtensionSet 1.1
Q_ADD_ DEFICITS	HRHAP00_ENHANCE_FIX2	Fixed Enhancement — Add Deficits from Position	As of Enterprise 4.7 Extension Set 2.0
ADD_CURRENT_ JF	HRHAP00_ENHANCE_FIX6	Fixed Enhancement — Add Current Job Family	As of ECC 6.0

Table 10.4 Standard BAdI Implementations for HRHAP00_ENHANCE_FIX and Their Release Availability

Fixed enhancements get triggered upon form creation. For example, the standard BAdI implementation HRHAP00_ENHANCE_FIX5 adds any courses within the LSO module that the employee is currently booked for. Implementation HRHAP00_ENHANCE_FIX2 allows you to add position "deficits" to an employee's appraisal document upon form creation. The system compares the employee's qualifications versus the qualifications on that employee's position and job to determine where deficiencies exist.

To include this enhancement in your template, select the appropriate filter at the template (VA) or criteria group (VB) level for **Fixed Enhancement** found on the **Columns** tab in the **Dynamic Settings** section.

10.2.7 HRHAP00_ENHANCE_FREE (Appraisal Document — Free Enhancement)

Like fixed enhancements, free enhancements allow important integration with other functionality, including the Qualification Catalog, Development Plans, and the LSO. The main difference between free enhancement and fixed enhancement is that a free enhancement is user-driven, whereas fixed enhancements are systematic. Free enhancements are not performed unless the user initiates them, whereas fixed enhancements are performed by the system automatically based on an event (e.g., form creation).

Table 10.5 lists the standard implementations for BAdI HRHAP00_ENHANCE_FREE and their release availability.

Enhancement Name	BAdI Implementation	BAdI Implementation Description	Availability
ADD_IND_DEVPLAN_STATION	HRHAP00_ENHANCE_FRE5	Free Enhancement — Add Development Plan Items	As of ECC 5.0
ADD_NEW_ELEMENT	HRHAP00_ENHANCE_FRE1	Free Enhancement — Add New Element	As of Enterprise 4.7 Extension Set 1.1
ADD_NEW_ELEMENT_UP_TO_7	HRHAP00_ENHANCE_FRE3	Free Enhancement — Add New Element (up to 7)	As of Enterprise 4.7 Extension Set 1.1
ADD_QUALIFICATION	HRHAP00_ENHANCE_FRE2	Free Enhancement — Add Qualification	As of Enterprise 4.7Extension Set 1.1
ADD_REQ_QUALIFICATION	HRHAP00_ENHANCE_FRE4	Free Enhancement — Add Requirements of Position	As of Enterprise 4.7 Extension Set 2.0

Table 10.5 Standard BAdI Implementations for HRHAP00_ENHANCE_FREE and Their Release Availability

Enhancement Name	BAdl Implementation	BAdl Implementation Description	Availability
ADD_TRAINING_TYPES	HRHAP00_ENHANCE_FRE6	Free Enhancement — Add Business Event Types	As of ECC 5.0
ADD_JOB_FAMILY	HRHAP00_ENHANCE_FRE7	Free Enhancement — Add Job Family	As of ECC 6.0
ADD_REQ_Q_FROM_JF	HRHAP00_ENHANCE_FRE8	Free Enhancement — Requirements of Job Families	As of ECC 6.0
ADD_Q_FROM_JF	HRHAP00_ENHANCE_FRE9	Add Required Qualifications from Job Family	As of ECC 6.0

Table 10.5 Standard BAdl Implementations for HRHAP00_ENHANCE_FREE and Their Release Availability (Cont.)

To include in your template, select the appropriate filter at the template (VA) or criteria group (VB) level for **Free Enhancement** found on the **Columns** tab in the **Dynamic Settings** section.

10.2.8 HRHAP00_ENHANCE_DEL (Appraisal Document — Delete Element)

BAdl HRHAP00_ENHANCE_DEL is used to control whether a particular user can delete an appraisal element. For example, a business requirement may be to allow a user the ability to remove an objective during the In Planning and In Review statuses. If you need to create your own filter, ask yourself two questions: 1) In which statuses should this element be removable? 2) Which user(s) are permitted to remove this element? After you have answered these, you can determine how to implement this BAdl.

Table 10.6 lists the standard implementations for BAdl HRHAP00_ENHANCE_DEL and their release availability.

Enhancement Name	BAdl Implementation	BAdl Implementation Description	Availability
DELETION_2	HRHAP00_ENHANCE_DEL1	Delete Element — Only In Planning	As of Enterprise 4.7 Extension Set 1.1
DELETION_2_3	HRHAP00_ENHANCE_DEL2	Delete Element — Only In Planning or In Review	As of Enterprise 4.7 Extension Set 1.1
DELETION_2_3_4	HRHAP00_ENHANCE_DEL3	Delete Element — In Planning, In Review, In Process	As of Extension 4.7 Set 1.1

Table 10.6 Standard BAdl Implementations for HRHAP00_ENHANCE_DEL and Their Release Availability

To include this enhancement in your template, select the appropriate filter at the criteria group (VB) and criterion (VC) level for **Deletion of an Element** found on the **Columns** tab in the **Dynamic Settings** section.

10.2.9 HRHAP00_FOLLOW_UP (Appraisal Document — Follow-Up Processing [Background])

SAP's follow-up processing functionality provides a way to perform actions after an appraisal document is completed. Most standard implementations perform updates against the employee's Qualification Catalog. In other words, after the appraisal is closed, the employee's qualification profile in Personnel Development is updated with the appropriate qualification and proficiency level indicated on the form. Starting in ECC 5.0, two additional enhancements — both incorporating the new job family object (JF) — have been included as standard implementations.

Table 10.7 lists the standard implementations for BAdI HRHAP00_FOLLOW_UP and their release availability.

Enhancement Name	BAdI Implementation	BAdI Implementation Description	Availability
ADJUST_POTENTIAL	HRHAP00_FOLLOW_UP_05	Follow-Up (Background) — Adjust Potential (Start Date)	As of ECC 6.0
ADJUST_POTENTIAL_2	HRHAP00_FOLLOW_UP_06	Follow-Up (Background) — Adjust Potential (End Date)	As of ECC 6.0
ADJUST_QUAL_WITH_NOTE_1	HRHAP00_FOLLOW_UP_03	Follow-Up Processing (Background) — Adjust Qualif+No (Start Date)	As of Enterprise 4.7 Extension Set 2.0
ADJUST_QUAL_WITH_NOTE_2	HRHAP00_FOLLOW_UP_04	Follow-Up Processing (Background) — Adjust Qualif+No (End Date)	As of Enterprise 4.7 Extension Set 2.0
ADJUST_QUALIFICATIONS	HRHAP00_FOLLOW_UP_01	Follow-Up Processing (Background) — Adjust Qualif. (Start Date)	As of Enterprise 4.7 Extension Set 1.1
ADJUST_QUALIFICATIONS_2	HRHAP00_FOLLOW_UP_02	Follow-Up Processing (Background) — Adjust Qualif. (End Date)	As of Enterprise 4.7 Extension Set 1.1

Table 10.7 Standard BAdI Implementations for HRHAP00_FOLLOW_UP and Their Release Availability

To include this enhancement in your template, select the appropriate check box found on the **Processing** tab (on the appraisal) in the **Follow-Up Processing** section.

10.2.10 HRHAP00_FOLLOW_UP_D (Appraisal Document — Follow-Up Processing [Dialog])

The HRHAP00_FOLLOW_UP_D BAdI operates similarly to its sister BAdI definition HRHAP00_FOLLOW_UP but differs in that changes are performed online (in a dialog box). When this option is implemented, an administrator must manually perform the follow-up activities via Transaction PHAP_ADMIN. After you have selected the appraisals you want to follow up on, you begin the follow-up procedures by highlighting the appropriate appraisal(s) and selecting **Appraisal Document • Start Follow-Up**. Note that no standard implementations exist for this definition.

10.2.11 HRHAP00_SMARTFORMS (Appraisal Document — Print Preview [Smartform])

Customers commonly change the look-and-feel of the printed appraisal document. If the standard PDF Smartform does not meet your requirements, you can create your own Smartform and integrate it within the appraisal document. A custom Smartform requires a technical resource, typically one skilled in ABAP programming. This BAdI is not the Smartform itself (that is done within Transaction SMARTFORMS) but rather provides the hook needed to integrate your custom-developed form into your appraisal template for printing purposes. After implementation, users who click on the **Print** button within the appraisal form will see the new customized form.

Users of ECC 6.0 also have the capability of using an Adobe Form-based form. BAdI HRHAP00_OFFLINE01 permits the use of the new offline appraisal functionality.

To include this enhancement in your template, select the appropriate filter for **Print Layout** found on the **Layout** tab in the **Further** section. This BAdI is available as of Extension 4.7 Set 1.1. The standard BAdI implementation STANDARD either renders Smartform HAP_TEMPLATE_01 (for those appraisals that have between 1 and 10 columns) or HAP_TEMPLATE_02 (for those appraisal that have more than 10 columns).

10.2.12 HRHAP00_BSP_TMPL (Appraisal Document —
Web Layout [BSP])

If you decide to make front-end user interface (UI) changes, BAdI HRHAHP00_ BSP_TMPL enables you to integrate your custom BSP application. The standard BAdI implementation STANDARD renders the standard BSP application HAP_ DOCUMENT. If you customize the frontend, the application will need to repointed to the custom BSP application, perhaps named Z_HAP_DOCUMENT or similar.

To include this enhancement in your template, select the appropriate filter for **Web Layout** found on the **Layout** tab in the **Further** section. This BAdI is available as of Extension 4.7 Set 1.1.

10.2.13 HRHAP00_OFFLINE (Appraisal Document — Offline)

BAdI HRHAP00_OFFLINE provides the ability for offline appraisal functionality. Offline appraisals allow employees to download an online version of their appraisal in PDF format using Adobe Forms. Employees can then enter their self-assessments or self-rate themselves using the configured value lists. Also, the standard functions of Adobe, such as spell check, are available. After employees have completed their edits offline, they can upload the modifications. For data integrity purposes, the appraisal is locked while employees have it "checked out." This enhancement is available as of ECC 6.0 only.

10.2.14 HRHAP00_DYN_EVENT (Appraisal Document —
Dynamic Cell Value Event)

BAdI HRHAP00_DYN_EVENT is used to perform dynamic logic at the cell value level. SAP provides one standard implementation, HRHAP00_DYN_NOTE, which makes a note required if a particular cell value is considered too low. This BAdI is available as of ECC 5.0.

10.3 BAdI Area A: Catalog

The BAdI area Catalog assists configuration specialists with the creation of categories and templates. These are more background activities that do not touch end users and therefore are not as frequently customized. The enhancement implementations provide a good reference for creating categories and templates.

10.3.1 HRHAP00_CATEG_EXMPLE (Catalog — Create Example Category)

BAdI HRHAP00_CATEG_EXMPLE allows a configuration specialist to create categories in PHAP_CATALOG using a predefined template. Category examples are defined for such categories that will house forms such as objective setting appraisals, checklists, and 360-degree feedback.

Table 10.8 lists the standard implementations for BAdI HRHAP00_CATEG_EXMPLE and their release availability.

Enhancement Name	BAdI Implementation	BAdI Implementation Description	Availability
CHECK_LIST	HRHAP00_CATEG_EXMPL5	Create Example Category — Checklist	As of Extension 4.7 Set 1.1
FEEDBACK_360	HRHAP00_CATEG_EXMPL3	Create Example Category — 360-degree Feedback	As of Extension 4.7 Set 1.1
OBJECTIVE_SETTING	HRHAP00_CATEG_EXMPL2	Create Example Category — Objective Setting	As of Extension 4.7 Set 1.1
REFERENCE	HRHAP00_CATEG_EXMPL4	Create Example Category — References	As of Extension 4.7 Set 1.1
STANDARD_APPRAISAL	HRHAP00_CATEG_EXMPL1	Create Example Category — Standard Appraisal	As of Extension 4.7 Set 1.1

Table 10.8 Standard BAdI Implementations for HRHAP00_CATEG_EXMPLE and Their Release Availability

10.3.2 HRHAP00_TMPL_EXAMPLE (Catalog — Create Example Templates)

Example templates are possible to define in the Appraisal Catalog. These templates, which are made available to your configuration specialist, can be used to provide default templates in configuration.

Table 10.9 lists the standard implementations for BAdI HRHAP00_TMPL_EXMPLE and their release availability:

Enhancement Name	BAdI Implementation	BAdI Implementation Description	Availability
OBJECTIVE_SETTING	HRHAP00_TMPL_OBJ_SET	Example — Objective Setting	As of Enterprise 4.7 Extension Set 1.1

Table 10.9 Standard BAdI Implementations for HRHAP00_TMPL_EXMPLE and Their Release Availability

Enhancement Name	BAdI Implementation	BAdI Implementation Description	Availability
PERFORMANCE_ FEEDBACK	HRHAP00_TMPL_PF	Example — Performance Feedback	As of Enterprise 4.7 Extension Set 1.1
POTENTIAL_JF	HRHAP00_TMPL_JF_POT	Example — Job Family Potential Assignment	As of ECC 6.0

Table 10.9 Standard BAdI Implementations for HRHAP00_TMPL_EXMPLE and Their Release Availability (Cont.)

10.3.3 HRHAP00_TMPL_WIZARD (Catalog — Create Templates Using Wizard)

BAdI HRHAP00_TMP_WIZARD allows you to define a wizard for creating templates in the Appraisal Catalog. This can be used in lieu of a template example (as shown in BAdI HRHAP00_TMPL_EXMPLE).

10.4 BAdI Area C: Appraisal Enhancements

As with the **Template and Behavior** BAdI area, the **Appraisal Enhancements** BAdI area is full of robust functionality that makes the performance management functionality so extensible. We will cover all the available BAdIs and the standard implementations by release.

10.4.1 HRHAP00_TMPL_GETLIST (Appraisal Document — Get Template List)

This BAdI enables you to return a list of all appraisals according to defined criteria. Depending on your business requirements, criteria from the appraisal header, for example, can be used to filter appraisal documents to the user. Several transactions are impacted by this BAdI, including PHAP_ ADMIN and PHAP_CHANGE.

10.4.2 HRHAP00_DOC_DEF_DN (Appraisal Document — Default Appraisal Document Name)

BAdI HRHAP00_DOC_DEF_DN allows you to manipulate the appraisal document's name. Without implementing this BAdI, your appraisal document's name will default as the name of your template (as defined in the configuration). Although this is fine for most customers, this BAdI enables you to dynamically generate a document name when the form is created. The standard implementation HRHAP00_DOC_DEF_DN01 appends the validity start and end dates to the title.

10.4.3 HRHAP00_DOC_DEF_D1 (Appraisal Document — Default Appraiser)

Defaulting header information into the appraisal document is one of the most common practices of appraisal creation. With BAdI HRHAP00_DOC_DEF_D1, you can default in the appraiser of the document based on certain criteria. Standard-delivered implementation HRHAP00_DOC_DEF_D101 defaults in the "chief manager" of the current user as the appraiser of the document.

10.4.4 HRHAP00_DOC_DEF_D2 (Appraisal Document — Default Appraisee)

Like BAdI HRHAP00_DOC_DEF_D1, you can default in the appraisee of a document based on certain criteria. Standard BAdI implementation HRHAP00_DOC_DEF_D201 defaults in the current user as the appraisee.

10.4.5 HRHAP00_DOC_DEF_DP (Appraisal Document — Default Part Appraisers)

You can use BAdI HRHAP00_DOC_DEF_DP to default in the part appraisers of your document. A popular use for this BAdI is when you need to default in other evaluators of the employee, such as a dotted- or dual-line manager. Upon form creation, part appraisers could be autopopulated based on certain organizational management data (e.g., custom relationships). SAP provides BAdI implementation HRHAP00_DOC_DEF_DP01, which defaults in both the employee and manager as part appraisers.

10.4.6 HRHAP00_DOC_DEF_DO (Appraisal Document — Default Further Participants)

BAdI HRHAP00_DOC_DEF_DO defaults in further participants to your document in the same way the preceding BAdIs do for the appraisee, appraiser, and part appraisers.

10.4.7 HRHAP00_DOC_DEF_DV (Appraisal Document — Default App. Document Validity Period)

The validity period of an appraisal is important for the process because it drives reporting. It's crucial that appraisal documents have a begin and end date because downstream functionality, such as compensation adjustments or qualification updates, could potentially need these validity dates. SAP provides BAdI implementation HRHAP00_DOC_DEF_DV01, which defaults the validity period based on when the document is created. If created before July 1, the validity period is set to the previous year (e.g., 01/01/2007-12/31/2007). If created on or after July 1, the validity period is set to the next year (e.g., 01/01/2008-12/31/2008). For many customers, a custom implementation is needed to default in a validity period that corresponds to their planning year.

10.4.8 HRHAP00_DOC_DEF_DE (Appraisal Document — Default Completion Period)

The completion period of the document (if used) can be defaulted based on certain criteria. The completion or execution period (as defined in the appraisal template) can be defaulted to the validity period of the document by using standard BAdI implementation HRHAP00_DOC_DEF_DE01.

10.4.9 HRHAP00_DOC_DEF_DR (Appraisal Document — Default Review Date)

The review date can be defaulted as well using an enhancement. SAP delivers BAdI implementation HRHAP00_DOC_DEF_DR01, which defaults in the review date as the system date.

10.4.10 HRHAP00_COL_OWNER (Appraisal Document — Column Owner)

BAdI HRHAP00_COL_OWNER provides you the ability to enhance or override the standard column owner configuration. Enhancements here will expand configuration settings available on the **Column Owner** column within the **Column Access** tab of the appraisal document. Additional column owners will appear in the **Column Owner** dropdown. You might this use functionality if you have set up delegation or proxy capability and want to have these users update or view appraisal information.

Table 10.10 lists the standard implementations for BAdI `HRHAP00_COL_OWNER` and their release availability.

Enhancement Name	BAdI Implementation	BAdI Implementation Description	Availability
AA	HRHAP00_COL_OWNER_AA	Column Owners Appraiser and Appraisee	As of Enterprise 4.7 Extension Set 2.0
AE	HRHAP00_COL_OWNER_AE	Column Owner Appraisee	As of Enterprise 4.7 Extension Set 2.0
AR	HRHAP00_COL_OWNER_AR	Column Owner Appraiser	As of Enterprise 4.7 Extension Set 2.0
OT	HRHAP00_COL_OWNER_OT	Column Owner Further Participants	As of Enterprise 4.7 Extension Set 2.0
PA	HRHAP00_COL_OWNER_PA	Column Owner Part Appraiser	As of Enterprise 4.7 Extension Set 2.0

Table 10.10 Standard BAdI Implementations for HRHAP00_COL_OWNER and Their Release Availability

10.4.11 HRHAP00_COL_ACCESS (Appraisal Document — Column Access)

The column access BAdI is one of the more common BAdIs implemented. It is often implemented when custom substatuses are being used within your template. With BAdI `HRHAP00_COL_ACCESS`, column access configuration (on the **Column Access** tab on the template) is enhanced. Figure 10.3 shows a custom table that supports an implementation of the column access BAdI. Notice the **Substatus** column within this table. This means that the BAdI can hide, display, enable, and so on a column based on a status and substatus combination. This is just one example of how a customer used the BAdI and custom table combination to enhance column access to the appraisal form.

10.4.12 HRHAP00_ATT_ACCESS (Document — Attachment(s) Authorization Handling)

Using BAdI `HRHAP00_ATT_ACCESS`, you can add authorization for how users can use the attachments functionality. You can influence whether a particular user can add, change, or delete an attachment. This BAdI is available as of Extension 4.7 Set 2.0.

Figure 10.3 Example of a Custom Table for Column Access

10.4.13 HRHAP00_BUT_ACCESS (Appraisal Document — Pushbutton Access)

Enhancing pushbutton access is often another important part of the SAP Performance Management solution. Using the HRHAP00_BUT_ACCESS BAdI, you can supplement and override pushbutton access settings maintained in the configuration (on the **Status Flow** tab). Figure 10.4 shows a custom table that can be maintained by a configuration specialist. Notice that begin and end dates are included in the table. This allows you to adjust when pushbuttons should be available throughout the process. For example, you may want to disable or hide a particular button from users during a certain period within the process when it makes the most sense. This BAdI is available as of Extension 4.7 Set 1.1.

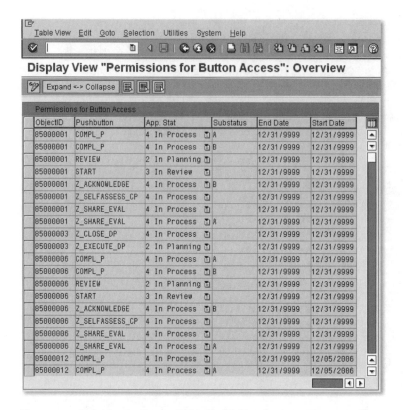

Figure 10.4 Example of a Custom Table for Pushbutton Access

10.4.14 HRHAP00_ACTION_LOG (Appraisal Document — Action Log)

BAdI HRHAP00_ACTION_LOG provides the ability to perform more detailed logging if required. This enhancement is meant to supplement the standard action log functionality available on the **Processing** tab's **Action Log** selection at the template level. Customer-specific information can be written to the application log based on audit and tracking requirements. The application log can be viewed using Transaction **SLG1** (Analyze Application log). Ensure that you search based on Object HRHAP00 (Appraisal Systems). This BAdI is available as of Extension 4.7 Set 1.1.

10.4.15 HRHAP00_DOC_BC (Appraisal Document — Business Check)

BAdI HRHAP00_DOC_BC is a powerful enhancement that can be used to perform customer-specific business logic checks on the appraisal document contents. The BAdI gets called anytime the appraisal document is created, changed, saved, or changes status and, therefore, is widely used in many implementations to add custom-specific logic.

As an example, if a weighting is used within your objective setting process, you may want to ensure that all objectives in total do not exceed 100%. Business rules such as this can be achieved by the use of this BAdI. This BAdI is available as of Extension 4.7 Set 1.1

10.4.16 HRHAP00_AUTHORITY (Appraisal Document — Authorization Check)

If the standard authorizations do not meet your security requirements, BAdI HRHAP00_AUTHORITY can be implemented to enhance your authorization needs. This enhancement enables further refinement of authorizations beyond the new authorization object P_HAP_DOC. Authorization management is discussed in detail in Chapter 13. This BAdI is available as of Extension 4.7 Set 1.1.

10.4.17 HRHAP00_DOC_DELETE (Appraisal Document — Delete)

BAdI HRHAP00_DOC_DELETE determines a customer-specific way of handling appraisal document deletion. Business rules may be in place to perform some follow-up process or notify a group or individual after deletion occurs. This BAdI is available as of Extension 4.7 Set 1.1.

10.4.18 HRHAP00_DOC_SAVE (Appraisal Document — Save Appraisal Document)

BAdI HRHAP00_DOC_SAVE enables customer-specific business rules to be executed when the user saves the appraisal document. The BAdI is called each time the **Save** button is clicked and when status changes occur. Information on the appraisal document, for example, can be saved to standard and custom tables if needed. This BAdI is available as of Extension 4.7 Set 1.1.

10.4.19 HRHAP00_MAX_P_APPER (Maximum Number of Part Appraisers)

BAdI HRHAP00_MAX_P_APPER restricts the number of part appraisers on an appraisal document. In most implementations, there will be no need for more than one or two part appraisers unless you are delivering a 360-degree feedback. SAP delivers two standard implementations: one for limiting the part appraisers to three and another for limiting to four.

Table 10.11 lists the standard implementations for BAdI HRHAP00_MAX_P_APPER and their release availability.

Enhancement Name	BAdI Implementation	BAdI Implementation Description	Availability
MAX_3_PART_APPRAISER	HRHAP00_MAX_P_APPER3	Maximum Number of Part Appraisers = 3	As of Enterprise 4.7 Extension Set 1.1
MAX_4_PART_APPRAISER	HRHAP00_MAX_P_APPER4	Maximum Number of Part Appraisers = 4	As of Enterprise 4.7 Extension Set 1.1

Table 10.11 Standard BAdI Implementations for HRHAP00_MAX_P_APPER and Their Release Availability

10.4.20 HRHAP00_ACC_HEADER (Appraisal Document — Header Data Access)

BAdI HRHAP00_ACC_HEADER enables access to the header of the appraisal document. Access can be enabled based on user and status. You might use this enhancement, for example, if you wanted to provide the ability for the appraiser (e.g., the manager) to search for and select part appraisers during a particular status or statuses. The two standard implementations allow the appraiser to change the part appraiser(s) when status is In Planning (status 2) or In Review (status 3) only (implementation HRHAP00_ACCESS_HDR_1) and when status is In Process (status 4) only (implementation HRHAP00_ACCESS_HDR_2).

Table 10.12 lists the standard implementations for BAdI HRHAP00_ACC_HEADER and their release availability.

Enhancement Name	BAdI Implementation	BAdI Implementation Description	Availability
PART_APPER_ACCESS	HRHAP00_ACCESS_HDR_1	Change Part Appraisers Before Appraisal	As of Enterprise 4.7 Extension Set 1.1
PART_APPER_ACCESS_2	HRHAP00_ACCESS_HDR_2	Change Part Appraisers During Appraisal	As of Enterprise 4.7 Extension Set 1.1

Table 10.12 Standard BAdI Implementations for HRHAP00_ACC_HEADER and Their Release Availability

10.5 BAdI Area E: Reporting

BAdI area E is dedicated to standard reporting in SAP. This area contains only two BAdIs: one for reports made available in Transaction PHAP_SEARCH and the other for default variants.

10.5.1 HRHAP00_REPORTING (Appraisal Document — Reporting)

The standard reporting capability within SAP's Performance Management solution is delivered via BAdI HRHAP00_REPORTING. Within this BAdI, reports are made available within the "report tree" of PHAP_SEARCH. Standard reports include a ranking list and analysis tool.

Table 10.13 lists the standard implementations for BAdI HRHAP00_REPORTING and their release availability.

Enhancement Name	BAdI Implementation	BAdI Implementation Description	Availability
ANALYZE	HRHAP00_REPORTING_03	Analyze	As of Enterprise 4.7 Extension Set 1.1
EXPORT_IN_EXCEL	HRHAP00_REPORTING_02	Export to Excel	As of Enterprise 4.7 Extension Set 1.1
RANKING_LIST	HRHAP00_REPORTING_00	Ranking List	As of Enterprise 4.7 Extension Set 1.1
SMARTFORMS	HRHAP00_REPORTING_01	Print	As of Enterprise 4.7 Extension Set 1.1

Table 10.13 Standard BAdI Implementations for HRHAP00_REPORTING and Their Release Availability

The standard-delivered reports and their capabilities and limitations are covered in detail in Chapter 12.

10.5.2 HRHAP00_REP_GEN_VAR (Appraisal Document — Reporting [Generic Variants])

BAdI HRHAP00_REP_GEN_VAR enables you to dynamically determine variants based on user for Transactions PHAP_SEARCH, PHAP_CHANGE, and PHAP_ADMIN. SAP delivers implementation HRHAP00_REP_GEN_VAR0, which delivers a generic variant. This BAdI is available as of Extension 4.7 Set 1.1.

10.6 BAdI Area X: Administrator

BAdI area X is reserved for administrative purposes. SAP provides one standard BAdI HRHAP00_ADMIN explained next.

10.6.1 HRHAP00_ADMIN (Appraisal Document — Admin. Functions)

BAdI HRHAP00_ADMIN allows you to integrate customer-specific applications within Transaction PHAP_ADMIN. After executing a selection criteria search in PHAP_ADMIN, the **Administrator Functions** becomes available to perform further processing. The button calls on this BAdI to perform the customized functionality. The button could launch a custom transaction, for example. BAdI HRHAP00_ADMIN is available as of Extension 4.7 Set 1.1.

10.7 BAdI Area Y: Add-On Application

BAdI area Y contains so-called "technical objects," meaning that these enhancements are only to be changed by SAP. This means the following BAdIs are for your reference only. Any customer-defined implementation of these BAdI should be performed with extreme caution.

10.7.1 HRHAP00_ADD_ON_APPL (Development: Add-On Application)

BAdI HRHAP00_ADD_ON_APPL defines the relationship between an add-on application and its corresponding category group in the Appraisal Catalog.

10.7.2 HRHAP00_CATALOG_ACT (Development: Catalog — Action)

BAdI HRHAP00_CATALOG_ACT allows for the inclusion of specific functions for template processing in the context menu of the Appraisal Catalog.

10.7.3 HRHAP00_INIT_CATALOG (Development: Catalog — On Initialization)

BAdI HRHAP00_INIT_CATALOG allows for the automation of catalog and template creation when a user first accesses the Appraisal Catalog.

10.7.4 HRHAP00_CATEG_CREATE (Development: Catalog — Category)

BAdI `HRHAP00_CATEG_CREATE` allows for the creation of categories in the Appraisal Catalog.

10.7.5 HRHAP00_TMPL_608 (Development: Applic. — Add-On Dependent Template Restriction)

BAdI `HRHAP00_TMPL_608` is a technical enhancement that supports BAdI `HRHAP00_TMPL_RESTR` discussed in detail later in this chapter.

10.7.6 HRHAP00_CHECK_CUSTOM (Development: Customizing — Check Tables and Settings)

BAdI `HRHAP00_CHECK_CUSTOM` performs checks on the tables and other customizing settings within the Performance Management solution. Among other activities, the PA (Personnel Appraisal) add-on component implementation (`HRHAP00_CHECK_CUST01`) performs consistency checks against tables such as T77780, T777E, T777I, T777Z, T778A, T77S0, T77HAP_COL, T77HAP_ROLE, T77HAP_VAL_CLS, T77HAP_EX, T77HAP_EX_AREA, T77MWBFCD, and T77MWBFCH.

10.8 BAdI Area Z: Further BAdIs

BAdI area Z is reserved for those BAdIs that do not fit into any of the other BAdI areas. The following sections present all six of these miscellaneous BAdIs.

10.8.1 HRHAP00_SELECTION (Appraisal Document — Object Selection [Role and To-Do List])

BAdI `HRHAP00_SELECTION` enables you to determine all objects that belong to a particular object. This BAdI is available as of Extension 4.7 Set 1.1.

10.8.2 HRHAP00_DEFAULT_OBJ (Runtime — Generate Default [User <-> Object])

This BAdI permits the conversion between the system user and any object, and vice versa, and creates a suitable default value. As an example, this BAdI could be implemented to return a position for a particular user. The system would return the position based on relationships between the objects, for example, user (US) to employee (P) and then employee (P) to position (S).

10.8.3 HRHAP00_WF_RULE_ID (Workflow Executor)

BAdI HRHAP00_WF_RULE_ID determines the actor required for a particular workflow ID. As discussed in Chapter 9, the workflow ID drives pushbutton access. SAP provides five standard implementations as shown in Table 10.14.

Enhancement Name	BAdI Implementation Description	BAdI Implementation	Availability
HRHAP00_WF_RULE_ID01	12300009	Workflow Executor — Appraiser	As of Enterprise 4.7 Extension Set 1.1
HRHAP00_WF_RULE_ID02	12300010	Workflow Executer — Appraisee	As of Enterprise 4.7 Extension Set 1.1
HRHAP00_WF_RULE_ID03	12300011	Workflow Executor — Part Appraiser	As of Enterprise 4.7 Extension Set 1.1
HRHAP00_WF_RULE_ID04	12300012	Workflow Executor — Further Participant	As of Enterprise 4.7 Extension Set 1.1
HRHAP00_WF_RULE_ID05	12300020	Workflow Executor — Higher-Level Manager	As of Enterprise 4.7 Extension Set 1.1

Table 10.14 Standard BAdI Implementations for HRHAP00_WF_RULE_ID and Their Release Availability

Additional workflow executors can be created if needed by your organization. For example, if delegates or proxies are part of your performance management process, you may need to create a custom workflow rule and reference it in this BAdI.

10.8.4 HRHAP00_GET_LIST_FLT (Appraisal Documents — Filter HRHAP_DOCUMENT_GET_LIST_XXL)

BAdI HRHAP_DOCUMENT_GET_LIST_XXL enables you to filter appraisal documents according to various criteria in overview lists from existing appraisal documents. The BAdI is called after the function module GET_LIST_XXL has been run. This function is used in the Administrator function only. The administrator creates variants to define certain selection criteria according to which appraisal documents can be filtered. This BAdI is available as of Extension 4.7 Set 2.0.

10.8.5 HRHAP00_DOC_STATNAME (Appraisal Document — Alternative for Status Names)

BAdI HRHAP00_DOC_STATNAME can replace the standard status names (In Preparation, In Planning, In Review, etc.) with customer-specific status names. All nine status names can be overridden. You can specify status name changes based on category group, category, and appraisal template. This BAdI is available as of Extension 4.7 Set 2.0.

Table 10.15 shows an example mapping of standard to customer-specific status names.

Status	Status Name	Customer Status Name
1	In Preparation	Document Creation
2	In Planning	Setting Objectives
3	In Review	Achieving Objectives
4	In Process	Processing Evaluation
5	Complete	Final

Table 10.15 Sample Mapping of Standard to Custom Status Names

10.8.6 HRHAP00_DOC_PREPARE (Appraisal Document — Prepare Appraisal Documents)

BAdI HRHAP00_DOC_PREPARE allows you to make available other programs to assist in preparing your appraisal documents. Standard programs include the following:

▶ A wizard feature that takes you through the creation of one or more templates in a restrictive fashion

▶ A program that prepares appraisal documents based on organizational unit selection

▶ A program that prepares appraisal documents based on organizational unit selection and BAdI HRHAP00_SELECTION

Table 10.16 lists the standard implementations for BAdI HRHAP00_DOC_PREPARE and their release availability.

Enhancement Name	BAdI Implementation	BAdI Implementation Description	Availability
PREPARE_1	HRHAP00_DOC_PREPARE1	Prepare Appraisal Docs with Template, Appraiser, Appraisee	As of Enterprise 4.7 Extension Set 2.0
PREPARE_2	HRHAP00_DOC_PREPARE2	Prepare Appraisal Docs with Organizational Units	As of Enterprise 4.7 Extension Set 2.0
PREPARE_3	HRHAP00_DOC_PREPARE3	Prepare Appraisal Docs with Restricted Templates	As of ECC 5.0

Table 10.16 Standard BAdI Implementations for HRHAP00_DOC_PREPARE and Their Release Availability

10.9 Integrating Custom BAdI implementations into Your Template

If the standard-delivered BAdIs do not provide the suitable enhancements needed to support your business processes, you will need to work with a developer resource to create your own BAdI implementation(s). Depending on its complexity, a customer-specific BAdI implementation can generally take anywhere from one hour to one week to develop and unit test. When the BAdI implementation is active, it does not automatically appear in the template. There are a few steps required before the enhancement can be included within your template.

> **Tip**
>
> An enhancement area is not the same as a BAdI area. Whereas a BAdI area groups similar BAdIs together, an enhancement area is essentially a reference to a BAdI definition. Enhancements within an enhancement area correlate to BAdI implementations.

Let's look at an example. Assume that you need to enhance BAdI HRHAP00_ENHANCE_DEL because the standard implementations (or enhancements) from SAP are not sufficient to meet your requirements.

After defining your requirements and writing up the functional specification for the enhancement, the ABAP developer then completes his development and "activates" the implementation. To include a custom BAdI implementation into your appraisal template, you must find the appropriate enhancement area within Transaction OOHAP_BASIC. First, highlight enhancement area **AJ Deletion of an Appraisal Element** as shown in Figure 10.5.

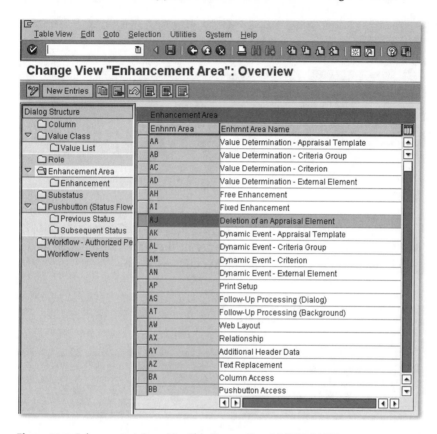

Figure 10.5 Enhancement Area AJ within Transaction OOHAP_BASIC

Second, double-click on the folder entitled **Enhancement** in the tree on the left navigation panel (see Figure 10.6). Next, select the **New Entries** button, and choose the appropriate customer-specific enhancement available on the dropdown.

If the enhancement does not appear, you may want to check with the developer to ensure that the implementation is active. Also, double-check to ensure that you are viewing the correct enhancement area. After you have done this, there is one more step before the enhancement is fully integrated (and available) into your appraisal document.

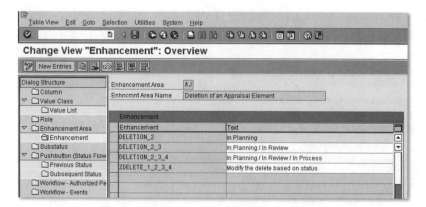

Figure 10.6 Enhancements (i.e., BAdI Implementations) within Enhancement Area AJ Deletion of an Appraisal Element

The last step is performed within the Appraisal Catalog (Transaction PHAP_ CATALOG). The new enhancement appears in the Appraisal Catalog at the category group level on the **Enhancements** tab (see Figure 10.7).

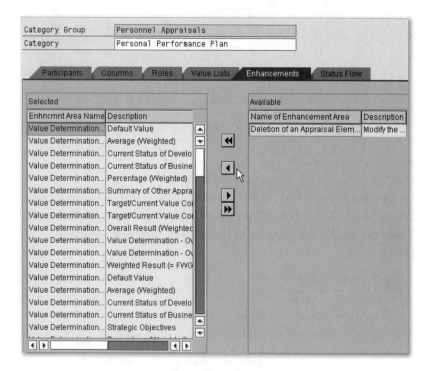

Figure 10.7 A View of the Enhancements Tab at the Category Group Level

The enhancement first appears on the right side in the **Available** section. To make the customization available within any underlying appraisal templates, highlight the enhancement and move the item to the left side in the **Selected** section by clicking on the left arrow button in the center of the screen.

10.10 Summary

In this chapter, each performance management BAdI definition and the associated standard implementations were covered in detail, including their release availability. BAdI areas, used to logically group together BAdIs definitions, are visible via program RHHAP_BADI_OVERVIEW. Some BAdIs come with standard implementations that can be implemented without the need of custom development. If custom BAdI implementations are needed, a configuration analyst must make the customizations available using the procedure outlined previously. Now, you can see how BAdIs make the solution extensible.

In the next chapter, we delve into portal configuration. The portal is a crucial component of the performance management delivery as most end users of the product access it via the SAP NetWeaver Portal.

Portal configuration in performance management can be a challenge due to the multitude of components involved in the system configuration, such as Object and Data Provider (OADP), BSP integration, and portal iViews. This chapter shows you what to expect from the SAP NetWeaver Portal during your performance management build.

11   Portal Configuration

Although you can implement SAP's Performance Management functionality without a portal, most clients decide to integrate the module into their current portal-based Manager and Employee Self Service (MSS and ESS) applications. The new Objective Setting and Appraisals component was designed to be web-based, although GUI functionality is available. The standard user interface for the application integrates seamlessly via a Single Sign-On (SSO) to the SAP NetWeaver Portal. This means that after a user logs in to the SAP Portal, he will not be prompted again for his username and password when accessing the performance management web pages.

11.1   Frontend

The performance management application is based on BSP (Business Server Pages) technology. This technology uses an SAP proprietary language called BSP to render .htm pages in a web browser, in the same way Microsoft's ASP and Java's JSP operate. BSP is no stranger to SAP HCM because it is used in other modules outside of Performance Management, including eRecruitment, the Learning Solution (LSO), and Personnel Cost Planning (PCP). Although BSPs are here to stay, SAP will be offering a WebDynpro frontend in the future for the Objective Setting and Appraisal module.

The standard-delivered BSP application HAP_DOCUMENT serves as the source for all web pages related to performance management. The standard frontend includes views for the appraisee, appraiser, part appraiser, and further participant. The frontend dynamically renders in a web browser based on the configured appraisal template performed in the backend SAP system. Some customers choose to enhance the look-and-feel of the web frontend by engaging the help of a BSP developer or by purchasing an alternative frontend from a third-party vendor.

We'll next discuss the various views available to the end users of the application, whether they are employees, managers, or other participants in the process. Each section references the appropriate BSP page used and any configuration needed on the portal and/or backend.

11.2 Appraisee Views

In most cases, the appraisee is the employee in an Objective Setting Appraisal scenario. Out-of-the-box, the appraisee has two views available on the portal: one displays appraisal documents currently In Process, and the other displays those that are Complete. These views are typically added to the Employee Self Service (ESS) area of the portal where employees can access their appraisal documents.

11.2.1 Appraisee's Inbox (Appraisals in Process)

This view provides the employee a list of all incomplete appraisal documents where the employee is the appraisee. This inbox will display any appraisal document in status In Preparation, In Planning, In Review, and In Process for the employee. Table 11.1 lists BSP application HAP_DOCUMENT and the name of the starting page for the appraisee's "in process" appraisals.

BSP Application	Page Name
HAP_DOCUMENT	documents_received_open2.htm

Table 11.1 BSP Application and Page Name for the Appraisee (i.e., Employee) Inbox

The appraisal inbox shows the following information: **Appraiser Type**, **Appraiser Name**, **Appraisal Document Name**, **Appraisal Document Type** (e.g., appraisal document versus part appraisal document), **Appraisal Status**, and **Period** and **To** dates (see Figure 11.1). Additions or changes to the verbiage or order of these elements will require customizations to the standard BSP application.

Clicking on the hyperlinked name of the **Appraisal Document** launches the form. If several documents are in process for a given employee, all forms with appear in the inbox as a separate line item. For those employees with many documents in process concurrently, scrolling is available through the pagination feature on the lower-left portion of the view.

> **Note**
>
> Using standard SAP functionality, the employee cannot initiate an appraisal document from this page (only the manager has this capability in their view). If your business process allows for employees to create appraisal documents, modifications need to be made to the standard BSP page.

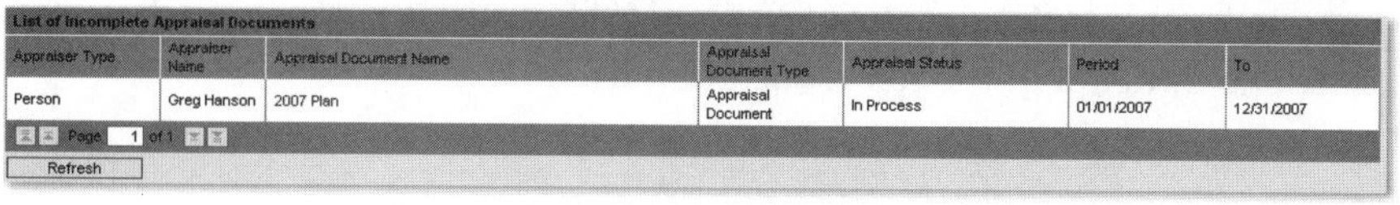

List of Incomplete Appraisal Documents							
Appraiser Type	Appraiser Name	Appraisal Document Name		Appraisal Document Type	Appraisal Status	Period	To
Person	Greg Hanson	2007 Plan		Appraisal Document	In Process	01/01/2007	12/31/2007

Page 1 of 1

Refresh

Figure 11.1 Appraisal Inbox for Appraisee, Showing Any Appraisal Documents in Process

11.2.2 Appraisee's Completed Appraisals

This view provides the employee with a list of all completed appraisal documents. This inbox displays any appraisal documents in status **Complete**, **Approved**, **Closed Approved**, **Rejected**, and **Closed Rejected** where the user is the appraisee. Table 11.2 lists BSP application HAP_DOCUMENT and the name of the starting page for the appraisee's completed appraisals.

BSP Application	Page Name
HAP_DOCUMENT	documents_received.htm

Table 11.2 BSP Application and Page Name for the Appraisee (e.g., Employee) Completed Inbox

As with the previous view, the appraisal inbox shows the following information: **Appraiser Type**, **Appraiser Name**, **Appraisal Document Name**, **Appraisal Document Type**, **Appraisal Status**, and **Period** from and **To** dates (see Figure 11.2).

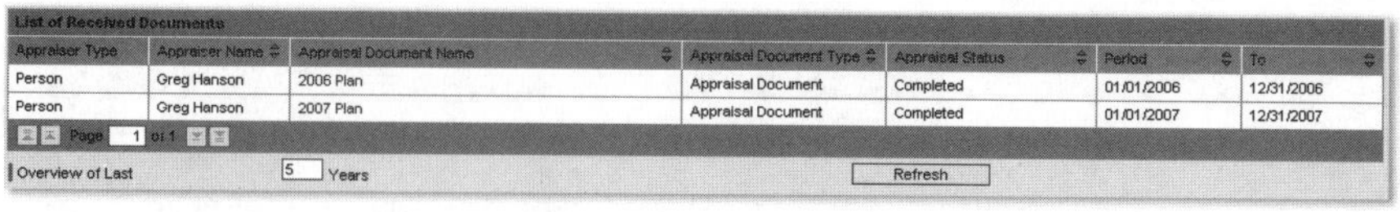

List of Received Documents							
Appraiser Type	Appraiser Name	Appraisal Document Name	Appraisal Document Type	Appraisal Status	Period	To	
Person	Greg Hanson	2006 Plan	Appraisal Document	Completed	01/01/2006	12/31/2006	
Person	Greg Hanson	2007 Plan	Appraisal Document	Completed	01/01/2007	12/31/2007	

Page 1 of 1

Overview of Last 5 Years

Refresh

Figure 11.2 Appraisal Inbox for Appraisee Showing Completed Appraisal Documents

As mentioned, this inbox only displays appraisals that have at least status Complete (status 5). All completed appraisal documents appear in this view and can be referenced at any time. At the bottom of the screen, the **Overview of Last <X> Years** option allows the user to filter based on number of years by inputting a number and clicking on the **Refresh** button.

11.3 Appraiser Views

In addition to the two standard views for the appraisee, SAP also includes three views for the appraiser: two from the HAP_DOCUMENT BSP application and one from the Manager Self Service (MSS) business package. Each view is described in detail in the following sections.

11.3.1 Appraiser's Inbox (Appraisals in Process)

This view provides the manager with a list of all incomplete appraisal documents where he is the appraiser. This inbox displays any appraisal document in status In Preparation, In Planning. In Review, and In Process. Table 11.3 lists BSP application HAP_DOCUMENT and the name of the starting page for the appraiser's "in process" appraisals.

BSP Application	Page Name
HAP_DOCUMENT	documents_todo.htm

Table 11.3 BSP Application and Page Name for the Appraiser (i.e., Manager) Inbox

As with the appraisee's inbox, the appraisal inbox shows the following information: **Appraisal Type**, **Appraisee Name**, **Appraisal Document Name**, **Appraisal Document Type**, **Appraisal Status**, and **Period From** and **To** dates (see Figure 11.3).

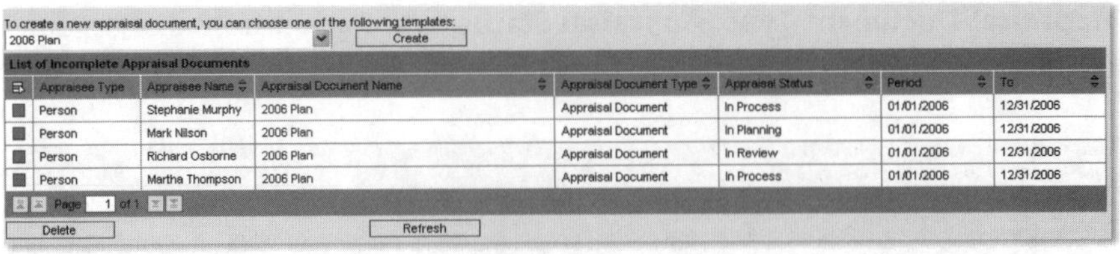

Figure 11.3 Appraisal Inbox for the Manager Showing Appraisal Documents Still in Process

Unlike the employee, however, the manager does have the ability to initiate appraisals within the appraisal inbox. The dropdown list shows all appraisal templates in Released status (those in Not Released or Archived status do not appear). To initiate an appraisal, the manager selects the appropriate template from the selection and clicks on the **Create** button. Depending on your business process, you may decide to prevent managers from initiating appraisal forms (appraisal forms may be administratively created en masse by an administrator or HR business partner, for example). If this is the case, modifications are needed to the BSP page to remove this Create functionality from managers.

Delete functionality is also available to delete appraisal documents. Obviously, this is a very powerful and dangerous option. Most customers decide either to remove this option from the screen (through a simple customization to the BSP) or restrict the delete capability by using the standard security authorization object P_HAP_DOC on the backend role for the manager.

11.3.2 Appraiser's Completed Inbox

This view provides the manager with a list of all completed appraisal documents where he is the appraiser. This inbox displays any appraisal documents in status Complete, Approved, Closed Approved, Rejected, and Closed Rejected. Table 11.4 lists BSP application HAP_DOCUMENT and the name of the starting page for the appraiser's completed appraisals.

BSP Application	Page Name
HAP_DOCUMENT	documents_created.htm

Table 11.4 BSP Application and Page Name for the Appraiser's Completed Inbox

As with the employee's Completed view, this appraisal inbox shows the following information: **Appraiser Type**, **Appraiser Name**, **Appraisal Document Name**, **Appraisal Document Type**, **Appraisal Status**, and **Period From** and **To** dates (see Figure 11.4). Like the appraisee view, users can filter appraisals based on the last X number of years.

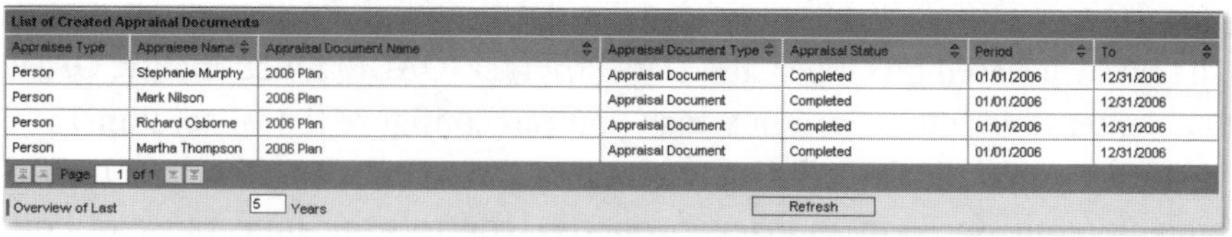

List of Created Appraisal Documents						
Appraisee Type	Appraisee Name ⇕	Appraisal Document Name ⇕	Appraisal Document Type ⇕	Appraisal Status ⇕	Period ⇕	To ⇕
Person	Stephanie Murphy	2006 Plan	Appraisal Document	Completed	01/01/2006	12/31/2006
Person	Mark Nilson	2006 Plan	Appraisal Document	Completed	01/01/2006	12/31/2006
Person	Richard Osborne	2006 Plan	Appraisal Document	Completed	01/01/2006	12/31/2006
Person	Martha Thompson	2006 Plan	Appraisal Document	Completed	01/01/2006	12/31/2006

Page 1 of 1

Overview of Last [5] Years — Refresh

Figure 11.4 Appraisal Inbox for the Manager Showing Completed Appraisal Documents

11.3.3 Status Overview (MBO TeamViewer)

This view, called Status Overview or the MBO TeamViewer, provides a manager with a *status overview* (by template and time period) of all appraisals for that manager's direct and indirect reports. As opposed to the views discussed until now, this view is the only Java-based iView in the Objective Setting and Appraisals solution. It can be incorporated into your SAP Enterprise or NetWeaver Portal by downloading the relevant MSS Business Package (see Table 11.5 for released availability). MSS Business Packages can be found online in the SAP Portal Content Portfolio located at *https:// www.sdn.sap.com/irj/sdn/contentportfolio*. The iView, whose technical name is com.sap.pct.hcm.teamviewer.mbo, can be used in any of the latest releases (Enterprise 4.7 Extension Set 1.1 and 2.0, ECC 5.0, and ECC 6.0).

Package Name	Package Release	Backend Compatibility
Business Package for Manager Self-Service (mySAP ERP)	1.0	ECC 6.0
Business Package for Manager Self-Service (mySAP ERP 2004)	60.1.2	ECC 5.0
Business Package for Manager Self-Service	60.1.20	4.7 and 4.6c

Table 11.5 Listing of MSS Business Packages, Their Release, and Their Backend Compatibility

The iView is grid-like (see Figure 11.5) — positioning a manager's direct (or direct *and* indirect) reports against appraisal progress. The manager's reports are listed on the vertical and the appraisal statuses are listed on the horizontal. The number in a cell of the grid reflects the number of appraisal documents that exist for that employee in that status based on the time period selected. It is also important to note that clicking on the number **0** in the **In Preparation** column allows the manager to initiate an appraisal document. This functionality is configurable. If you decide not to allow managers to create appraisal documents via this iView, you can hide this column or change the configuration to not permit the manager from doing so.

The iView is based on Object and Data Provider (OADP) functionality. OADP is an extensible framework in which you can configure fields, columns, and views for portal display. The view group of the iView, HAP_STATUS (a configurable option stored in an iView property), controls the appearance of both the dropdown values and the columns rendered on the screen for the iView. The iView is extensible as columns can be removed and column text can be changed. The views Directly Reporting Employees and All Employees can be configured differently, and additional views can be added. For example, clients with dual- or dotted-line manager relationships may benefit from adding additional views to return their view of the organization data bring rendered on the screen. These appraisal templates (in Released status) are available in the dropdown menu next to the word **Display**.

| Status Overview | | | | | | | | | |

Display 2007 Plan
for Directly Reporting Employees
from 1/1/2006 To 12/31/2006 Start

Description	% Complete	In Preparation	In Planning	In Review	In Process	Completed	Approved	Closed Approved	Rejected	Closed Rejected
Jason Turner	40.00		1							
Betsy Clark	80.00	0			1					
Zach Nilson	60.00			1						
Larry Milestone	60.00			1						
Peter Norsberg	60.00			1						
Hilary Norton	80.00	0			1					
Katie Morris	40.00		1							

Figure 11.5 Status Overview iView (Also Called MBO TeamViewer)

Tip

Appraisal templates can be filtered using BAdI HRHAP00_TMPL_RESTR (discussed in Chapter 13) or by using standard SAP authorizations (discussed in Chapter 16) within the Status Overview iView.

The **From** and **To** dates allow you to select the object and column data within the same time period. If an employee transfers into a manager's organization, and the manager wants to view that employee's appraisal from a previous year, you could not handle this using previous versions of the iView. SAP recognized the limitations of this logic and addressed it in *SAP Note 953371: TeamViewer MBO: Selection Period for Object and Column Data*. The iView now comes with a new parameter called ObjectProvisionSydate, which, if set to Yes, returns all of the manager's employees for the current system date. The **From** and **To** dates in the iView only pertain to the column selection (i.e., the appraisal documents).

11.4 Part Appraiser View

The part appraiser may or may not play a role in your business process. For those customers who do use Part Appraiser functionality, you need to provide part appraisers the ability to view part appraisal documents via the part appraiser inbox.

11.4.1 Part Appraiser Inbox (Appraisal in Process)

The part appraiser view is actually the same as the manager's inbox (documents_todo.htm). This inbox displays any part appraisal documents in status In Preparation, In Planning, In Review, and In Process, where the user is the part appraiser. Once closed, the part appraisal cannot view the completed document.

Out-of-the-box part appraisal documents are only visible using this inbox. This might pose a problem if some of your part appraisers are not managers (e.g., if you are seeking peer or subordinate feedback). In these cases, customers can either give the manager's inbox to employees (which may be a problem if you do not want these users to be able to initiate documents), or customers can create a customized view for those employees who are part appraisers but not also managers.

11.5 Further Participants View

If your process includes the need for further participants, a separate view is available. Further participants provide additional input into an employee's appraisal, such as a project manager.

11.5.1 Further Participant Inbox (Appraisal in Process and Completed)

This view provides a further participant with access to any appraisal documents for which he is the further participant, regardless of appraisal status.

Note that when creating this BSP-based iView, the iView parameter MODE should be set as X. This will allow the further participant to edit the document. (iView parameters are discussed in the next section.). Table 11.6 lists BSP application HAP_DOCUMENT and the name of the starting page for the further participant's appraisals.

BSP Application	Page Name
HAP_DOCUMENT	documents_where_participated.htm

Table 11.6 BSP Application and Page Name for the Further Participant Inbox

The views in the previous sections outline the standard available in the BSP application HAP_DOCUMENT. If modifications are needed to any BSP pages, it's best to create a Z version of the HAP_DOCUMENT BSP application (e.g., Z_HAP_

DOCUMENT) where you can modify the BSP pages as needed for functionality and look-and-feel changes. This will protect your customizations from patching and upgrade efforts. Of course, any SAP Notes that pertain to the standard BSP pages need to be reviewed and incorporated into your customized BSP pages.

11.6   Helpful Technical Hints

In this section, we discuss helpful technical hints including how to create BSP-based iViews, how to test BSP pages from the backend system, how to determine the need for custom iViews, and how to activate BSP pages in the system.

11.6.1   How to Create BSP-Based iViews

If you plan on using any of the five BSP pages discussed previously, documents_received_open2.htm, documents_received.htm, documents_todo.htm, documents_created.htm, and documents_where_participated.htm, you need to create iViews to house each of these in the portal. To do this, a portal-knowledgeable resource must create a BSP-based iView for each of the views.

You need a portal resource to log on to the SAP NetWeaver Portal as a content administrator. Within the Portal Content folder, navigate to the appropriate folder to create the iView (see Figure 11.6).

Figure 11.6 Creating a BSP-based iView from the Portal Content Studio Available within the Content Administrator Role

The iView Wizard will step you through the process of creating an iView. To create a BSP-based iView that will house a performance management BSP page, perform the following steps:

1. In Step 1 (Template Selection) of the wizard, select the option **SAP BSP iView**, and click on the **Next** button.

2. In Step 2 (General Properties), input the appropriate iView **Name, iView ID, iView ID Prefix, Master Language**, and **Description,** and click on the **Next** button.

3. In Step 3 (Selection of Application Variant), select **BSP** as the BSP Definition type.

4. In Step 4 (Application Parameter), select the appropriate **System** (which should be known by a portal administrator), and specify the **Application Namespace** and **Customer Namespace** (default values are fine). Select **HAP_DOCUMENT** for **Business Server Pages (BSP) Application**, and select the appropriate **Start Page** (e.g., documents_received_open2.htm) as shown in Figure 11.7.

5. In Step 5 (Summary), review your information, and click the **Finish** button to create the iView.

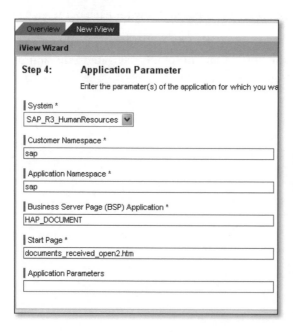

Figure 11.7 Step 4 of the iView Wizard for iView Creation

After an iView is created, you should assign it to the appropriate page or workset for incorporation into the portal. You need to create a BSP-based iView for each of the views you decide to use within your portal. Most implementations have at least four views (two for employees and two for managers) and possibly more depending on if part appraisers and further participants are part of the process.

11.6.2 How to Test BSPs from the SAP Backend

Throughout the build part of your project, you may want to test your configuration changes without using the portal. This ultimately saves you time because you do not need to log in and out of the portal constantly or worry about caching issues. To do this, you can launch the BSP pages directly from the backend. Transaction PHAP_START_BSP allows you to preview a particular BSP page (see Figure 11.8). To view a web page, select the appropriate .htm page from the dropdown. Additionally, you can alter any parameter values in the middle section. Clicking the **Refresh URL** button refreshes the web address located in the lower portion of the screen.

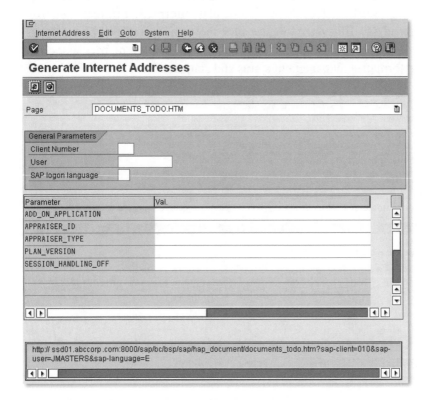

Figure 11.8 Transaction PHAP_START_BSP

Tip

You can also launch web pages from Transaction SE80 (if you have access). You need to identify the BSP application in the Repository Browser and use the wrench button (F8) to launch the selected BSP page. This transaction is meant for developers and should not be used by process or configuration resources.

11.6.3 Custom iViews

Depending on time, resources, and business needs, custom iViews can be built to deliver additional, company-specific functionality on the portal. Whether it's providing visibility to metrics for managers or analytics or reporting for senior executives, a customized snapshot of appraisal information may be of utmost importance. As technology becomes easier to deploy and maintain, and as more and more resources become knowledgeable with Java, .NET, BSP, and WebDynpro, customers will inevitably gravitate toward providing customized iViews on the portal to please their stakeholders. Powerful statistics and metrics can be presented to the end user — even for those customers who do not have Business Intelligence (BI). This is achieved by developing user-intuitive iViews that display information in real time from the backend SAP HR system. Figure 11.9 shows an example of how one customer developed a customized portal iView to display metrics associated with performance management status and statistics.

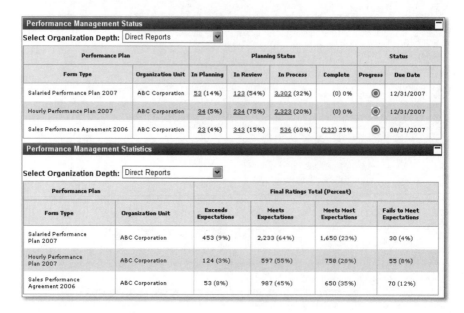

Figure 11.9 A Custom iView — Performance Management Dashboard, Showing Key Metrics and Summary Information by Direct and Direct/Indirect Reports for a Manager

11.6.4   Activation of BSP Pages

Activating the HAP_DOCUMENT BSP application and other BSP applications that support the baseline BSP environment are important first steps for your Basis and/or portal resource. Before you can view any standard-delivered BSP pages, you need to perform activation on all BSP pages needed as a prerequisite. *SAP Note 517484, Inactive Services in the Internet Communication Framework*, provides detailed information on which services need activation for the baseline services to work properly. The SAP Note lists each BSP application and what specific services need to be activated. Activation occurs using Transaction SICF (Maintain Service). A Basis resource usually performs this task.

BSP application HAP_DOCMENT must be activated for the performance management BSPs to work (see Figure 11.10). The service for the HAP_DOCUMENT BSP can be found in the following path: *sap\bc\bsp\sap*. If you have created a custom BSP application, you'll need to activate services for that BSP application.

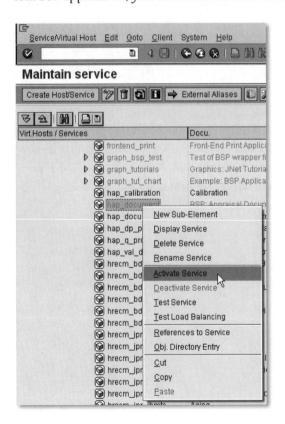

Figure 11.10 Activating BSP Service HAP_DOCUMENT in Transaction SICF

11.6.5 Browser Support of BSP Pages

SAP Note 598860, Browsers Supported by BSP, describes which web browsers support BSP technology. According to the information provided by SAP, clients typically experience fewer problems when using Microsoft's Internet Explorer web browser, but support from Firefox, Mozilla, and others is available. Some web browser issues come in the form of JavaScript errors. Your portal team should be aware of BSP support and your corporate policy for web browser usage.

11.7 Summary

In this chapter, we covered the portal side of the implementation. Each actor involved in the performance management process in SAP, including the appraisee, appraiser, part appraiser, and further participants, has its own portal view. These views allow access to appraisal documents at appropriate points in the process.

We also reviewed some important technical information regarding BSP technology, iView creation, and other technical "gotchas." It's important to remember that a successful implementation is always contingent on available portal and Basis resources.

Now that we have covered the configuration and development aspects of implementation, the next chapter discusses the operational side, that is, how to support the functionality after it has gone live. Administrative and reporting capabilities are discussed in detail in the next chapter.

After go-live, production maintenance activities will certainly challenge your support organization. Knowing the administrative and reporting capabilities available in the application will better prepare you for post go-live support. In this chapter, both basic and advanced administration and reporting transactions are described to aid in the operational success of your implementation.

12 Administrative and Reporting Capabilities

This chapter explores the operational side of the performance management process from the general administration of the appraisal forms to the reporting capabilities inherent within the tool. We will review several important procedures that can help your organization support the performance management product after the application is in your production environment. In addition, we will cover appraisal preparation, review popular administrative procedures, and describe the out-of-the-box reporting capabilities in the standard system, including the latest calibration tool.

12.1 Appraisal Preparation

As you learned in Chapter 8, appraisal forms are "prepared" (i.e., created) by administrators at the outset of the process so that eligible employees and their managers can automatically receive forms in their respective inboxes. Typical appraisal preparation involves both creating and processing the form through the first status (In Preparation). During this time, the appraisal header of the document is created. Most header information (such as the appraisee, appraiser, part appraiser, validity dates, etc.) is defaulted in during the preparation stage, but that depends on the BAdIs that you have included within your appraisal template (see Chapter 10 on the available BAdIs to assist with header creation). The preparation process, using Transaction PHAP_PREPARE, is discussed in detail next.

12.1.1 Transaction PHAP_PREPARE

Transaction PHAP_PREPARE allows administrators to prepare appraisals. Appraisals can be created individually or en masse using various options. As discussed in Chapter 10, the transaction makes available programs identified in BAdI HRHAP00_DOC_PREPARE. In ECC 6.0, three BAdIs are available (see Figure 12.1):

▶ HRHAP00_DOC_PREPARE1
  Prepare Appraisal Docs with Template, Appraiser, Appraisee

▶ HRHAP00_DOC_PREPARE2
  Prepare Appraisal Documents Using Organizational Unit

▶ HRHAP00_DOC_PREPARE3
  Prepare Appraisal Docs with Restricted Templates

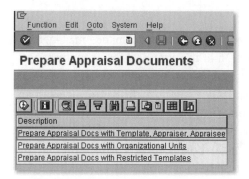

Figure 12.1 Standard Delivered Options for Preparation within Transaction PHAP_PREPARE

Using the first option, **Prepare Appraisal Docs with Template, Appraiser, Appraisee**," a wizard is provided to guide the user through the completion of the preparation process. The wizard's step-by-step screens query the user for information such as template, validity period and name of the appraisal document. This information is then used to create the appraisal document, including its header.

This option is dependent upon identifying the appraisee or appraiser as its **Base Object**. In other words, a unique appraiser or appraisee needs to be specified during the wizard's operation as a reference for appraisal creation. A document for an appraisee, for example, can be easily created using the wizard by selecting the appraisee as the **Base Object** and following the wizard steps. Likewise, documents can be created for all direct reports of a manager using this approach. After selecting the appraiser as the **Base Object**, the **Manager** role should be used to determine the manager's subordinates for the **Target Objects**. Figure 12.2 shows the wizard within the step **Determine Base Object**.

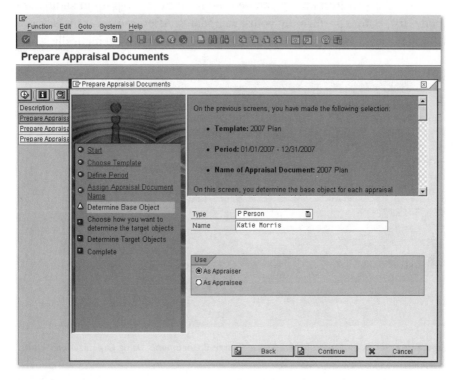

Figure 12.2 Preparation Wizard, Allowing Creation of Form(s) Based on Appraiser or Appraisee Assignment

The second option available for appraisal preparation, **Prepare Appraisal Documents Using Organizational Unit**, enables you to prepare appraisal documents by organizational units and template ID. This program, RHXHAP_APP_DOC_PREPARE_ORG, is available on Transaction PHAP_PREPARE via the BAdI HRHAP00_DOC_PREPARE. This program is typically used to create appraisal documents en masse. The selection screen, shown in Figure 12.3, allows you to enter a root organizational unit (**Root Object ID**) and an appraisal template ID in the **Objects** section. The start and end date period for data selection is provided in the **Validity Period** section via the fields **Start date of DSP** and **End date of DSP**. In the **Further Options** area, three check boxes provide additional functionality. If **Last Appraisal Template** is checked, appraisal creation will be based on the last appraisal document, and therefore no appraisal ID is required. The **Skip Preparation** option allows you to skip the first status In Preparation. This is typically checked for most implementations because the preparation process should fully prepare the document through until the In Review (status 2) or In Process (status 3) status. Last, the **Test Run** option can be used to run the program in simulation mode first, before performing your live updates. After update, appraisals satisfying the criteria specified in the selection are created systematically.

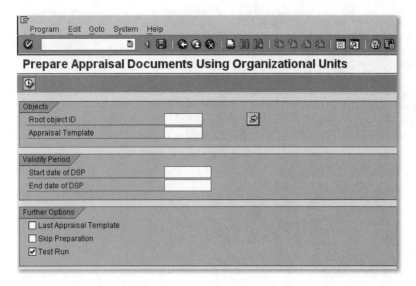

Figure 12.3 Selection Screen for Preparing Appraisal Documents Using Organizational Units

The third standard option available, **Prepare Appraisal Docs with Restricted Templates,** is similar to the preceding program but with an important distinction. Although the selection screen for the program RHXHAP_APP_DOC_PREPARE is exactly the same as the previous program, this program allows you to restrict the selection of **Appraisal Templates** to include particular employee groups.

If you know which employees' appraisal documents need to be prepared, you can use an employee attribute such as an employee's job to restrict the number of appraisal templates offered for selection.

If you do not know which employees' appraisal documents need to be prepared, the appraisal template is offered first. Input help restricts the employees available for selection to include only those employees who, according to their employee attributes, can be considered for the appraisal template.

Some customers implementing SAP Performance Management realize the limitations with the standard programs and decide to create a custom program with more flexible options for appraisal creation. For example, you may want the ability to prepare appraisals based on more than just organizational unit(s). A program can be created to handle this additional functionality that can then be incorporated into the PHAP_PREPARE transaction via BAdI HRHAP00_DOC_PREPARE. An example is shown in Figure 12.4.

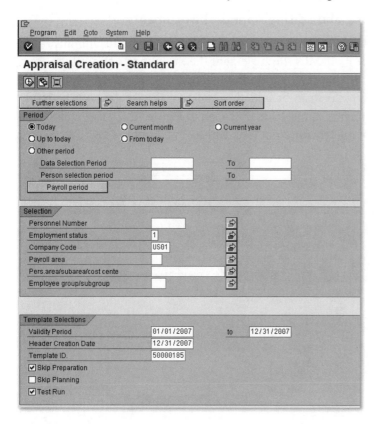

Figure 12.4 Custom Program for Appraisal Preparation, Including Key Data Elements for Selection

In this particular program, the selection screen contains familiar selection screen options, including **Employee group/subgroup, Pers. area, Pers. area/subarea/cost center, Employment Status, Payroll Area,** and so on. A **Template ID**, **Validity Period**, and **Header Creation Date** (date at which to base the header information off of) can be selected on the selection screen.

12.2 Administration

PHAP_ADMIN is one of the most important transactions in SAP Performance Management. Administrators can perform a wide range of functions, including the ability to change appraisal data, delete appraisal documents, reset statuses, and perform follow-up processing, among other things. The following sections explain the functions available to the administrator in detail.

12.2.1 Creating and Editing Appraisal Documents

Appraisal documents can be created and changed within administrative Transaction PHAP_ADMIN. Both element (i.e., row) notes and values (from value lists) can be changed by the administrator from the backend using this transaction. Objectives can be added or deleted, header data can be modified, and attachments can be added. As seen in Figure 12.5, an appraisal document has a completely different look-and-feel within the GUI.

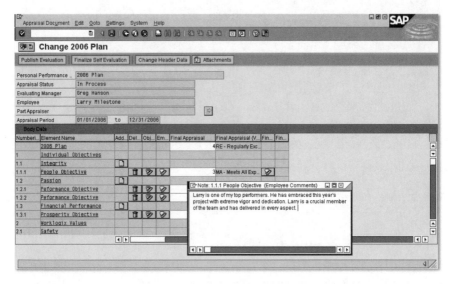

Figure 12.5 Administrator Access for Changing Appraisal Elements, Including Notes and Values

Most administrators need to be trained on how to use the functionality because the interface does require some getting used to. All functions that are available on the web-based form can also be accessed here, including all pushbuttons, attachments, saving, and printing.

12.2.2 Changing Appraisal Statuses

Within the PHAP_ADMIN Transaction, you can change the status of one or more appraisal documents. To change status, select the document or documents you need to change status on, and select **Appraisal Document** •

Change Status. A pop-up will appear (see Figure 12.6) with four options: **Target Status, Target Substatus, Reset Workflow,** and **Workflow Event**. The **Target Substatus** option is based on what is selected for **Target Status**. For example, selecting the status **In Process** allows the selection of the substatus **Part Appraisal In Process**. Also, workflow events can be initiated again if desired by selecting the option **Rest Workflow** and identifying the appropriate workflow event from the dropdown list.

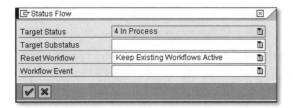

Figure 12.6 Change the Status Flow of the Appraisal Document

12.2.3 Deleting an Appraisal Document

An administrator can delete appraisal documents if given access via authorization object P_HAP_DOC (see Chapter 13 "Authorization Management"). Caution must be used when granting access for deleting appraisal documents given the importance and sensitivity of performance evaluations. Reference *SAP Note 938404: Administrator Authorization to Delete Appraisal Documents* for recent corrections within the deletion functionality.

12.2.4 Unlocking Appraisal Documents

Appraisal locking is an important concept. Whenever a user accesses an appraisal, the document becomes "locked." When the appraisal is locked, no other user can edit the document; others can only display it. This is for data integrity purposes because you do not want appraisal information to be changing while a manager is writing his assessment of the employee's performance, for example. To unlock one or more documents, select **Goto • Locked Appraisal Documents** from Transaction PHAP_ADMIN. Within that transaction, you can highlight one or more rows (i.e., appraisals) and select the **Unlock** button.

The support organization should be ready to address appraisal locking issues by developing procedures to handle them. The organization should also consider providing intuitive training aides for end users on the application to minimize the occurrence of appraisal locking.

> **Tip**
>
> You may need to unlock appraisal documents, if a user did not exit out of the appraisal properly. To avoid this problem, train users on how to use the **Exit** button within the appraisal document. Many users simply save their work within the appraisal and then close the portal browser window, without exiting from the appraisal document first. By doing so, the appraisal does not unlock. Any subsequent users, including the user who did not exit out of the document properly, who access the document will now be locked out and will be notified that the document is locked and cannot be edited. Administrator intervention is needed at this point.

12.2.5   Access to BAdI Implementations

Choosing **Utilities • BAdI Overview** within Transaction PHAP_ADMIN enables administrators to access program RHHAP_BADI_OVERVIEW (covered in Chapter 10). The list of BAdI implementations allows administrative users to understand which BAdIs have been implemented.

12.2.6   Checking Customizing

The ability to verify that all configuration settings are valid and complete is provided within the PHAP_ADMIN Transaction by choosing **Utilities • Check Customizing**. This is the same program RHHAP_CUSTOMIZING_CHECK that was discussed in Chapter 8.

12.2.7   Starting Follow-up Processing

Follow-up processing uses logic defined in BAdIs HRHAP00_FOLLOW_UP and HRHAP00_FOLLOW_UP_D to perform any customer-specific actions after the appraisal is complete (or approved, if the approval process is activated within the template). One of the more common follow-up processes is to impart a qualification on an employee based on a skills assessment. A skill assessment might require the manager to rate an employee on some qualifications, skills, or competencies. These qualifications can then be systematically updated using follow-up processing. To start follow-up processing, select the document or documents you want to follow up on, and select **Appraisal Document • Follow-Up Processing**.

A pop-up dialog box (see Figure 12.7) identifies the follow-up processing that will be performed. The checkbox on the right indicates whether any follow-up has previously occurred. Follow-up processing can be performed as many times as needed. This is helpful if data on a completed appraisal needs to be corrected and reprocessed.

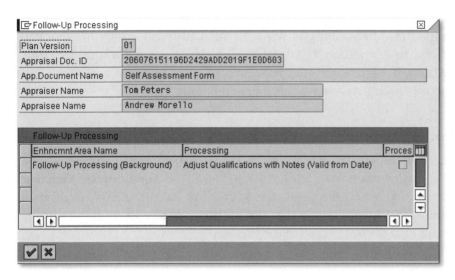

Figure 12.7 Follow-Up Processing (Performed in the Background)

12.2.8 Anonymous Appraisals Information

Information on anonymous appraisals is available from Transaction PHAP_ ADMIN by choosing **Goto • Anonymous Appraisals**. You can also access this directly from Transaction PHAP_ANON. The transaction provides a list of anonymous entries in the event this information needs to be "married" to the actual appraisal document (see Figure 12.8).

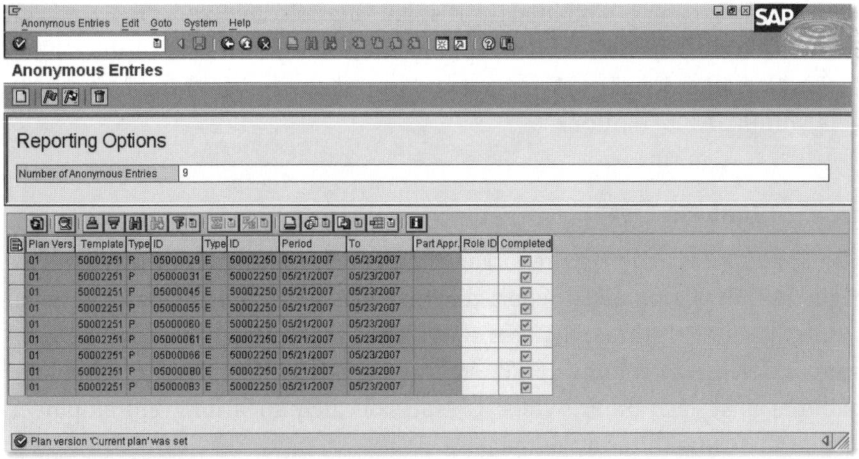

Figure 12.8 Anonymous Appraisal Table Listing the Appraisal Template and the Anonymous Personnel Number and Appraisal

When anonymous appraisals are saved in the system, the appraiser and appraisee information gets stored in this table (visible only to those with access to Transaction PHAP_ANON) but do not appear within the PHAP_ADMIN Transaction. In this way, you can lock down which users can have access to sensitive anonymous appraisal information.

12.2.9 Additional Functionality

Further administrative functionality can be provided to administrators with the implementation of BAdI HRHAP00_ADMIN. The **Administrator Functions** button located on the results screen of PHAP_ADMIN allows customers to define their own administrator functionality. No sample BAdI implementations exist for this in the standard system.

12.3 Reporting

SAP offers several reports within the Performance Management module, including a web-based calibration tool and a series of standard BI queries. Besides the analytical information available within the PHAP_ADMIN Transaction, reports can be accessed via another Transaction PHAP_SEARCH. The reports are listed in the report tree and are available based on BAdI implementation HRHAP00_REPORTING. This provides the mechanism to add customer-specific reports to the report tree.

The standard reports, Ranking List, Display Smart Form, Export to Excel, and Analysis, are discussed in detail. Special attention is also paid to the Online Calibration functionality. A separate section discusses the BI content available within SAP's solution.

12.3.1 Ranking List

The Ranking List, the first report in the PHAP_SEARCH reporting tree (see Figure 12.9), is a standard report that provides a view of all appraisal documents listed with the appraisee, status and final "value," that is, the final appraisal value of column FAPP. Multiple appraisal templates can be compared against each other, which is especially helpful if different employee groups are using different templates.

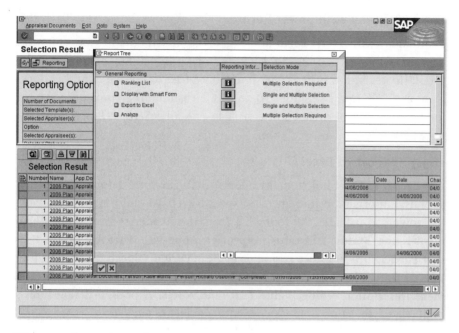

Figure 12.9 Report Tree within Transaction PHAP_SEARCH

The default sort of the Ranking List report is based on final appraisal value descending (see Figure 12.10). The data output could be sorted differently, but additional information, such as validity period and self-assessment ratings, needs to be customized for inclusion in the report.

Ranking List for Appraisal Documents

Plan Vers.	Name	Type	Name	Type	Appraisee Name	App. Stat	Value	Value Text
01	2006 Plan	P	Greg Hanson	P	Jason Turner	Completed	4	RE - Regularly Exceeds Expectations
01	2006 Plan	P	Katie Morris	P	Stephanie Murphy	Completed	4	RE - Regularly Exceeds Expectations
01	2006 Plan	P	Greg Hanson	P	Betsy Clark	Completed	4	RE - Regularly Exceeds Expectations
01	2006 Plan	P	Greg Hanson	P	Larry Milestone	Completed	4	RE - Regularly Exceeds Expectations
01	2006 Plan	P	Katie Morris	P	Martha Thompson	Completed	3	MA - Meets All Expectations
01	2006 Plan	P	Greg Hanson	P	Hilary Norton	Completed	3	MA - Meets All Expectations
01	2006 Plan	P	Greg Hanson	P	Katie Morris	Completed	3	MA - Meets All Expectations
01	2006 Plan	P	James Martin	P	Greg Hanson	Completed	2	MM - Meets Mosts Expectations
01	2006 Plan	P	Katie Morris	P	Mark Nilson	Completed	2	MM - Meets Mosts Expectations
01	2006 Plan	P	Greg Hanson	P	Peter Norsberg	Completed	2	MM - Meets Mosts Expectations
01	2006 Plan	P	Greg Hanson	P	Zach Nilson	Completed	1	FM - Fails to Meet Expectations
01	2006 Plan	P	Katie Morris	P	Richard Osborne	Completed	1	FM - Fails to Meet Expectations

Figure 12.10 Ranking List Report

12.3.2   Display with Smart Form

The **Display with Smart Form** link enables administrators to view and print appraisal documents. The Adobe PDFs can be printed immediately or to the spool. However, the system does not allow a user to save an appraisal document as a PDF to the desktop. To do this, a custom program is necessary or the purchase of PDF writer software such as Adobe Acrobat Professional.

12.3.3   Export to Excel

The **Export to Excel** functionality allows administrators to download certain appraisal information into an Excel spreadsheet. The information available for download includes the following from the **Header** section: **App. Document Name, Status, Substatus, Appraiser, Appraisee, Part Appraiser, Further Participants, Validity Period, Execution Period, Objective Set Date, and Review Date.** The following are also available under the **Body** section: **Element Description, Value, Value Text,** and **Notes.** A pop-up dialog box is available for selection of these elements (see Figure 12.11).

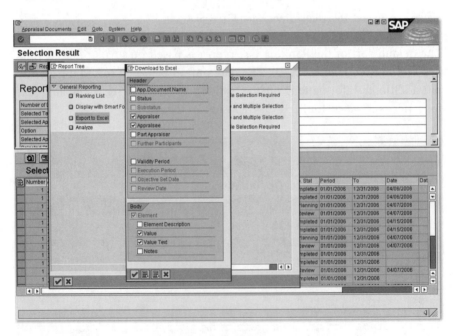

Figure 12.11 Export to Excel Functionality — Export Options

This report comes with two restrictions. First, if the appraisal document has more than 20 elements, it cannot be downloaded. Think of an element as a row on the appraisal document (in technical terms, this equates to criteria groups and criteria). If you attempt to download a form with more than 20 elements, a message will be displayed "Appraisal document contains more than 20 elements; download not possible" as shown in Figure 12.12.

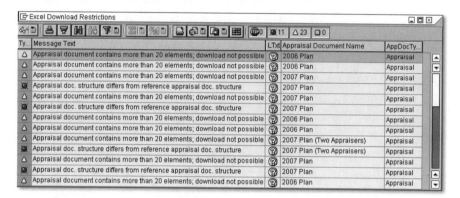

Figure 12.12 Excel Download Restrictions

The second restriction deals with the appraisal's structure. With the standard export functionality, you cannot compare appraisals with different "structures" (meaning number of appraisal elements). This includes appraisal documents with free enhancements because appraisals may differ in their composition (for example, different employees will have varying amounts of objectives). If you attempt to download forms with different structures, a message will be displayed "Appraisal doc. structure differs from reference appraisal doc. structure."

The structures of the appraisal can be validated against a reference appraisal. A reference document can be set by selecting a line and choosing **Edit • Set as Reference**. If you do not set a reference, the system uses the first appraisal document in the output of PHAP_SEARCH as the reference appraisal. If these restrictions are too limiting, you can make customizations to allow for customer-specific requirements.

12.3.4 Analysis

The last standard option available in the reporting tree, **Analysis**, provides basic analytical capabilities. The **Analysis** functionality is not meant to replace BI, but it does function in a similar manner by allowing the user to filter through the columns and rows of one or more appraisal documents. Both the values and notes of the forms can be viewed and exported to Microsoft Excel and other formats. Some customers find the usability of the tool to be a challenge and do not leverage the functionality (see Figure 12.13).

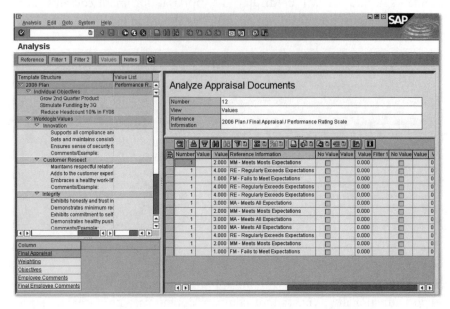

Figure 12.13 Reporting Option Analysis within Transaction PHAP_SEARCH

12.3.5 Calibration

As of ECC 5.0, a web-based calibration tool is available. The Calibration functionality is only available from a web browser and will most likely be integrated into your SAP NetWeaver Portal. The users of this application will depend on how formal or informal your company's calibration process is. In some organizations, the tool may be a good fit for HR generalists/business partners, whereas for others, rolling out to line managers and/or senior executives may be another idea. Most customers decide to only roll out to a small HR population and not to line managers.

End users will need to be trained to use the online tool. On the selection screen, users first need to select each of the following: **Template**, **Validity Period** (to and from), and **Appraisal Status** to filter from. Appraisee selection can then be performed based on appraisee identification (i.e., a direct search for the appraisee(s)), appraiser assignment of the appraisee, or organizational unit assignment of the appraisee. Figure 12.14 shows a selection of organizational units from the HR department of a company based on certain filter criteria.

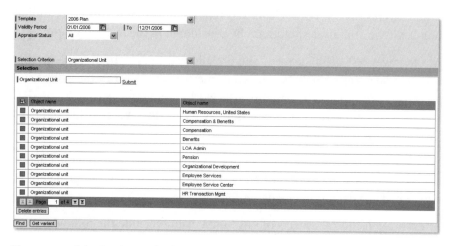

Figure 12.14 Selection Screen for the Calibration Functionality

After retrieving your results list, you can pare it down by highlighting the relevant items(s) you want to remove and clicking on the **Delete Entries** button. After selecting one of more items from the results list, clicking on the **Find** button will bring you to the **Table View** and **Graphic** area for display. One or two dimensions can be viewed. A dimension can be the template (VA), criteria group (VB), or criterion (VC). In Figure 12.15, a two-dimensional view was selected. The first dimension is **2006 Plan**, returns the overall appraisal level score. This dimension is compared against the second dimension, **Financial Performance**, which returns its own criteria group level score.

Dimensions

| First Dimension | 2006 Plan |
| Second Dimension | 1.3 Financial Performance |

Table View / Graphic

	Appraisee Type	Appraisee Name	Appraiser Type	Appraiser Name	Appraisal Status	Period	To	First Dimension	Value Text		Seco
■	Person	Zach Nilson	Person	Greg Hanson	Completed	01/01/2006	12/31/2006	1.000	FM - Fails to Meet Expectations		0.00
■	Person	Betsy Clark	Person	Greg Hanson	Completed	01/01/2006	12/31/2006	4.000	RE - Regularly Exceeds Expectations		0.00
■	Person	Larry Milestone	Person	Greg Hanson	Completed	01/01/2006	12/31/2006	4.000	RE - Regularly Exceeds Expectations		0.00
■	Person	Katie Morris	Person	Greg Hanson	Completed	01/01/2006	12/31/2006	3.000	MA - Meets All Expectations		0.00
■	Person	Greg Hanson	Person	James Martin	Completed	01/01/2006	12/31/2006	2.000	MM - Meets Mosts Expectations		0.00
■	Person	Hilary Norton	Person	Greg Hanson	Completed	01/01/2006	12/31/2006	3.000	MA - Meets All Expectations		0.00
■	Person	Jason Turner	Person	Greg Hanson	Completed	01/01/2006	12/31/2006	4.000	RE - Regularly Exceeds Expectations		0.00
■	Person	Peter Norsberg	Person	Greg Hanson	Completed	01/01/2006	12/31/2006	2.000	MM - Meets Mosts Expectations		0.00
□											
□											

Page 1 of 1

Delete entries

Save list

○ Standard
⦿ User-Specific

Variant [ ]
Save as Variant

Figure 12.15 Example of Calibration Report Output in Table View

When the results are output, you can remove documents from the calibration list if the appraisee should not be considered in the calibration process.

At the lower left of the screen, you are allowed to save both **User-Specific** and **Standard Variants**. By saving your query, you can rerun the calibration report at a later time. The variants here work in the same way as in the GUI — a user-specific variant is only visible by its creator, whereas the standard variant is visible by all users.

Within the calibration list, you can display and change appraisal documents if needed. This may come in handy during dynamic calibration meetings where updates need to be made on-the-fly.

A few more technical aspects of this functionality include the following:

► The calibration graphs within the alternate **Graphic** view are based on SAP NetWeaver Internet Graphic Services (IGS). To use the calibration graphs, a Basis resource must configure the TCP/IP connection IGS_RFC_DEST_MBO in Transaction SM59.

► To incorporate this functionality into your portal, a portal resource must help you create a BSP-based iView to house the start page (search.htm) of the BSP application HAP_CALIBRATION. For help on creating a BSP iView, see Chapter 11.

12.3.6 Business Intelligence Queries

SAP's Business Intelligence (BI) solution delivers nine queries. (For more about these queries, visit *http://help.sap.com*.) Available queries include the following:

► **Status Overview of Appraisal Documents**
Determines the current degree of completion (in percent) of appraisal documents for an organizational unit, for example.

► **Appraisal Average for Overall Appraisal**
Determines the average appraisal value for the end result of the selected appraisal document irrespective of criteria group or criterion.

► **Appraisal Average for Criterion**
Determines the average appraisal value for a specific criterion within a criteria group.

► **Average of All Dimensions for Overall Appraisal**
Determines the average values for the dimensions Target, Current Value, and Appraisal in relation to the final result of the appraisal document.

▸ **Average of All Dimensions for Criterion**
Determines the average values for the dimensions Target, Current Value, and Appraisal in relation to a specific criterion within a criteria group.

▸ **Time Series for Appraisal Documents**
Determines the current calendar year and the previous two calendar years.

▸ **Appraisal Distribution for Overall Appraisal**
Analyzes the distribution of appraisal values in relation to the final result of the appraisal document. Also, determines the number of appraisal documents with a particular value.

▸ **Appraisal Distribution for Criterion (Quality Scale)**
Displays the distribution of appraisal values, target values, and actual values for an individual row (criterion) in the appraisal document.

▸ **Appraisal Distribution for Criterion (Point Scale)**
Displays the distribution of appraisal values in relation to a criterion with a point scale within a criteria group.

As with any BI implementation, custom dataSources, InfoSets, and queries can (and will most likely) be created to extract additional or customer-specific information from the system. Often, BI queries provide the analytics that senior managers are looking for, so it is a good idea to consider implementing it, if you do not already have it in-house.

12.4 Summary

In this chapter, we covered the operational areas within the SAP Performance Management solution, including its reporting and administrative capabilities. The administrative elements, handled mostly within Transaction PHAP_ADMIN, will provide your administrators full back-office management of your personnel appraisals, including changing appraisal values, changing status, and even deleting appraisal documents.

From a reporting perspective, a report tree with several out-of-the-box reports is available via the PHAP_SEARCH Transaction as well as more robust offerings such as an online calibration tool and BI queries. With these reports, you can provide key stakeholders with the information they need to become more efficient and effective in their day-to-day work.

In the next chapter, we discuss one of the most important elements of any implementation: authorization management. The security on the appraisal document in the portal and in backend system is discussed in detail.

Security authorizations in the new performance management functionality offer enhanced abilities for clients to restrict user access to appraisal forms and elements on the form. This chapter considers these, as well as those clients who are using (or considering) structural authorizations.

13 Authorization Management

Proper authorization management in the new SAP Performance Management solution relies on a solid knowledge of existing R/3 security concepts. The introduction of a new authorization object, P_HAP_DOC and the ongoing interplay between standard and structural authorizations proves challenging to implement for many companies. In addition, column access (and row access, beginning with ERP 2005) at the appraisal form level provides an additional layer of authorizations available for clients to implement.

This chapter explores authorization management within the module: standard, structural, and those available on the form itself. Data stored within the Performance Management module may be some of the most sensitive in your organization and, therefore, knowing what security is available is paramount to a successful implementation. The following information serves to kick-start your security design. It is imperative that you work with your HR security resource when designing the authorizations needed for this module.

13.1 Essential Authorization Objects in Performance Management

As stated previously, a security resource with familiarity with HR authorizations needs to spend a sufficient amount of time architecting the best possible design. This is especially true if your organization has implemented structural authorizations. Before discussing the challenges associated with integrating structural authorizations into your overall security model, an overview of the standard authorization objects is needed. All core HR authorization objects, such as P_PERNR and P_ORGIN, are needed to implement Performance Management. In addition, a new object, P_HAP_DOC, was created to specifically control access to appraisal templates.

In the standard system, SAP delivers the following R/3 security roles, which can be copied to your customer namespace and altered according to your specific security requirements via Transaction PFCG (Role Maintenance):

▶ SAP_HR_HAP_ADMINISTRATOR (Administrator — Objective Setting and Appraisals) for administrators of the performance management application

▶ SAP_HR_HAP_EMPLOYEE (Employee Generic — Appraisals and Objective Setting Agreements) for employees (or appraisees) in the process

▶ SAP_HR_HAP_MANAGER (Manager Generic — Appraisals and Objective Setting Agreements) for managers (or appraisers) in the process

The employee and manager roles include access to transaction codes, such as PHAP_CHANGE and PHAP_CREATE. In most implementations, however, access to R/3 transactions for managers and employees are unnecessary because your implementation will be delivered via the SAP Enterprise or NetWeaver Portal. Administrators, on the other hand, will be granted access to many performance management transaction codes to fulfill the tasks associated with their duties.

Each authorization object is described in the following sections with examples and tips for use in your customer-defined roles. Although these objects are used in other modules, they are described in relation to the access needed for the performance management process.

13.1.1 S_TCODE and P_TCODE

Authorization objects S_TCODE and P_TCODE are used to control access to transaction codes in the SAP system. Whereas S_TCODE is the standard authorization check for transactions used across all SAP modules, P_TCODE is an HR-specific check required for some HR transaction codes such as PHAP_CHANGE, PHAP_ADMIN, and other important transactions such as PA30 and PA40. Figure 13.1 shows an example implementation of authorization objects S_TCODE and P_TCODE.

All performance management transactions either start with the PHAP or OOHAP prefix. OOHAP Transactions, such as OOHAP_BASIC and OOHAP_VALUE_TYPE, are typically ones used by the systems analyst during the configuration of the forms. PHAP Transactions are a mix of administrative (e.g., PHAP_ADMIN and PHAP_ANON) and user (e.g., PHAP_CREATE and PHAP_CHANGE) transaction codes. If you are implementing the self-service aspect of performance management through the SAP Enterprise or NetWeaver Portal, access to PHAP_CREATE and PHAP_CHANGE are unnecessary and unwanted for your employee and manager roles.

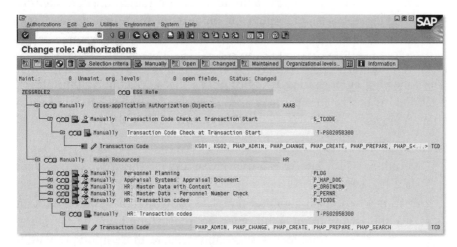

Figure 13.1 Authorization Objects S_TCODE and P_TCODE Granting Access to Transactions PHAP_ADMIN and PHAP_SEARCH among Others

For a full list of performance management transactions, see Appendix A "Performance Management Transaction Codes."

13.1.2 P_PERNR

Authorization object P_PERNR is used to control access to a user's (i.e., employee's) own HR data. P_PERNR restricts access based on infotype and subtype. If you have already implemented employee self-service, then this authorization object is already a part of your employee role.

Chances are, your security resource will not need to change this object very much with the employee and manager self-service profiles if your company has already implemented ESS. It is a good idea, however, to review the existing authorizations to ensure that all employees will have access to their own data, which they need during the performance management process.

13.1.3 PLOG

For new implementations of performance management, updates are needed to authorization object PLOG. At the very least, you need to add objects VA (appraisal template), VB (criteria groups), and VC (criteria) for infotypes 5020 through 5026, and subtypes 5020, A605, A606, A607, B605, B606, and B607 with varying read/write permissions depending on the role. For end users (employees and managers), you might want to grant read-only access to objects VA, VB, and VC, whereas administrators (in the production environment) and those specialists responsible for customizing (in the development environment) might get wider access. Figure 13.2 shows an example implementation of authorization object PLOG.

The following authorization fields comprise the PLOG authorization object. Each field is described separately and highlighted with important information on usage.

- **Infotype (INFOTYP)**
  Determines which infotypes a user has access to. The group of infotypes 1000, 1001, 5020, 5021, 5022, 5023, 5024, 5025, and 5026 on objects VA, VB, and VC is where most appraisal template configuration resides. Without read authorization to these infotypes, no information from the configuration can be read. Infotypes in PLOG only refer to those infotypes within Personnel Development (and not Personnel Administration).

- **Planning Status (ISTAT)**
  Determines which planning statuses a user has access to. Appraisal documents can be either in status 3 (Submitted) or status 4 (Approved). This equates to Not Released (status 3) and Released (status 4) in the performance management configuration, as configured in PHAP_CATALOG. Most end users (i.e., employees and managers) will only have access to those documents in status 4 because only released appraisal forms will be in a production environment. Typically, only your performance management configuration specialists would have access to forms that are still in process (i.e., Not Released) during the design of the form.

- **Object Type (OTYPE)**
  Determines which object types a user has access to. Objects VA (appraisal template), VB (criteria groups), and VC (criteria) need to be included within your performance management profiles. However, depending on the number of free or fixed enhancements (see Chapter 10 for discussion on enhancements), you might also need access to other objects in Personnel Development. These might include qualifications (object type Q) and the Qualifications Catalog (object type QK) if you are integrating with the qualification or competency management/development; DC (Curriculum Type), EC (Curriculum), F (Location), and G (Resource) if you are integrating with the LSO (Learning Solution) or Training and Events module; and BL (Development Plan Group) and B (Development Plan) if you are integrating with the Development Plan functionality.

> **Note**
>
> Keep in mind that any custom PD objects that you have created and might be referencing or including on the appraisal form need to be included as part of PLOG authorizations. For example, if you have created a custom object for Goal (and let's say you have named it ZG), you need to include the ZG object in PLOG for users to have access to read or write to it.

▸ **Plan Version** (PLVAR)

Determines which plan versions a user has access to. Plan version 01 (Active plan) is the default plan version and should be the only plan version used in your process. Using other plan versions should be avoided. Plan versions ** and .: should never be used.

▸ **Function Code** (PPFCODE)

Determines what permissions the user has read, write, and delete access to. Most likely, you will use one or more of the following function codes in your implementation: AEND (Change), DEL (Delete), DISP (Display), and INSE (Insert).

▸ **Subtype** (SUBTYP)

Determines which subtypes a user has access to. Values for subtype go hand-in-hand with those infotypes identified in your infotype authorization field (INFOTYP), discussed earlier. For example, subtypes A605, A606, A607, B605, B606, and B607 are all important relationships among VA, VB, and VC objects and need to be included in the PLOG authorization. Subtypes in PLOG only refer to subtypes within Personnel Development (and not Personnel Administration).

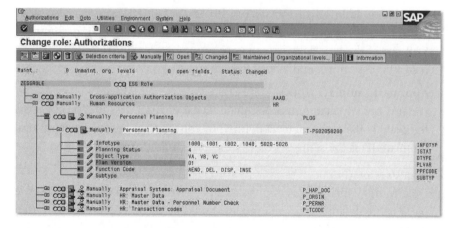

Figure 13.2 Authorization Object PLOG Granting Access to Standard PD Objects VA, VB, and VC

13.1.4 P_HAP_DOC

P_HAP_DOC is a new authorization object within the Objective Setting and Appraisals functionality. P_HAP_DOC is a mandatory authorization for implementing appraisals and must be used in conjunction with P_PERNR, PLOG, and P_ORGIN or P_ORGINCON (described below). Figure 13.3 shows an example implementation of authorization object P_HAP_DOC.

Additionally, P_HAP_DOC includes the capability to integrate with an authorization profile configured in the structural authorizations module. For more information on this, refer to Section 13.2.2.

The following authorization fields comprise the P_HAP_DOC authorization object:

► **Activity (ACTV)**
Determines what operations (or "activities") a user can perform on an appraisal form. Available options are 02 (Change), 03 (Display), and 06 (Delete). Notice there is no Create activity. Without change authorization, an appraisee or appraiser is unable to create an appraisal.

► **Appraisal Category ID (HAP_CAT)**
Determines which catalog ID a user has access to. The appraisal category ID is the eight-digit ID category defined in your configuration. In addition to Transaction PHAP_CATALOG, you can also view your categories via Transaction OOHAP_CATEGORY.

► **Appraisal Category Group ID (HAP_CAT_G)**
Determines which catalog group ID a user has access to. The appraisal category group ID is the eight-digit ID category group defined in your configuration. In addition to transaction PHAP_CATALOG, you can also view your category groups via Transaction OOHAP_CAT_GROUP. Standard SAP out-of-the-box delivers category groups 1 (Personnel Appraisals), 10 (Learning Solution), and 100 (E-Recruiting).

► **Appraisal Template ID (HAP_TEMPL)**
Determines which appraisal template ID a user has access to. The appraisal template is the eight-digit ID defined in your configuration. The appraisal template ID is the same as the VA object ID of the form.

► **Plan Version (PLVAR)**
Determines which plan versions a user has access to. Plan version 01 (Active plan) is the default plan version and should be the only plan version used in your process. Using other plan versions should be avoided. Again, plan versions ** and .: should never be used under any circumstances.

▶ **Authorization Profile** (PROFL)

Identifies the authorization profile to be used (this is optional). If structural authorizations are used in your organization, you can integrate an authorization profile directly in P_HAP_DOC through this authorization field. Any profile defined in table T77PR can be used (access through Transaction OOSB).

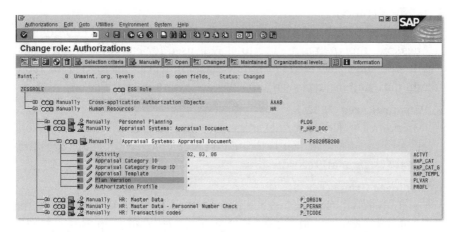

Figure 13.3 New Authorization Object P_HAP_DOC Configured with Open Access

13.1.5 P_ORGIN/P_ORGINCON

P_ORGIN and P_ORGINCON are very important authorization objects because they permit users to access HR data on other employees. Both provide the same function but differ in one important way: P_ORGINCON includes an authorization profile. For those clients seeking a context-sensitive solution, P_ORGINCON enables the use of structural authorizations in the overall profile. A discussion on the use of context-sensitive authorizations is beyond the scope of this book.

Both objects provide a way to restrict access based on infotype, subtype, personnel area, personnel subarea, and organizational key. The following authorization fields comprise the P_ORGIN and P_ORGINCON authorization object (see Figure 13.4).

▸ **Authorization Level (AUTHC)**
Determines the access level a user is granted. Available options are M (search help), R (read record), S (write locked record; unlock if the last person to change the record is not the current user), E (write locked record), D (change lock indicator), W (write record), and * (all operations).

▸ **Infotype (INFTY)**
Determines which infotypes a user has access to. This is the infotype in question. Infotype range 0000 to 0999 is used for employee master data, infotype range 2000 to 2999 for time data, infotypes 4000 to 4999 for applicant data, and infotypes 9000 to 9999 are customer-specific.

▸ **Personnel Area (PERSA)**
Determines which personnel areas a user has access to. This is the personnel area (field PERSA) that is located on an employee's IT0001 (Organizational Assignment) record.

▸ **Employee Group (PERSG)**
Determines which employee groups a user has access to. This is the employee group (field PERSG) that is located on an employee's IT0001 (Organizational Assignment) record.

▸ **Employee Subgroup (PERSK)**
Determines which employee subgroup a user has access to. This is the employee subgroup (field PERSK) that is located on an employee's IT0001 (Organizational Assignment) record.

▸ **Organizational Key (VDSK1)**
Determines which organizational keys a user has access to. This is the organizational key (field VDSK1) that is located on an employee's IT0001 (Organizational Assignment) record.

Additionally, `P_ORGINCON` includes one other very important field:

▶ **Authorization Profile** (`PROFL`)
Identifies the authorization profile to be used. If structural authorizations are used in your organization, you can integrate an authorization profile directly in `P_ORGINCON` through this authorization field. Any profile defined in table T77PR can be used (access through Transaction OOSB).

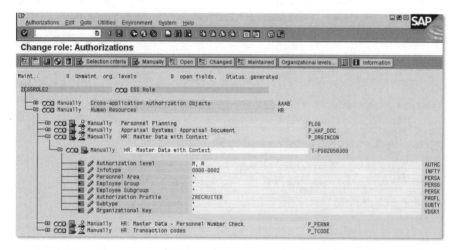

Figure 13.4 Context-sensitive Authorization Object P_ORGINCON Granting Access to Read and Search Access to Infotypes 0000, 0001, and 0002 with Structural Profile ZRECRUITER

Section 13.2 discusses the use of structural authorizations using the authorization profiles described in the `P_HAP_DOC` and `P_ORGINCON` authorization objects.

13.1.6 Summary of Standard Authorizations for Performance Management

Table 13.1 lists an overview of the authorization objects discussed previously that are essential to the performance management application.

Authorization Object(s)	Use
S_TCODE and P_TCODE	Used for transaction checks. S_TCODE is used for all transactions, whereas P_TCODE is used as an additional check for some HR transactions, for example, PHAP_ADMIN and PA40.
P_PERNR	Used to control access to user's own HR data such as basic pay (IT0008).

Table 13.1 Authorization Objects for PM and Their Intended Use

Authorization Object(s)	Use
PLOG	Used to control access to personnel development (PD) objects, such as VA (appraisal template), VB (criteria groups), VC (criteria), and O (organizational units), including custom objects.
P_HAP_DOC	Used to control access to appraisal documents, configured in the Appraisal Catalog.
P_ORGIN / P_ORGINCON	Used to control access to personnel infotype data, including employee actions (infotype 0000), organizational assignment (infotype 0001), and personal data (infotype 0002). Can include authorization profiles (i.e., structural authorizations) if P_ORGINCON is used.

Table 13.1 Authorization Objects for PM and Their Intended Use (Cont.)

13.1.7 Activation Switches in T77So

To activate the authorization objects P_PERNR, P_ORGIN, and P_ORGINCON for use in your system, ensure that the proper switches have been activated in system table T77SO.

For P_PERNR, switch AUTSW/PERNR needs value 1 to activate; for P_ORGIN, switch AUTSW/ORGIN needs value 1 to activate; and for P_ORGINCON, switch AUTSW/INCON needs value 1 to activate. Figure 13.5 shows authorization objects P_PERNR and P_ORGIN being used, but not P_ORGINCON.

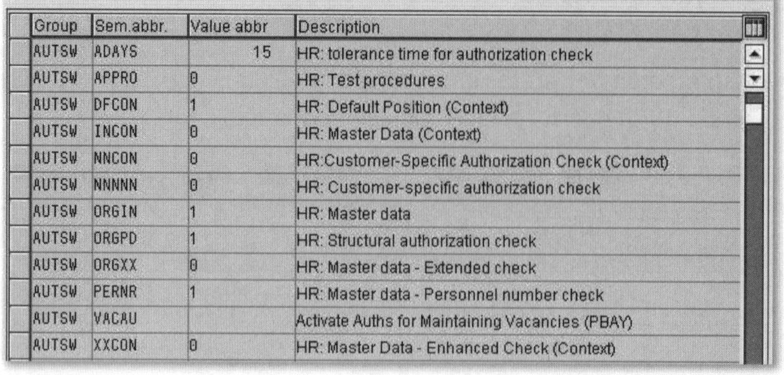

Group	Sem.abbr.	Value abbr	Description
AUTSW	ADAYS	15	HR: tolerance time for authorization check
AUTSW	APPRO	0	HR: Test procedures
AUTSW	DFCON	1	HR: Default Position (Context)
AUTSW	INCON	0	HR: Master Data (Context)
AUTSW	NNCON	0	HR:Customer-Specific Authorization Check (Context)
AUTSW	NNNNN	0	HR: Customer-specific authorization check
AUTSW	ORGIN	1	HR: Master data
AUTSW	ORGPD	1	HR: Structural authorization check
AUTSW	ORGXX	0	HR: Master data - Extended check
AUTSW	PERNR	1	HR: Master data - Personnel number check
AUTSW	VACAU		Activate Auths for Maintaining Vacancies (PBAY)
AUTSW	XXCON	0	HR: Master Data - Enhanced Check (Context)

Figure 13.5 System Table T77S0, Group AUTSW

For more information on the authorization objects discussed here, refer to the book *SAP Security and Authorizations* by Mario Linkies and Frank Ott (SAP Press, 2006).

13.2 Using Structural Authorizations in Performance Management

This section discusses implementing structural authorization security in addition to the standard authorization. Implementing structural authorization is not a requirement for deployment for performance management but rather serves as additional means of securing data. Some customers are under the mistaken belief that structural authorization is a prerequisite for self-service functionality on the portal. This is not the case. Structural authorizations should only be considered when there is a strong business reason to do so.

13.2.1 Overview

If structural authorizations are currently being used in your company, the following section is very important for your implementation. If structural authorization is not currently being used, but you are considering implementing because of performance management, you need to consider the following points carefully. As most practitioners know, implementing structural authorization is a major shift in your approach to R/3 security.

13.2.2 Using Structural Authorizations in Performance Management But Not in Personnel Administration

Structural authorizations in the Performance Management module are unique in that you have the option of activating the functionality only for this module. In other words, structural restrictions can be made for accessing appraisals only, but in the Personnel Administration module, no checks are performed. To do this, you must activate switch HAP00/AUTHO in table T77S0 by placing an X as the value (see Figure 13.6). Additionally, because no structural authorizations checks need to be performed in Personnel Administration, you use authorization object P_ORGIN for your infotype checks (and not P_ORGINCON, which includes an authorization profile).

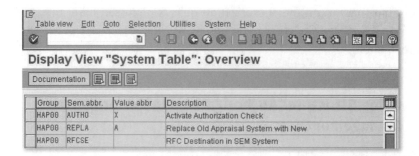

Figure 13.6 System Table T77S0, Group HAP00 Showing Semantic Abbreviation AUTH0, Used for Determining Structural Profile Use in PM

When the HAP00/AUTH0 switch is turned on, a structural profile *must* be entered in the authorization field PROFL for authorization object P_HAP_DOC. Additionally, the user must have an entry in table T77UA (see Figure 13.7).

Note

If an entry is not made in table T77UA or the user has a * in the authorization profile field, he will have access to all appraisals, even if you have defined an authorization profile in the P_HAP_DOC object.

Change View "User Authorizations": Overview

User name	Auth.profile	Start date	End date	Exclusion	Display Objects
JMTEST1	ZMANAGER	08/17/2006	12/31/9999	☐	ℹ
SAP*	ALL	01/01/1900	12/31/9999	☐	ℹ
STUDENT01	ZMANAGER	08/17/2006	12/31/9999	☐	ℹ
STUDENT02	ZMANAGER	08/17/2006	12/31/9999	☐	ℹ
STUDENT02	ZPERFMGMT	08/17/2006	12/31/9999	☐	ℹ
STUDENT03	ZPERFMGMT	08/17/2006	12/31/9999	☐	ℹ

Figure 13.7 Table T77UA (User Authorizations) for Structural Authorizations

Also, be sure that the correct authorization profile is defined in P_HAP_DOC itself. If the HAP00/AUTH0 switch is turned on, and no authorization profile (or a wrong authorization profile) is defined in P_HAP_DOC, users with the identified authorization profile will be unable to access appraisals.

> **Note**
>
> For more information on structural authorizations in performance management, see the document "Authorizations in Performance Management," available on the SAP Service Marketplace at *http://service.sap.com/erp-hcm*. On the left navigation panel, select **Talent Management** • **Employee Performance Management** • **Media Center**.

13.2.3 Using Structural Authorizations in Both Performance Management and Personnel Administration

If you currently use structural authorizations, presumably you will want to continue to use them when you implement the Performance Management module. This means that the system will use structural restrictions in both your Personnel Administration and Performance Management modules.

As described previously, switch HAP00/AUTHO should be activated, and the PROFL authorization field of authorization object P_HAP_DOC should have the appropriate authorization profile. You may or may not be using the context-sensitive solution (P_ORGINCON).

Because the appraisal form and the elements of the form itself are PD objects, it is also very important to include them in your authorization profile(s). Figure 13.8 shows a custom evaluation path Z_APPR, which identifies all elements of an appraisal document, including the template (VC object), criteria group (VB objects), and criteria (VC objects). The evaluation path will return all appraisal elements (meaning VA, VB, and VC objects) based on a given template as root object.

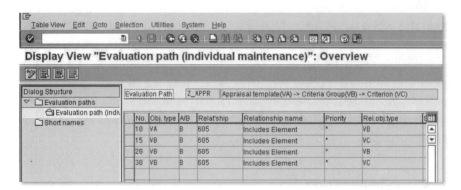

Figure 13.8 Custom Evaluation Path Z_APPR Identifying All Elements (VA, VB, and VC) of an Appraisal Document

After a custom evaluation path is created, a custom authorization profile needs to be created to identify those elements that will be accepted in a structural user's profile. Figure 13.9 shows custom authorization profile ZAPPR, which identifies all appraisal templates (VC object), criteria groups (VB objects), and criteria (VC objects) for the profile. Note that any fixed or free enhancement (see Chapter 10) cannot be identified via an evaluation path and must be explicitly maintained in the profile. In Figure 13.9, line 15, object type VC, object ID 85200001 is an example of this.

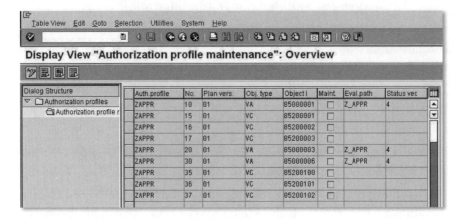

Figure 13.9 Custom Authorization Profile ZAPPR Using Evaluation Path Z_APPR for Identification of All Appraisal Templates and Form Elements

13.3   Appraisal Level Security

In addition to the standard and structural R/3 security described previously, SAP also provides additional security at the appraisal level. This security, defined in infotype 5023, is configured via Transaction PHAP_CATALOG. As described in detail in Chapter 8, configuration of the **Column Access** tab provides an additional level of form-specific security for all participants in the process, including appraisers, appraisees, part appraisers, and further participants. Beginning in ECC 6.0, clients can restrict based on rows (or elements) of the form.

13.3.1   Column Access

As discussed in Chapter 9, column access for a form is configured via the Appraisal Catalog (Transaction PHAP_CATALOG). Each appraisal document has a **Column Access** tab at the appraisal form level (VA element) containing an inventory of all columns available for the template. Each column is listed with a column owner (see Figure 13.10).

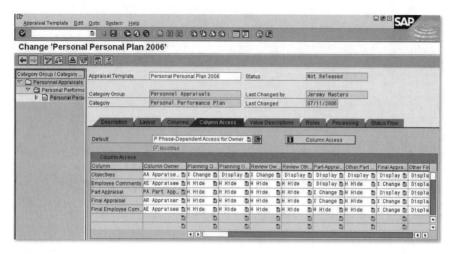

Figure 13.10 A View of the Column Access Tab in an Appraisal Form

The column owner is identified based on the configured roles (see Chapters 8 and 9 for more information on roles). Standard functionality allows the following roles to be identified as owners of a column: Appraisee (AE), Appraiser (AR), Appraiser, Appraisee (AA), Further Participants (OT), and Part Appraisers (PA).

Each appraisal status (In Planning, In Review, etc.) has two columns: the first signifying the access level for the column owner, and the second signifying the access level for all other parties involved during the process (for that status). For example, in Figure 13.11, the **Objectives** column (the first row in this configuration) is owned by both the appraiser and appraiser (role = AA). Additionally, during the Planning phase (status 1 In Planning), the planning owner (both appraiser and appraiser) can change the contents of this column. However, all other participants in the process (e.g., a part appraiser or further participant) can only display its contents.

In addition to the standard column access configuration, the column access BAdI, HRHAPP00_COL_OWNER, provides a robust way to dynamically restrict and grant access to columns based on some customer-defined criteria. This is especially useful when additional substatuses are configured. This is because custom substatuses are not configurable on the **Column Access** tab in configuration. Therefore, a different means of column access must be achieved via a user exit (see Figure 13.12).

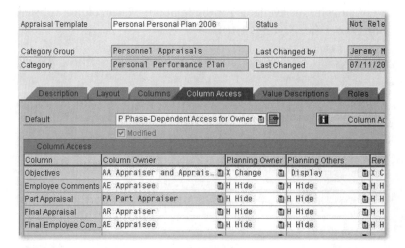

Figure 13.11 View of Column Control for the In Planning Status (Status 1)

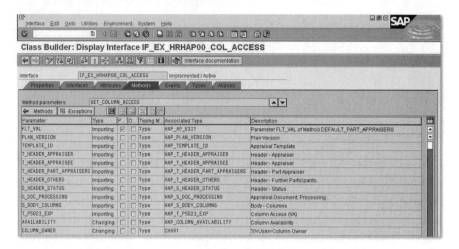

Figure 13.12 Method GET_COLUMN_ACCESS of BAdI HRHAP00_COL_ACCESS

It is best not to hard-code values within a user exit. Figure 13.13 shows an example of a custom table for column access. This table shows how you could restrict access to templates based on custom-defined substatuses. In the following example, substatuses A and B are seen for appraisal document 50000054. Each column (Column ID) is listed with its availability (H=Hide, [blank]=Display, and X=Change) based on the status/substatus and role of the user (APEE=Appraisee, APER=Appraiser, and PAPR=Part Appraiser). Again, this is an example of how you could use the column access BAdI. A benefit of this design is that business rules can be easily maintained through configuration each year, rather than programmatically hard-coded.

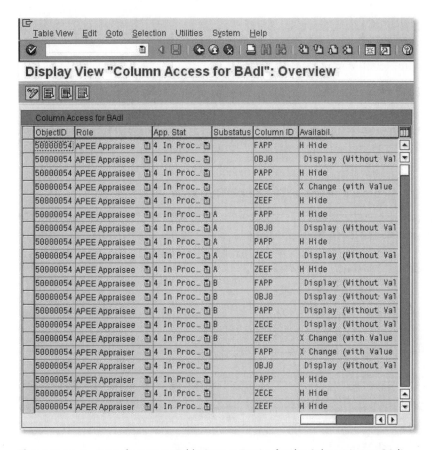

Figure 13.13 An Example Custom Table Storing Entries for the Column Access BAdI

Row access, before ECC 6.0, is not available. Starting from ECC 6.0, row access (meaning the ability to completely hide a row from a user per status) is available. This adds another layer of robust authorization to your template.

13.3.2 Roles

Roles are available to provide another level of security access but specifically for part appraisal documents. Roles, which are configured in Transaction OOHAP_BASIC, are used to restrict part appraisals at the level of individual elements (VA or VB objects). For example, roles allow you to distinguish between a manager's part appraisal authorizations and an employee's part appraisal authorizations in relation to part appraisal columns in the same appraisal template. The system determines the user's role at runtime. Some standard roles include the following:

> ▶ Manager (MA)

> ▶ Self (ME)

> ▶ Higher-level Manager (MB)

Roles are frequently misunderstood as providing column and row access for the appraisal document. Knowing what roles can restrict and when they can be used in your template will go a long way toward a clean implementation, specifically if you use Part Appraisal functionality.

13.3.3 Appraiser Authority Check Override

A flag in the configuration is available on the appraisal template entitled **No Authorization Check for Appraiser** (see Figure 13.14). This flag determines whether or not the user has access to the appraiser (i.e., the appraiser's personnel number) of the document.

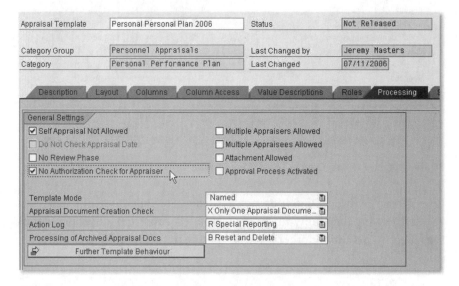

Figure 13.14 Processing Tab on an Appraisal Template where the Flag No Authorization Check for Appraiser Is Checked

As discussed in Chapter 8, this indicator is of particular value if you have implemented structural authorizations. If you have used function module RH_GET_MANAGER_ASSIGNMENT within an authorization profile that you have granted to all managers, the managers in your organization will be unable to view their own appraisals unless this indicator is set. This is because the structural profile has excluded the user's own manager from their overall profile. To sidestep this authorization, ensure that the **No Authorization Check for Appraiser** checkbox is selected.

13.4 BAdI HRHAP00_AUTHORITY — Appraisal Document Authorization Check

SAP provides a customer-defined way of defining authorizations to appraisal documents via the use of BAdI HRHAP00_AUTHORITY. If implemented, this BAdI (whose interface is shown in Figure 13.15) can be used to fully replace the standard authorization checks in the system.

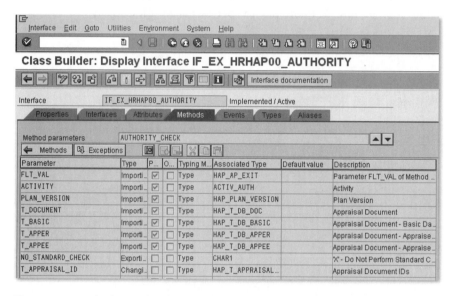

Figure 13.15 Method AUTHORITY_CHECK of BAdI HRHAP00_AUTHORITY

You should use this BAdI only if really necessary. In most implementations, appraisal security can be handled via a combination of R/3 security roles and appraisal level security (i.e., column and row access). If role maintenance is anticipated to become a burden (or if your R/3 role definition does not satisfy the granularity in which you want to define your appraisal security), then using this user exit may makes sense for your organization.

13.5 Summary

We have covered a wide range of authorization topics that will provide you the necessary security for your performance management implementation. Whether or not you use structural authorizations, the design of security within performance management is complex because of the various layers that range from standard R/3 security roles, to appraisal element column and row access, to the available security-related BAdIs.

In the next chapter, we discuss our final topic: the integration between the Performance Management and Compensation Management modules. This topic is particularly popular in today's strategic HR initiatives, as many companies look to enforce their "pay for performance" philosophy.

One of the most powerful aspects of the SAP HR system is its robust capability to integrate with other modules. The Performance Management module is no different, offering key integration with one of the most frequently sought-after modules: Compensation Management. This chapter details the integration touch points between the Compensation Management and Performance Management modules within SAP, with special emphasis on eligibility and guidelines.

14 Integration with Compensation Management

With more and more companies seeking "pay for performance," it is no wonder discussions around performance management and compensation management go hand in hand. Although SAP's Performance Management module can be implemented without integration with the Compensation Management module, many customers seeking to maximize the most return on investment should look to integrate the two processes.

To take full advantage of the latest SAP functionality, clients should implement the new Compensation Management functionality (application component PA-EC), popularly known as Enterprise Compensation Management (ECM). (The old compensation functionality application component PA-CM will not be discussed in this chapter.) The new module comes with enhanced features for budgeting, including a new web frontend for managing budgets before and during the planning process, as well as an entirely new framework for compensation planning. New infotypes, transactions, and processes have been introduced in the ECM module.

For this integration to work seamlessly, configuration must be performed in both the Performance Management module and in the Compensation Management module. We will first discuss the appraisal configuration needed for integration.

14.1 Appraisal Configuration

Minimal configuration is needed within the appraisal catalog (Transaction PHAP_CATALOG) for the Compensation Management module to retrieve performance management information such as final rating(s) and weightings. In the next section, we review the importance of appraisal statuses and how the configuration inherent in your appraisal template will drive integration.

14.1.1 Importance of Appraisal Status

Chapter 8 described appraisal statuses in detail. Depending on your performance management process, you may or may not need to leverage the additional appraisal statuses for approvals (statuses 6 through 9). Some customers decide to use the approval statuses within the module to explicitly track approved and rejected appraisals, whereas others keep it simpler and only require the appraisal to reach status Completed (status 5) before process completion. The **Approval Process Activated** indicator (located on the **Processing** tab of the template) enables the appraisal to use these additional statuses (see Figure 14.1). If the indicator is checked in the template, then the appraisal can use the additional statuses for approval: **Approved** (6), **Closed Approved** (7), **Rejected** (8), and **Closed Rejected** (9).

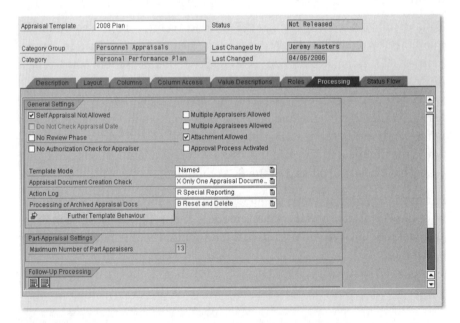

Figure 14.1 Appraisal Template's Processing Tab with the Approval Process Activated" Indicator Unchecked

If your template is using these approval statuses, the appraisal information becomes available to compensation management only when the document reaches statuses **Approved** (6) or **Closed Approved** (7). If your template does not need formal approval statuses configured, the appraisal information becomes available to compensation when the document is in status **Completed** (5). This behavior is due to standard SAP programming. Function module HRHAP_PA_CMP_DOC_VALUE_READ, which is read by several programs within the system, is hard-coded to function this way. Performance ratings displayed on the portal (e.g., in the Compensation Planning worksheet) use the standard function module HR_ECM_UI_DISP_APPRAISAL, which only displays the appraisal rating if the preceding logic is true. For those customers seeking more flexibility on when performance ratings can be available for compensation, enhancements can be made to the system to allow the ratings to be transparent throughout the compensation planning process, for example.

Figure 14.2 shows view V_TWPC_COL. In this view, column EC_APPRAISAL, entitled **Rating**, uses the standard function module HR_ECM_UI_DISP_APPRAISAL to display the performance rating. (All columns starting with prefix **EC** are pertinent to ECM functionality).

A custom function module can be created (based on the standard), which allows the appraisal document's performance score to be available throughout the appraisal process. This is beneficial because some companies do not want to be so restrictive with when the performance rating is accessible to compensation. For example, companies that hold calibration meetings may want to permit ratings to be "fluid" in the process as changes to performance scores could change after sessions cease. Of course, this is just one example of how you can enhance the standard functionality based on your unique business requirements. You can add additional logic to retrieve criteria group or criteria level ratings and weightings if these items are needed for compensation display or calculations. For example, if competencies are rated within the appraisal form, and these ratings need to be visible on the compensation planning worksheet, custom development is required.

Now that we have looked at the performance management side, let's discuss compensation management configuration. Compensation management configuration is more complex than performance management from an integration perspective because more setup is involved within the IMG.

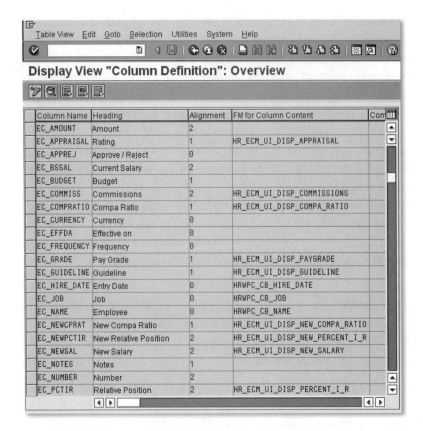

Figure 14.2 Table View V_TWPC_COL with Entry EC_APPRAISAL, which Uses the Standard Function Module HR_ECM_UI_DISP_APPRAISAL

14.2 Compensation Configuration

For integration with the Performance Management module, several items need configuration within the Compensation Management module. As mentioned previously, the information presented here exclusively covers the new ECM compensation framework. Integration with the old Compensation Management module is viable, and several clients *are* currently doing this. However, today, it is more common to see the new ECM and Performance Management modules integrated. Using the newer modules allows you to use more standard functionality out-of-the-box.

The next section covers both the eligibility and guideline configuration needed to link the two modules. The configuration is found within the ECM area of the IMG under **Personnel Management • Enterprise Compensation**

Management • **Compensation Administration**. We first discuss how to configure compensation eligibility, and then we cover compensation guidelines.

14.2.1 Eligibility

You can control compensation plan eligibility based on appraisal information such as performance rating minimums and maximums. The first step in configuring eligibility is to create *appraisal rules* in the IMG. Appraisal rules identify which appraisal template and template elements (criteria group and criteria) should be evaluated by the system as well as the minimum and maximum performance ratings needed to become eligible.

To define appraisal rules, navigate in the IMG to **Personnel Management** • **Enterprise Compensation Management** • **Compensation Administration Eligibility** • **Define Appraisal Rules** (see Figure 14.3).

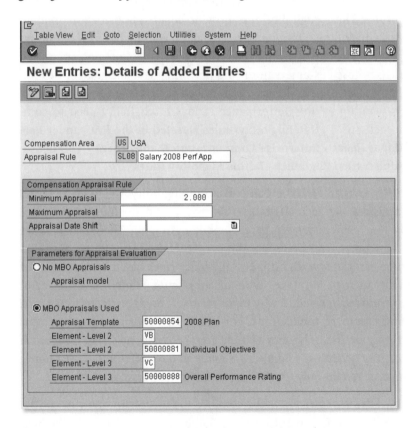

Figure 14.3 Compensation Appraisal Rule Using an MBO Template

Each appraisal rule is uniquely identified by **Compensation Area** so that the same appraisal rule could mean different things depending on the chosen compensation area. The **Compensation Appraisal Rule** section stores the minimum and maximum appraisal scores as well as the **Appraisal Date Shift** field. This date is important if eligibility dates within the Compensation Management module do not coincide with the eligibility dates of the appraisal form.

Example

If compensation eligibility is based on a January 1st date, but the appraisal document is only valid from January 1st to December 31st *of the previous year*, then an appraisal date shift of one day should be used to align the eligibility requirements with your compensation and performance management programs.

After defining appraisal rules, you need to integrate them into compensation eligibility rules. These eligibility rules provide detailed information on eligibility criteria, including minimum service, salary, waiting periods, minimum working hours, and the appraisal rule. The appraisal rule is not a required entry because those customers not using performance management or linking eligibility to an appraisal form do not need such a rule. However, those customers wanting to link performance ratings to eligibility need to complete IMG activity "Define Eligibility Rules" located in the IMG under **Personnel Management • Enterprise Compensation Management • Compensation Administration Eligibility • Define Eligibility Rules**.

Figure 14.4 shows an example **Compensation Eligibility Rule** with a configured **Appraisal Rule**. Each eligibility rule may vary depending on the compensation area, eligibility variant and eligibility grouping. These concepts are beyond the scope of this book, but the basic premise is that many appraisal rules can be associated with different eligibility rules based on a number of different factors (e.g., employee type, location, etc.). Eligibility variants and eligibility groupings provide a way to associate different compensation plans to different employee populations. For example, senior executives at your company may be the only ones eligible for the company's restricted stock plan. Eligibility groupings and variants allow you to differentiate this population and ensure that only executives are eligible for that stock plan.

If eligibility business rules prove too complex to satisfy with standard configuration, BAdI `HRECM00_ELIGIBILITY` is available to implement (with the help of an ABAP resource). In this enhancement, customer-specific business rules can be programmed to return whether the employee is eligible or not for a compensation plan. If a BAdI is used, the configuration explained previously may not be needed or may need to be modified to accommodate its development.

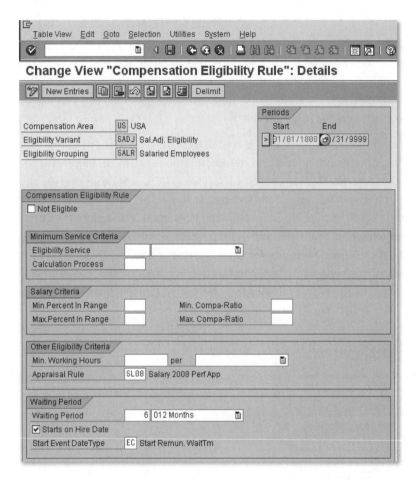

Figure 14.4 Example Eligibility Rule Configured with an Appraisal Rule

After completing the preceding steps, you can see how compensation eligibility (based on appraisal rules) can be implemented within your compensation management process. In addition to making the appraisal influence the employee's eligibility, the system also allows guidelines to be suggested based on performance ratings. In the next section, compensation guideline configuration is discussed in detail.

14.2.2 Guidelines

Performance ratings that influence compensation guidelines is one of the most popular integration scenarios in talent management systems today. SAP has provided this integration out-of-the-box and provides flexible ways of determining guidelines based on several factors, including performance rating.

To calculate a guideline or guidelines, the system uses a matrix. In cases where only one criterion is used to determine a guideline (e.g., if only the performance rating was used as the basis for determining guidelines), a one-dimensional matrix is created. Using standard configuration, you can define up to three dimensions in your matrix.

The first step in creating a matrix is to define what SAP calls "methods" for each matrix dimension. Several predefined methods are available, including one for Compa-ratio (CRAT), Length of service (SERV), Appraisal (APPR), and MBO Appraisal (MBOA). The standard methods can be reviewed and additional ones defined in the IMG by choosing **Personnel Management · Enterprise Compensation Management · Compensation Administration · Guidelines · Matrix · Define Methods for Matrix Dimensions**. See Figure 14.5 for the standard methods available. Method APPR evaluates the old appraisal models, whereas the MBOA evaluates the new performance management functionality. We'll discuss the latter in this chapter.

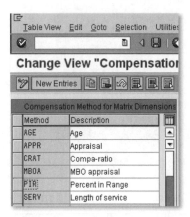

Figure 14.5 Standard Matrix Dimension Methods

Behind each method is a BAdI implementation. For the MBOA method, BAdI implementation HRECM00_MATR_MBOAPPR was created. The standard logic within this BAdI retrieves the appropriate rating from the employee's appraisal document in question. It uses the function module HRHAP_PA_CMP_DOC_VALUE_READ to read the appraisal result. As with the Standard Eligibility functionality discussed earlier in this chapter, the logic inherent within this programming only returns a rating if the appraisal document is in Complete status (if the approval process has not been activated) or if it's in Approved or Closed Approved status (if the approval process has been activated).

When setting up your guideline rules, you should first define your matrix dimensions by choosing **Personnel Management • Enterprise Compensation Management • Compensation Administration • Guidelines • Matrix • Define Matrix Dimensions** in the IMG (see Figure 14.6).

Start by selecting the proper dimension method. In our business scenario, we will configure a matrix dimension based on dimension method MBOA. The Method Parameter field defines the appraisal template (VA), criteria group (VB), or criterion (VC) that should be evaluated within the Performance Management module.

The **Unit of Meth. Result** should be ignored in this scenario because it's not used in this dimension method. **Dimension Date Shift** acts similarly to the Date Shift functionality within the eligibility configuration. The guideline Date Shift functionality allows for guideline effective dates to coincide with the validity period of the appraisal document.

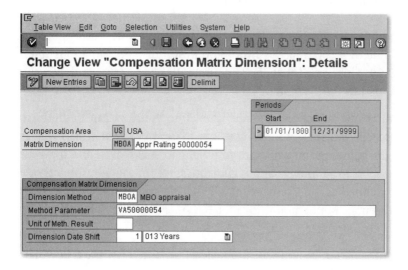

Figure 14.6 Defining a Compensation Matrix Dimension for an MBO Appraisal Document

After defining one or more **Matrix Dimensions**, you must next define the individual segments that will eventually comprise the overall matrix. To define a Matrix Dimension segment, navigate in the IMG by choosing **Personnel Management** • **Enterprise Compensation Management** • **Compensation Administration** • **Guidelines** • **Matrix** • **Define Matrix Dimension Segments**.

Each segment should be defined with a description (e.g., 3- MA [Meets All Expectations]) and a **Minimum/Maximum Result**. In Figure 14.7, **Segment 3** constitutes an appraisal rating of a 3 because both the **Minimum Result** and **Maximum Result** values are configured as 3.

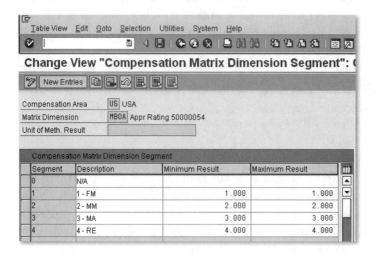

Figure 14.7 Example of Matrix Dimension Segments

The minimums and maximums could span ranges as well. For example, a **Segment** value of 3 could have a **Minimum Result** of 3.00 and a **Maximum Result** of 3.99. This means that any appraisal rating between 3 and 4 (exclusive) is mapped to the 3 **Segment** value.

After defining one or more segments, guideline matrices can be defined. Within this step, you specify the dimensions to use in each matrix as well as what type of guideline information you want to make available for your compensation plan. Compensation guidelines for merit adjustments are commonly defined as a percentage (e.g., 3%). The system allows guidelines by both percentage and amount for monetary plans but only guidelines by number for non-monetary plans (e.g., stock options).

Guideline information can only be defined within one set of the following:

▶ **Default Amount, Minimum Amount, and Maximum Amount**
  For example, a default amount of $1000, a minimum amount of $500, and a maximum amount $2000.

▶ **Default Percent, Minimum Percent, and Maximum Percent**
  For example, a default percentage of 3%, a minimum percentage of 2%, and a maximum percentage of 4%.

▶ **Default Number, Minimum Number, and Maximum Number**
  For example, a default number of 50 stock units, a minimum number of 0 stock units, and a maximum number of 200 stock units.

As stated previously, up to three dimensions can be used within your matrix in the standard configuration. In our example, let's say that the guideline is based on both the employee's appraisal and compa-ratio — a two-dimensional matrix. To configure the guideline matrix, navigate in the IMG by choosing **Personnel Management • Enterprise Compensation Management • Compensation Administration • Guidelines • Matrix • Define Guideline Matrices.**

Based on plan guideline rules, you should select the appropriate matrix relevance indicator(s). You may select only a default, a minimum, and maximum, or all three. The example in Figure 14.8 shows a configured **Guideline Matrix** ZSAL called MbO and Compa Matrix, which has the **MBO** and **Compa-Ratio** dimensions defined as being applicable for default, minimum, and maximum guideline *percentage* values only.

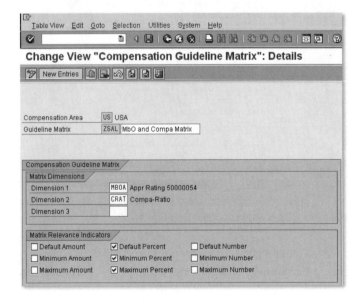

Figure 14.8 Compensation Guideline Matrix Definition

After defining your matrix, including its dimensions and segments, it's time to actually assign matrix values (i.e., percentages, amounts, numbers) to the grid. To do this, go to the IMG activity by choosing **Personnel Management • Enterprise Compensation Management • Compensation Administration • Guidelines • Matrix • Assign Matrix Values**.

In this step, each segment dimension is defined for each indicator (default, minimum, and maximum) based on validity period. Figure 14.9 shows a matrix with sample values. Depending on the number of dimension segments and actual dimensions being configured, your matrix can be very large based on the number of permutations that could exist.

> **Note**
>
> In edit mode, any values of 0 appear to be blank even though the table will store them correctly as 0s.

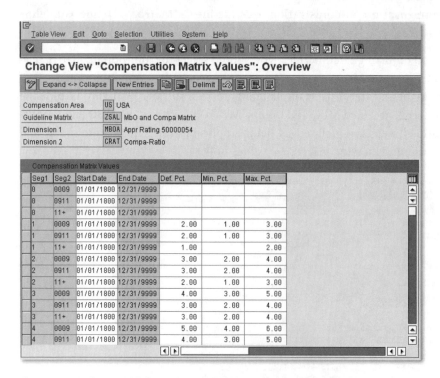

Figure 14.9 Defining Guideline Values within the Compensation Matrix

The next step is to assign your matrix to a compensation guideline variant. You do this by choosing **Personnel Management • Enterprise Compensation**

Management • Compensation Administration • Guidelines • Define Guidelines. The **Guideline Variant** is comprised of the **Compensation Area**, **Guideline Grouping**, **Guidel. Matrix**, and a **Proration Rule** (if applicable). Figure 14.10 shows our example guideline matrix ZSAL.

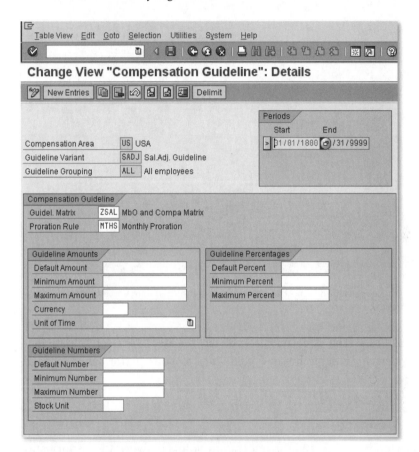

Figure 14.10 Guideline Variant Definition, Including the Guidel. Matrix

The final step is to assign the guideline variant to one or more compensation plans (see Figure 14.11). This is done by choosing **Personnel Management • Enterprise Compensation Management • Compensation Administration • Plan Attributes • Assign Compensation Plan Attributes**.

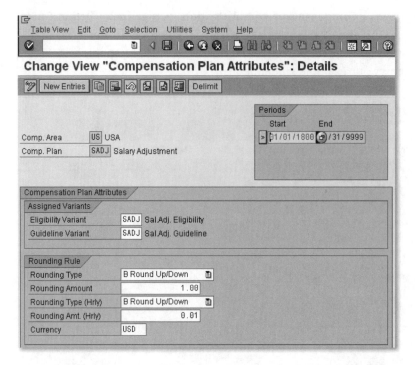

Figure 14.11 Compensation Plan Attributes, Including the Guideline Variant and Eligibility Variant

Congratulations! You have now completed the necessary configuration to link compensation eligibility and guidelines to your performance management data.

14.2.3 Summary

In this chapter, we covered the integration points between the Performance Management and Compensation Management modules. Compensation eligibility and compensation guidelines are two key integration components. As discussed, standard functionality can be modified to account for any customer-specific business requirements. Customers can expect to increase their return on investment by marrying these two modules seamlessly in their integrated landscape.

This concludes our coverage of the SAP Performance Management Module. We hope that you have found the information easy to understand and that it will be helpful in your own implementation.

Appendix

A   Performance Management Transaction Codes

Table A.1 lists important transaction codes used within the performance management application. All transaction codes starting with PHAP_* and OOHAP_* are used within the solution. Transaction codes with suffix _PA (e.g., PHAP_CATALOG_PA) references the PA add-on application, meaning that those transactions restrict visibility to appraisal templates for Personnel Administration only.

Transaction Code	Transaction Code Name	Transaction Code Description	Applicable For
PHAP_CATALOG and PHAP_CATALOG_PA	Appraisal Template Catalog	Provides access to the Appraisal Catalog.	Configurators
PHAP_ADMIN and PHAP_ADMIN_PA	Administrator — Appraisal Document	Performs administrative transactions such as changing appraisal ratings and comments. Administrator can also create appraisals, delete appraisals, and change appraisal status/substatus.	Administrators
PHAP_CREATE and PHAP_CREATE_PA	Create Appraisal	Creates an individual appraisal document.	Employees/Managers (if SAP backend is used)
PHAP_SEARCH and PHAP_SEARCH_PA	Evaluate Appraisal Document	Runs evaluations or reports (only display function). Creates ranking lists, exports documents to Microsoft Excel, and uses analysis tool.	Administrators

Table A.1 Performance Management Transaction Codes Listed with Transaction Code Name, Description and Applicable Users of the Transaction

Transaction Code	Transaction Code Name	Transaction Code Description	Applicable For
PHAP_CHANGE and PHAP_CHANGE_PA	Change Appraisal Document	Changes appraisal documents. Changes previously created appraisal documents, for example, adds or deletes objectives.	Employees/Managers (if SAP backend is used)
PHAP_PREPARE and PHAP_PREPARE_PA	Prepare Appraisal Documents	Creates appraisal documents via implemented BAdIs. Prepares several appraisal documents using a wizard or using organizational units.	Administrators
PHAP_START_BSP	Generate Internet Addresses	Allows you to construct and launch a URL for the appraisal document based on BSP application HAP_DOCUMENT. *Available as of Extension 4.7 Set 2.0.*	Developers; Configurators
PHAP_ANON	Appraisal Documents — Anonymous	Displays anonymous documents.	Administrators
OOHAP_BASIC	Basic Appraisal Template Settings	Performs configuration changes for templates, including columns, value lists, roles, enhancements, substatuses, pushbuttons, authorized persons, and workflow events.	Configurators

Table A.1 Performance Management Transaction Codes Listed with Transaction Code Name, Description and Applicable Users of the Transaction (Cont.)

Transaction Code	Transaction Code Name	Transaction Code Description	Applicable For
OOHAP_CAT_ GROUP	Category Group Settings	Performs configuration changes for category groups including changes to category group name, allowed object types, status/substatus, authorized persons, workflow events, and associated categories.	Configurators
OOHAP_CATEGORY	Appraisal Category Settings	Performs configuration changes for categories, including changes to category name, allowed appraisers, allowed appraisees, allowed part appraisers, allowed further participants, columns, value lists, enhancements, roles, status/substatus, authorized persons, workflow events, and associated categories.	Configurators
OOHAP_SETTINGS_ PA	PA: Settings	Gives access to two important T77S0 table entries: HAP00 REPLA and HAP00 RFCSE.	Configurators
OOHAP_VALUE_ TYPE	Standard Value Lists	Performs scale (i.e., value list) configuration. Allows you to configure value lists, values, and value descriptions regardless of value type (i.e., quantity, quality, etc.).	Configurators

Table A.1 Performance Management Transaction Codes Listed with Transaction Code Name, Description and Applicable Users of the Transaction (Cont.)

Transaction Code	Transaction Code Name	Transaction Code Description	Applicable For
SICF	HTTP Service Hierarchy Maintenance	Enables activation of BSP service HAP_DOCUMENT and others. For your Basis team.	Developers
SE80	ABAP Development Workbench	Allows for customizations of BSP application. For your development support team.	Developers

Table A.1 Performance Management Transaction Codes Listed with Transaction Code Name, Description and Applicable Users of the Transaction (Cont.)

B Performance Management Objects and Infotypes

Tables B.1 through B.3 provide a listing of Personnel Development (PD) objects and infotypes used within the Performance Management module. Like other modules within the HCM suite, Performance Management uses PD objects and infotypes to deliver its functionality. All appraisal templates and underlying structures are stored in HRP* infotypes.

Object	Object Name	Purpose in Performance Management
VA	Appraisal Template	Holds all appraisal-level information, including status flow and column access configuration
VB	Appraisal Criteria Group	Holds criteria group information, including description, columns, value descriptions, and roles
VC	Appraisal Criterion	Holds criteria information, including description, columns, value descriptions, and roles
Q	Qualification	Tracks skills and competencies
D	Business Event Type	Tracks business event types such as classroom training and eLearning

Table B.1 Performance Management Objects

Infotype	Infotype Description	Storage
HRP1000	Object	Contains the name of the appraisal form
HRP1001	Relationships	Contains linkages between the appraisal template (VA) and criteria groups (VB) and criteria (VC) elements via the A/B605 ("Includes Element") relationship. Additionally, stores sorting and element weighting information for the element.
HRP1002	Description	Contains the web layout and description stored on the **Description** tab
HRP1048	Proficiency Description	Contains the proficiency description and language key on the **Value Description** tab

Table B.2 Performance Management Infotypes

Info-type	Infotype Description	Storage
HRP5020	Category Assignment	Contains category group ID and category ID
HRP5021	Layout Definition	Contains information on the **Layout** tab, including links, header enhancement, text replacement, and numbering
HRP5022	Column/Cell Definition	Contains cell information from the **Column** tab, including value input, value list, note, and text layout, among other column information
HRP5023	Column Access	Contains column access information such as column ID, column owner, and column access matrix that is stored on the **Column Access** tab
HRP5024	Role Assignment	Contains role information relevant for the part appraisal document (e.g., Self, Manager, etc.) stored on the **Roles** tab
HRP5025	Processing	Contains information on **Processing** tab, including general settings, template mode, action log, further template behavior, part appraisal settings, and follow-up processing.
HRP5026	Status Switch	Contains information on the **Status Flow** tab, including status, substatus, and pushbuttons.

Table B.2 Performance Management Infotypes

HRHAP* tables store the actual performance management appraisal information. All appraisals In Process and Completed are stored in these tables.

Infotype	Infotype Description
HRHAP	Appraisal Document
HRHAP_ACT_LOG	Action Log — Additional Data
HRHAP_ANON	Anonymous Appraiser Assignments
HRHAP_APPEE	Appraisee Assignment
HRHAP_APPER	Appraiser Assignment
HRHAP_BASIC	Basic Element Data
HRHAP_FINAL	Cell Values of Final Appraisal Column
HRHAP_FURTHER	Values of Additional Participants Column
HRHAP_OBJECT	Cell Values of Objective Columns
HRHAP_OTHERS	Additional Participant Assignment

Table B.3 Performance Management Tables

Infotype	Infotype Description
HRHAP_P	Reference Appraisal
HRHAP_P_APPER	Part Appraiser Assignment
HRHAP_P_D	Reference Appraisal (Structure)
HRHAP_P_E	Reference Appraisal (Data)
HRHAP_P_T	Reference Appraisal Names
HRHAP_PART	Cell Values of Part Appraisal Columns
HRHAP_PROCESS	Processed Appraisal Functions
HRHAP_SEM_OBJ	Strategic Objectives from SEM System
HRHAP_T	Appraisal Document Name

Table B.3 Performance Management Tables

C Performance Management BAdIs

Tables C.1 through C.52 provide a listing of all Business Add-Ins (BAdIs) available for customer use in the Performance Management module. BAdIs provide a robust way of enhancing the R/3 system by allowing customers to implement specific businesses rules according to business needs. For a more detailed explanation of all BAdIs and how to integrate them into your appraisal templates, refer to Chapter 10.

Concerning BAdI implementations, note that:

▶ Any BAdI implementation available as of Enterprise 4.7 Extension Set 1.1 is also available in Enterprise 4.7 Extension Set 2.0, ECC 5.0, and ECC 6.0.

▶ Any BAdI implementation available as of Enterprise 4.7 Extension Set 2.0 is also available in ECC 5.0 and ECC 6.0.

▶ Any BAdI implementation available as of ECC 5.0 is also available in ECC 6.0.

C.1 BAdI Area: Template Definition and Behavior

Enhancement Name	BAdI Implementation	BAdI Implementation Description	Availability
D	HRHAP00_VALUE_TYPE_D	Date	As of Extension 4.7 Set 1.1
E	HRHAP00_VALUE_TYPE_D	Status of Development Plan Item	As of ECC 5.0
M	HRHAP00_VALUE_TYPE_M	Quantity Scale	As of Extension 4.7 Set 1.1
N	HRHAP00_VALUE_TYPE_N	Irregular Quality Scale	As of Extension 4.7 Set 1.1
O	HRHAP00_VALUE_TYPE_O	Options	As of Extension 4.7 Set 1.1
Q	HRHAP00_VALUE_TYPE_Q	Quality Scales	As of Extension 4.7 Set 1.1

Table C.1 HRHAP00_VALUE_TYPE (Appraisal Document — Value List)

Enhancement Name	BAdI Implementation	BAdI Implementation Description	Availability
S	HRHAP00_VALUE_TYPE_S	Numeric Value	As of Extension 4.7 Set 1.1
T	HRHAP00_VALUE_TYPE_T	Status of Business Event Types	As of ECC 5.0
C	HRHAP_VALUE_TYPE_C	Currency (TCURC)	As of ECC 5.0
U	HRHAP_VALUE_TYPE_CU	Unit of Measurement (T006)	As of ECC 5.0

Table C.1 HRHAP00_VALUE_TYPE (Appraisal Document — Value List) (Cont.)

Enhancement Name	BAdI Implementation	BAdI Implementation Description	Availability
ALTWEIGHT	HRHAP00_VAL_DET_012	Value Determination — Default Value	As of Extension 4.7 Set 2.0
AVERAGE	HRHAP00_VAL_DET_001	Value Determination — Average (Weighted)	As of Extension 4.7 Set 1.1
CURRENT_ PROFICIENCY	HRHAP00_VAL_DET_006	Value Determination — Current Proficiency	As of Extension 4.7 Set 1.1
CURRENT_ STATUS	HRHAP00_VAL_DET_013	Value Determination — Status of Development Plan Item	As of ECC 5.0
CURRENT_ TRAINING_TYPE_ STATUS	HRHAP00_VAL_DET_014	Value Determination — Status of Business Event Type	As of ECC 5.0
NOTE_INIT	HRHAP00_VAL_DET_008	Value Determination — Note Pre-assignment	As of Extension 4.7 Set 2.0
ORG_OBJECTIVES	HRHAP00_VAL_DET_005	Value Determination — Strategic Objectives	As of Extension 4.7 Set 1.1
PERCENTAGE	HRHAP00_VAL_DET_003	Value Determination — Percentage (Weighted)	As of Extension 4.7 Set 1.1
PERFORMANCE_ MATRIX	HRHAP00_VAL_DET_004	Value Determination — Performance Overview	As of Extension 4.7 Set 1.1
SUM_UP_ APPRAISAL_ RESULTS	HRHAP00_VAL_DET_011	Value Determination — Summary of Other Appraisal Documents	As of Extension 4.7 Set 2.0

Table C.2 HRHAP00_VAL_DET (Appraisal Document — Value Determination)

Enhancement Name	BAdI Implementation	BAdI Implementation Description	Availability
TARGET_ACTUAL_ COMPARISON	HRHAP00_VAL_DET_009	Value Determination – Targ/Act.Comp. in % with Overfulfillment	As of Extension 4.7 Set 2.0
TARGET_ACTUAL_ COMPARISON_2	HRHAP00_VAL_DET_010	Value Determination — Targ/Act.Comp. in % w/o Overfulfillment	As of Extension 4.7 Set 2.0
TOTAL	HRHAP00_VAL_DET_002	Value Determination — Total (Weighted)	As of Extension 4.7 Set 1.1
WEIGHTED_ RESULT	HRHAP00_VAL_DET_007	Value Determination — Weighted Result (=FWGT * FAPP)	As of Extension 4.7 Set 1.1

Table C.2 HRHAP00_VAL_DET (Appraisal Document — Value Determination) (Cont.)

Enhancement Name	BAdI Implementation	BAdI Implementation Description	Availability
DISPLAY_DOCUMENTS_ SUM_UP_CALC	HRHAP00_LINK_005	Link — Display Documents in Validity Period	As of Extension 4.7 Set 2.0
DISPLAY_IND_DEVEL- OPMENT	HRHAP00_LINK_006	Link — Display Individual Development	As of ECC 5.0
DISPLAY_MANAGER_ APPRAISAL	HRHAP00_LINK_004	Link — Manager's Document	As of Extension 4.7 Set 2.0
DISPLAY_PREVIOUS_ APPRAISAL	HRHAP00_LINK_003	Relationship — Display Last Document	As of Extension 4.7 Set 2.0
DISPLAY_QUALIFICA- TIONS	HRHAP00_LINK_002	Link — Display Qualifications	As of Extension 4.7 Set 1.1
DISPLAY_SCORECARD	HRHAP00_LINK_001	Link — Display Scorecard	As of Extension 4.7 Set 1.1

Table C.3 HRHAP00_LINK (Appraisal Document — Relationships)

Enhancement Name	BAdI Implementation	BAdI Implementation Description	Availability
PERSONNEL_ HEADER_DATA	HRHAP00_ADD_ HEADER_1	Additional Header Data — Personnel Header Data	As of Extension 4.7 Set 1.1

Table C.4 HRHAP00_ADD_HEADER (Appraisal Document — Additional Header Data)

Enhancement Name	BAdI Implementation	BAdI Implementation Description	Availability
APPRAISER_AND_APPRAISEE	HRHAP00_TEXT_SUBST01	Text Replacement — Names of Appraiser and Appraisee	As of Extension 4.7 Set 1.1

Table C.5 HRHAP00_TEXT_SUBST (Appraisal Document — Text Replacement)

Enhancement Name	BAdI Implementation	BAdI Implementation Description	Availability
ADD_BOOKED_TRAININGS	HRHAP00_ENHANCE_FIX5	Fixed Enhancement — Add Booked Courses	As of Extension 4.7 Set 2.0
ADD_IND_DEVELOPMENT	HRHAP00_ENHANCE_FIX3	Fixed Enhancement — Add Development Plan Items	As of Extension 4.7 Set 2.0
ADD_MAND_TRAINING	HRHAP00_ENHANCE_FIX4	Fixed Enhnancement — Add Required Business Event Types	As of Extension 4.7 Set 2.0
ADD_REQUIREMENTS	HRHAP00_ENHANCE_FIX1	Fixed Enhancement — Add Position Requirements	As of Extension 4.7 Set 1.1
Q_ADD_DEFICITS	HRHAP00_ENHANCE_FIX2	Add Deficits from Position	As of Extension 4.7 Set 2.0
ADD_CURRENT_JF	HRHAP00_ENHANCE_FIX6	Fixed Enhancement — Add Current Job Family	As of ECC 6.0

Table C.6 HRHAP00_ENHANCE_FIX (Appraisal Document — Fixed Enhancement)

Enhancement Name	BAdI Implementation	BAdI Implementation Description	Availability
ADD_IND_DEVPLAN_STATION	HRHAP00_ENHANCE_FRE5	Free Enhancement — Add Development Plan Items	As of ECC 5.0
ADD_NEW_ELEMENT	HRHAP00_ENHANCE_FRE1	Free Enhancement — Add New Element	As of Extension 4.7 Set 1.1
ADD_NEW_ELEMENT_UP_TO_7	HRHAP00_ENHANCE_FRE3	Free Enhancement — Add New Element (up to 7)	As of Extension 4.7 Set 1.1
ADD_QUALIFICATION	HRHAP00_ENHANCE_FRE2	Free Enhancement — Add Qualification	As of Extension 4.7 Set 1.1
ADD_REQ_QUALIFICATION	HRHAP00_ENHANCE_FRE4	Free Enhancement — Add Requirements of Position	As of Extension 4.7 Set 2.0

Table C.7 HRHAP00_ENHANCE_FREE (Appraisal Document — Free Enhancement)

Enhancement Name	BAdI Implementation	BAdI Implementation Description	Availability
ADD_TRAINING_TYPES	HRHAP00_ENHANCE_FRE6	Free Enhancement — Add Business Event Types	As of ECC 5.0
ADD_JOB_FAMILY	HRHAP00_ENHANCE_FRE7	Free Enhancement — Add Job Family	As of ECC 6.0
ADD_REQ_Q_FROM_JF	HRHAP00_ENHANCE_FRE8	Free Enhancement — Requirements of Job Families	As of ECC 6.0
ADD_Q_FROM_JF	HRHAP00_ENHANCE_FRE9	Add Required Qualifications from Job Family	As of ECC 6.0

Table C.7 HRHAP00_ENHANCE_FREE (Appraisal Document — Free Enhancement) (Cont.)

Enhancement Name	BAdI Implementation	BAdI Implementation Description	Availability
DELETION_2	HRHAP00_ENHANCE_DEL1	Delete Element — Only In Planning	As of Extension 4.7 Set 1.1
DELETION_2_3	HRHAP00_ENHANCE_DEL2	Delete Element — Only In Planning or In Review	As of Extension 4.7 Set 1.1
DELETION_2_3_4	HRHAP00_ENHANCE_DEL3	Delete Element — In Planning, In Review, In Process	As of Extension 4.7 Set 1.1

Table C.8 HRHAP00_ENHANCE_DEL (Appraisal Document — Delete Element)

Enhancement Name	BAdI Implementation	BAdI Implementation Description	Availability
ADJUST_POTENTIAL	HRHAP00_FOLLOW_UP_05	Follow-Up (Background) — Adjust Potential (Start Date)	As of ECC 6.0
ADJUST_POTENTIAL_2	HRHAP00_FOLLOW_UP_06	Follow-Up (Background) — Adjust Potential (End Date)	As of ECC 6.0
ADJUST_QUAL_WITH_NOTE_1	HRHAP00_FOLLOW_UP_03	Follow-Up Processing (Background) — Adjust Qualif+No (StarDate)	As of Extension 4.7 Set 2.0
ADJUST_QUAL_WITH_NOTE_2	HRHAP00_FOLLOW_UP_04	Follow-Up Processing (Background) — Adjust Qualif+No (End Date)	As of Extension 4.7 Set 2.0

Table C.9 HRHAP00_FOLLOW_UP (Appraisal Document — Follow-Up Processing [Background])

Enhancement Name	BAdI Implementation	BAdI Implementation Description	Availability
ADJUST_QUALIFI-CATIONS	HRHAP00_FOLLOW_UP_01	Follow-Up Processing (Background) — Adjust Qualif (Start Date)	As of Extension 4.7 Set 1.1
ADJUST_QUALIFICATIONS_2	HRHAP00_FOLLOW_UP_02	Follow-Up Processing (Background) — Adjust Qualif (End Date)	As of Extension 4.7 Set 1.1

Table C.9 HRHAP00_FOLLOW_UP (Appraisal Document — Follow-Up Processing [Background]) (Cont.)

No standard implementations exist.

Table C.10 HRHAP00_FOLLOW_UP_D (Appraisal Document — Follow-Up Processing [Dialog])

Enhancement Name	BAdI Implementation	BAdI Implementation Description	Availability
STANDARD	HRHAP00_SMARTFORMS01	Smartform — Standard Template	As of ECC 6.0
SMARTFORM	HRHAP00_SMARTFORMS02	Print Appraisal Documents — Old (with Smartforms)	As of Extension 4.7 Set 1.1

Table C.11 HRHAP00_SMARTFORMS (Appraisal Document — Print Preview [Smartform])

No standard implementations exist.

Table C.12 HRHAP00_BSP_TMPL Appraisal Document — Web Layout (BSP)

Enhancement Name	BAdI Implementation	BAdI Implementation Description	Availability
STANDARD	HRHAP00_OFFLINE01	Offline Appraisal Document — Standard Template	As of ECC 6.0

Table C.13 HRHAP00_OFFLINE Appraisal Document — Offline

Enhancement Name	BAdI Implementation	BAdI Implementation Description	Availability
DYNAMIC_NOTE	HRHAP00_DYN_NOTE	Dynamic Event — Mandatory Note for Low Valuation	As of ECC 6.0

Table C.14 HRHAP00_DYN_EVENT Appraisal Document — Dynamic Cell Value Event

C.2   BAdI Area A: Catalog

Enhancement Name	BAdI Implementation	BAdI Implementation Description	Availability
CHECK_LIST	HRHAP00_CATEG_EXMPL5	Create Example Category — Checklist	As of Extension 4.7 Set 1.1
FEEDBACK_360	HRHAP00_CATEG_EXMPL3	Create Example Category — 360-degree Feedback	As of Extension 4.7 Set 1.1
OBJECTIVE_SETTING	HRHAP00_CATEG_EXMPL2	Create Example Category — Objective Setting	As of Extension 4.7 Set 1.1
REFERENCE	HRHAP00_CATEG_EXMPL4	Create Example Category — References	As of Extension 4.7 Set 1.1
STANDARD_APPRAISAL	HRHAP00_CATEG_EXMPL1	Create Example Category — Standard Appraisal	As of Extension 4.7 Set 1.1

Table C.15 HRHAP00_CATEG_EXMPLE (Catalog — Create Example Category)

Enhancement Name	BAdI Implementation	BAdI Implementation Description	Availability
OBJECTIVE_SETTING	HRHAP00_TMPL_OBJ_SET	Example — Objective Setting	As of Extension 4.7 Set 1.1
PERFORMANCE_FEEDBACK	HRHAP00_TMPL_PF	Example — Performance Feedback	As of Extension 4.7 Set 1.1
POTENTIAL_JF	HRHAP00_TMPL_JF_POT	Example — Job Family Potential Assignment	As of ECC 6.0

Table C.16 HRHAP00_TMPL_EXAMPLE (Catalog — Create Example Templates)

Enhancement Name	BAdI Implementation	BAdI Implementation Description	Availability
TMPL_WZ_EASY	HRHAP00_TMPL_WIZARD1	Simple Template Creation	As of Extension 4.7 Set 1.1

Table C.17 HRHAP00_TMPL_WIZARD (Catalog — Create Templates Using Wizard)

C.3 BAdI Area C: Appraisal Enhancements

No standard implementations exist.

Table C.18 HRHAP00_TMPL_GETLIST (Appraisal Document — Get Template List)

Enhancement Name	BAdI Implementation	BAdI Implementa-tion Description	Availability
STANDARD	HRHAP00_DOC_DEF_DN01	Default Appraisal Document Name — Add Period Information	As of Extension 4.7 Set 1.1

Table C.19 HRHAP00_DOC_DEF_DN (Appraisal Document — Default Appraisal Document Name)

Enhancement Name	BAdI Implementation	BAdI Implementa-tion Description	Availability
DEFAULT_MANAGER	HRHAP00_DOC_DEF_D101	Default Manager as Appraiser	As of Extension 4.7 Set 1.1

Table C.20 HRHAP00_DOC_DEF_D1 (Appraisal Document — Default Appraiser)

Enhancement Name	BAdI Implementation	BAdI Implementa-tion Description	Availability
DEFAULT_MYSELF	HRHAP00_DOC_DEF_D201	Default Myself as Appraisee	As of Extension 4.7 Set 1.1

Table C.21 HRHAP00_DOC_DEF_D2 (Appraisal Document — Default Appraisee)

Enhancement Name	BAdI Implementation	BAdI Implementa-tion Description	Availability
DEFAULT_APPER_ AND_APPEE	HRHAP00_DOC_DEF_DP01	Default Appraiser and Appraisee as Part Appraisers	As of Extension 4.7 Set 1.1

Table C.22 HRHAP00_DOC_DEF_DP (Appraisal Document — Default Part Appraisers)

No standard implementations exist.

Table C.23 HRHAP00_DOC_DEF_DO (Appraisal Document — Default Further Participants)

Enhancement Name	BAdI Implementation	BAdI Implementation Description	Availability
STANDARD	HRHAP00_DOC_DEF_DV01	Default Validity Period — Process Dependent	As of Extension 4.7 Set 1.1
LAST_APPRAISAL	HRHAP00_DOC_DEF_DV02	Reflect Default Validity Period of Last Appraisal Document	As of ECC 6.0

Table C.24 HRHAP00_DOC_DEF_DV (Appraisal Document — Default App. Document Validity Period)

Enhancement Name	BAdI Implementation	BAdI Implementation Description	Availability
STANDARD	HRHAP00_DOC_DEF_DE01	Default Execution Period — Validity Period	As of Extension 4.7 Set 1.1

Table C.25 HRHAP00_DOC_DEF_DE (Appraisal Document — Default Completion Period)

Enhancement Name	BAdI Implementation	BAdI Implementation Description	Availability
STANDARD	HRHAP00_DOC_DEF_DR01	Default Review Date = SY-DATUM	As of Extension 4.7 Set 1.1

Table C.26 HRHAP00_DOC_DEF_DR (Appraisal Document — Default Review Date)

Enhancement Name	BAdI Implementation	BAdI Implementation Description	Availability
AA	HRHAP00_COL_OWNER_AA	Column Owners Appraiser and Appraisee	As of Extension 4.7 Set 2.0
AE	HRHAP00_COL_OWNER_AE	Column Owner Appraisee	As of Extension 4.7 Set 2.0
AR	HRHAP00_COL_OWNER_AR	Column Owner Appraiser	As of Extension 4.7 Set 2.0
OT	HRHAP00_COL_OWNER_OT	Column Owner Further Participants	As of Extension 4.7 Set 2.0
PA	HRHAP00_COL_OWNER_PA	Column Owner Part Appraiser	As of Extension 4.7 Set 2.0

Table C.27 HRHAP00_COL_OWNER (Appraisal Document — Column Owner)

No standard implementations exist.

Table C.28 HRHAP00_COL_ACCESS (Appraisal Document — Column Access)

No standard implementations exist.

Table C.29 HRHAP00_ATT_ACCESS (Document — Attachment(s) Authorization Handling)

No standard implementations exist.

Table C.30 HRHAP00_BUT_ACCESS (Appraisal Document — Pushbutton Access)

No standard implementations exist.

Table C.31 HRHAP00_ACTION_LOG (Appraisal Document — Action Log)

No standard implementations exist.

Table C.32 HRHAP00_DOC_BC (Appraisal Document — Business Check)

No standard implementations exist.

Table C.33 HRHAP00_AUTHORITY (Appraisal Document — Authorization Check)

No standard implementations exist.

Table C.34 HRHAP00_DOC_DELETE (Appraisal Document — Delete)

No standard implementations exist.

Table C.35 HRHAP00_DOC_SAVE (Appraisal Document — Save Appraisal Document)

Enhancement Name	BAdI Implementation	BAdI Implementation Description	Availability
MAX_3_PART_APPRAISER	HRHAP00_MAX_P_APPER3	Maximum Number of Part Appraisers = 3	As of Extension 4.7 Set 1.1
MAX_4_PART_APPRAISER	HRHAP00_MAX_P_APPER4	Maximum Number of Part Appraisers = 4	As of Extension 4.7 Set 1.1

Table C.36 HRHAP00_MAX_P_APPER (Maximum Number of Part Appraisers)

Enhancement Name	BAdI Implementation	BAdI Implementation Description	Availability
PART_APPER_ACCESS	HRHAP00_ACCESS_HDR_1	Change Part Appraisers Before Appraisal	As of Extension 4.7 Set 1.1
PART_APPER_ACCESS_2	HRHAP00_ACCESS_HDR_2	Change Part Appraisers During Appraisal	As of Extension 4.7 Set 1.1

Table C.37 HRHAP00_ACC_HEADER (Appraisal Document — Header Data Access)

C.4 BAdI Area E: Reporting

Enhancement Name	BAdI Implementation	BAdI Implementation Description	Availability
ANALYZE	HRHAP00_REPORTING_03	Analyze	As of Extension 4.7 Set 1.1
EXPORT_IN_EXCEL	HRHAP00_REPORTING_02	Export to Excel	As of Extension 4.7 Set 1.1
RANKING_LIST	HRHAP00_REPORTING_00	Ranking List	As of Extension 4.7 Set 1.1
SMARTFORMS	HRHAP00_REPORTING_01	Print	As of Extension 4.7 Set 1.1

Table C.38 HRHAP00_REPORTING Appraisal Document — Reporting

Enhancement Name	BAdI Implementation	BAdI Implementation Description	Availability
(No filter)	HRHAP00_REP_GEN_VAR0	Appraisal Document Reporting — Generic Variants	As of Extension 4.7 Set 1.1

Table C.39 HRHAP00_REP_GEN_VAR (Appraisal Document — Reporting [Generic Variants])

C.5 BAdI Area X: Administrator

No standard implementations exist.

Table C.40 HRHAP00_ADMIN (Appraisal Document — Admin. Functions)

C.6   BAdI Area Y: Add-On Application

Enhancement Name	BAdI Implementation	BAdI Implementation Description	Availability
LSO	HRHAP00_ADD_ON_LSO	Learning Solution	As of ECC 5.0
PA	HRHAP00_ADD_ON_PA	Development: Add-On Application Personnel Development	As of ECC 5.0

Table C.41 HRHAP00_ADD_ON_APPL (Development: Add-On Application)

No standard implementations exist.

Table C.42 HRHAP00_CATALOG_ACT (Development: Catalog — Action)

Enhancement Name	BAdI Implementation	BAdI Implementation Description	Availability
PA	HRHAP00_INIT_CTLG_01	Creation of Catalogs and Templates (If None Exist)	As of ECC 5.0

Table C.43 HRHAP00_INIT_CATALOG (Development: Catalog — On Initialization)

Enhancement Name	BAdI Implementation	BAdI Implementation Description	Availability
PA	HRHAP00_CATEG_CREATE	Implementation of Category Creation	As of ECC 5.0

Table C.44 HRHAP00_CATEG_CREATE (Development: Catalog — Category)

No standard implementations exist.

Table C.45 HRHAP00_TMPL_608 (Development: Applic. — Add-On Dependent Template Restriction)

Enhancement Name	BAdI Implementation	BAdI Implementation Description	Availability
PA	HRHAP00_CHECK_CUST01	Customizing: Additional Checks for PA	As of Extension 4.7 Set 1.1

Table C.46 HRHAP00_CHECK_CUSTOM (Development: Customizing — Check Tables and Settings)

C.7   BAdI Area Z: Further BAdIs

Enhancement Name	BAdI Implementation	BAdI Implementation Description	Availability
COLLEAGUE	HRHAP00_SELECTION_CO	Coworker	As of Extension 4.7 Set 1.1
CUSTOMER	HRHAP00_SELECTION_CE	External Customer	As of Extension 4.7 Set 1.1
HIGHER_MANAGER	HRHAP00_SELECTION_MB	Higher-Level Manager	As of Extension 4.7 Set 1.1
MANAGER	HRHAP00_SELECTION_MA	Manager	As of Extension 4.7 Set 1.1
MYSELF	HRHAP00_SELECTION_ME	Self	As of Extension 4.7 Set 1.1
SUBORDINATE	HRHAP00_SELECTION_SU	Subordinate	As of Extension 4.7 Set 1.1

Table C.47 HRHAP00_SELECTION (Appraisal Document — Object Selection [Role and To-Do List])

Enhancement Name	BAdI Implementation	BAdI Implementation Description	Availability
Person	HRHAP00_DEF_OBJ_P	Person	As of Extension 4.7 Set 1.1
User	HRHAP00_DEF_OBJ_US	User	As of Extension 4.7 Set 1.1

Table C.48 HRHAP00_DEFAULT_OBJ (Runtime — Generate Default [User <-> Object])

Enhancement Name	BAdI Implementation Description	BAdI Implementation	Availability
HRHAP00_WF_RULE_ID01	12300009	Workflow Executor — Appraiser	As of Extension 4.7 Set 1.1
HRHAP00_WF_RULE_ID02	12300010	Workflow Executer — Appraisee	As of Extension 4.7 Set 1.1
HRHAP00_WF_RULE_ID03	12300011	Workflow Executor — Part Appraiser	As of Extension 4.7 Set 1.1

Table C.49 HRHAP00_WF_RULE_ID (Workflow Executor)

Enhancement Name	BAdI Implementation Description	BAdI Implementation	Availability
HRHAP00_WF_RULE_ID04	12300012	Workflow Executor — Further Participant	As of Extension 4.7 Set 1.1
HRHAP00_WF_RULE_ID05	12300020	Workflow Executor — Higher-Level Manager	As of Extension 4.7 Set 1.1

Table C.49 HRHAP00_WF_RULE_ID (Workflow Executor) (Cont.)

Enhancement Name	BAdI Implementation	BAdI Implementation Description	Availability
CREATED	HRHAP00_GET_LIST_001	Filter- Synchronize (Part) Appraisal Docs Status Completed	As of ECC 5.0
TODO_LIST	HRHAP00_GET_LIST_002	Filter — Create To-Do List (Including Anonymous App.)	As of ECC 5.0

Table C.50 HRHAP00_GET_LIST_FLT (Appraisal Documents — Filter HRHAP_DOCUMENT_GET_LIST_XXL)

Enhancement Name	BAdI Implementation	BAdI Implementation Description	Availability
(No filter)	HRHAP00_STATNAME_01	Alternative Status Names	As of Extension 4.7 Set 2.0

Table C.51 HRHAP00_DOC_STATNAME (Appraisal Document — Alternative for Status Names)

Enhancement Name	BAdI Implementation	BAdI Implementation Description	Availability
PREPARE_1	HRHAP00_DOC_PREPARE1	Prepare Appraisal Docs with Template, Appraiser, Appraisee	As of Extension 4.7 Set 2.0
PREPARE_2	HRHAP00_DOC_PREPARE2	Prepare Appraisal Docs with Organizational Units	As of Extension 4.7 Set 2.0
PREPARE_3	HRHAP00_DOC_PREPARE3	Prepare Appraisal Docs with Restricted Templates	As of ECC 5.0

Table C.52 HRHAP00_DOC_PREPARE (Appraisal Document — Prepare Appraisal Documents)

D   Additional Resources

This appendix lists some recommended websites, information repositories, and user communities that may help you gain a better understanding of SAP's Performance Management offerings as well as SAP's HCM solution as a whole. We recommend the following resources for your discovery, exploration, and enjoyment!

D.1   Solution Documentation on SAP Service Marketplace

Solution documentation for the Performance Management module is available on SAP's **Service Marketplace** website for registered users.

> **Note**
>
> For those that do not have a username and password, talk with one of your Basis/technical resources on how to obtain a username and password for the Service Marketplace.

To download product documentation in the Media Library, follow these steps (see Figure D.1):

1. Go to *http://service.sap.com/erp-hcm* in your web browser.

2. On the left navigation panel, under **SAP ERP • SAP ERP Human Capital Management • Talent Management • Employee Performance Management**, click on **Media Library** for access to documents such as the following:

   ▸ Performance Management BAdI List

   ▸ Authorizations in Performance Management

   ▸ "What's New" Documents for Enterprise 4.7, ECC 5.0, and ECC 6.0

   ▸ Integration Documentation

   ▸ Comparisons with Previous SAP Appraisal Functionality

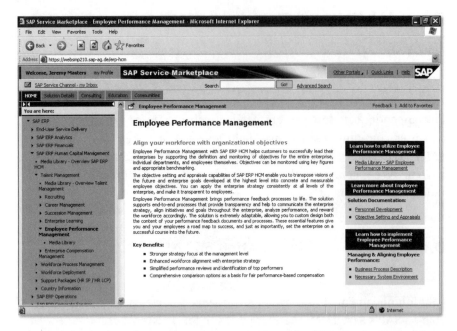

Figure D.1 Employee Performance Management Section within SAP's Service Markeplace

D.2 SAP Online Help

SAP's online help is often overlooked as a great resource for documentation. It's always helpful to ground yourself with SAP's standard documentation. SAP posts the latest, revised help documentation online on this site. To read the documentation on SAP's help website, follow these steps:

1. Go to *http://help.sap.com* in your web browser.

2. On the **SAP Solutions** tab, click on **SAP ERP**.

3. Open the documentation by clicking on the available language you prefer. (The latest documentation as of this book's release is SAP Enhancement Package 2 for SAP ERP 6.0 available in English and German.)

4. Another window launches with the SAP Library. Click on **SAP ERP** in the left navigation panel.

5. Expand the **Human Resources** folder in the left navigation panel.

6. Click on the **Personnel Management (PA)** folder.

7. Click on **Objective Setting and Appraisals**. This is the standard online documentation of the Performance Management module.

D.3   SAP Notes on SAP Service Marketplace

The SAP Notes section of the Service Marketplace is typically where SAP customers go when they are looking to troubleshoot an issue. This site, previously called OSS (Online Service System), provides important bug fixes for SAP customers and is the lifeline to a lot of project implementations (see Figure D.2).

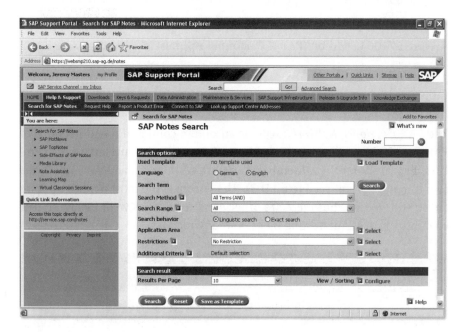

Figure D.2 SAP Notes Main Search Page

We suggest that you pay a visit to this support site when the pressure is off. You will be surprised at how much you can learn perusing through these Notes. SAP Notes can be accessed directly by going to *http://service.sap.com/notes* in your web browser. Most Performance Management related Notes are categorized under application area CA-GTF-AP-AP or PA-PD-AP.

Some important SAP Notes that you should considering referencing for Performance Management include the following:

▶ Note 497777: FAQ Composite SAP Note: Appraisal System

▶ Note 496485: General Questions and Information

▶ Note 496487: Configuration

▶ Note 496502: Application — Appraisals

▶ Note 496788: Application — Appraisals in the Internet/Web

▶ Note 496789: Customer-Specific Enhancement Options

▶ Note 497769: Information on the Releases (Change/Enhancement)

▶ Note 497772: Terminology and Translation

▶ Note 497773: Add-on Application — Information and Specifications

▶ Note 633982: Integration — SEM

▶ Note 571064: Add-on (PA) — Personnel Appraisals

D.4   SAP Developer Network (SDN)

The *SAP Developer Network* (SDN) is an online community and network of SAP practitioners: developers, configurators, and other project team members. Registration is free. Members can post, respond to, and view questions found in the Forum (see Figure D.3). The Forum is the most popular spot by far on the website, but there are other great features as well, including free eLearning classes, interesting blogs, and downloads.

Figure D.3 Forum Search on SAP's SDN (SAP Developer Network) Wesbite

A new community, called BPX (Business Process Expert Community), is an up-and-coming repository for business process expertise and knowledge sharing. Both SDN and BPX are online communities worth participating in.

D.5   Annual Conferences

Two conferences are most popular for SAP HR practitioners: the SAP HR conference and SAPPHIRE/ASUG.

Every year, Wellesley Information Services (the publisher of *SAP Insider*) sponsors the HR conference where SAP partners, exhibitors, and customers come to listen to speakers, share best practices, and see what new functionality is coming down the road. The conference is a great place to network, hear what others are doing, and have fun. The website for the HR 2008 conference is *http://www.saphr2008.com/*.

SAP recently combined its annual user conference ASUG (Americas' SAP Users' Group) with their annual SAPPHIRE conference. This conference is geared for both current and prospective clients. For more information on the conference, visit *http://www.sapsapphire.com/*.

D.6   HR Expert

Wellesley Information Services also publishes *HR Expert*, which is a newsletter that covers essential SAP HR concepts, tips, and best practices. The articles focus on case studies and "real-world" experiences. You can find a lot of good material on the website (requires a paid subscription) at *http://www.hrexpertonline.com/* (see Figure D.4).

There are two great *HR Expert* articles that are relevant for performance management:

"Workflow-Enable Your Performance Management" by Dr. Martina Schuh and Maurice Hagen from SAP AG is an excellent resource to learn more about statuses, substatuses, and workflow notifications within the Performance Management module. The article was published in the April 2004 issue.

Also, a three-part series entitled "Protect Sensitive Data in Performance Management with Authorizations" by Bianka Piehl, Maurice Hagen, and Martina Schuh from SAP AG published in July, August, and October of 2005 is a good white paper on authorization management within the module.

Figure D.4 HR Expert Website, Including the Current Issue and a Full Archive

D.7 User Communities

Two user communities are popular for networking events, knowledge sharing/harvesting, and round-table discussions.

ASUG (Americas' SAP Users' Group) is a customer-driven community of SAP professionals and partners. More than 45,000 individuals and 1,700 companies are represented within the community, which makes it a great place for networking. Visit the website at *http://www.asug.com/*.

SHRM (The Society for Human Resource Management) is the world's largest association devoted to human resource management. Founded in 1948 and representing more than 210,000 individual members, SHRM currently has more than 550 affiliated chapters and members in more than 100 countries. Visit their website at *http://www.shrm.org/*.

E   About the Authors

Christos Kotsakis

 Christos Kotsakis is Vice President of Information Technology at Starwood Hotels and Resorts Worldwide, which together with its subsidiaries, operates as a hotel and leisure company worldwide. Prior to joining Starwood Hotels and Resorts, Mr. Kotsakis was an associate partner in the Human Capital Management practice at IBM Global Business Services where he led the design and implementation of large-scale, global HR transformation projects using SAP HR. In the past 10 years, Mr. Kotsakis has managed more than a dozen project teams, spanning across HR functionality, including Performance Management, Compensation Management, and eRecruitment. He also has extensive experience in software development; self-service technology; enterprise portal implementations; including the SAP NetWeaver Portal, and related technologies. You can reach him via email at christos.kotsakis@emedianet.com.

Jeremy Masters

 Jeremy Masters is an author, speaker, and SAP HR subject matter expert. Mr. Masters is also the cofounder and managing partner of Worklogix, which provides SAP HR professional services and software solutions to fortune 1000 companies. Mr. Masters has been an SAP HR practitioner for over 10 years, spending his early years with Price Waterhouse, PwC Consulting, and IBM. He has been involved in over 16 projects, many of them global in scope. Mr. Masters has been helping clients implement performance management systems for the past 6 years. Besides Performance Management, he has worked with much of the new self-service functionality, including Compensation Management, Personnel Cost Planning, Succession Planning, and eRecruitment in both the SAP R/3 system and the SAP Enterprise Portal. You can reach him via email at jmasters@worklogix.com.

Index

Integrate the Cross-Application Time Sheet with SAP HR, FI, PS, PM, CS and MM

Master employee time management from various decentralized locations

96 pp., 2006, 68,– Euro / US$ 85.00
ISBN 978-1-59229-063-5

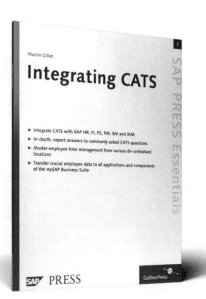

Integrating CATS

www.sap-hefte.de

Martin Gillet

Integrating CATS

SAP PRESS Essentials 7

One of the most important aspects of the Cross Application Time Sheet (CATS) is its integration with other SAP modules. This unique new guide provides readers with exclusive advice and best practices for integrating CATS with other key SAP modules. First, learn the fundamentals of CATS. Then, discover the concepts, practical applications and possible enhancements for CATS. You will quickly advance your mastery of CATS as you uncover little known tips, practical examples, and concise answers to your most frequently asked questions. Full of practical guidance and real-world scenarios, this book is for anyone interested in CATS.

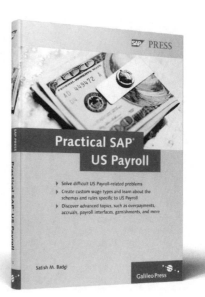

Practical SAP US Payroll

www.sap-press.com

Satish Badgi

Practical SAP US Payroll

„Practical US Payroll" has everything you need to
implement a successful payroll system. Readers will
learn how to create custom wage types, process
deductions for benefits and garnishments, handle
accruals, report and process taxes, and process
retroactive payrolls. From the hands-on, step-by-step
examples to the detailed wage type tables in the
appendix, this book is your complete guide to the
US Payroll system.

Best Practices for Payroll, Time Management, Personnel Administration, and much more

Expert advice for integrating Personnel Planning and SAP Enterprise Portal

Based on R/3 Enterprise and mySAP ERP HCM 2004

629 pp., 2006, 69,95 Euro / US$
ISBN 1-59229-050-7

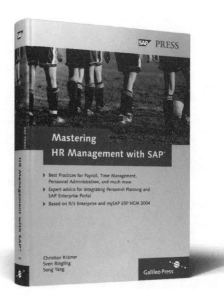

Mastering HR Management with SAP

www.sap-press.com

C. Krämer, S. Ringling, Song Yang

Mastering HR Management with SAP

Get a step-by-step guide to the entire personnel management process, from recruiting, to personnel controlling, and beyond. This book comes complete with practical examples regarding user roles, and covers all of the new enhancements, improved features and tools that have been introduced with R/3 Enterprise. Uncover the ins and outs of e-recruiting, organizational management, personnel administration, payroll, benefits, quality assurance, rolebased portals, and many others too numerous to list. The book is based on Release 4.7 (R/3 Enterprise), and mySAP ERP 2004 (HCM)

How to get most from your SAP
HR systems

552 pp., 2004, 69,95 Euro / US$ 69,95
ISBN 978-1-59229-024-6

HR Personnel Planning and Development Using SAP

www.sap-press.com

Christian Krämer, Christian Lübke, Sven Ringling

HR Personnel Planning and Development Using SAP

How to get the most from your SAP HR systems

This compelling new reference book gives you a comprehensive view of the most important personnel planning and development functionality within SAP. Whether you need to implement, customize, or optimize your HR systems, the real-world insights this book provides will help you master the concepts essential for effective personnel planning and development. This book will help you leverage the many HR options and processes supported by SAP and gives you practical examples and key metrics to help you measure your success.